CONSTITUTIONAL CONVENTIONS AND THE HEADSHIP OF STATE: AUSTRALIAN EXPERIENCE

ABOUT THE AUTHOR

Born in the outback of Queensland, Dr Donald Markwell was Rhodes Scholar for Queensland in 1981, and Fellow and Tutor in Politics at Merton College, Oxford, from 1986 to 1997. As a visiting professor at Victoria University, Melbourne, and subsequently, he worked closely with Sir Zelman Cowen on his memoirs. Dr Markwell served as Warden of Trinity College, University of Melbourne, from 1997 to 2007, and as a Professorial Fellow of the Centre for Public Policy and the Department of Political Science at the University of Melbourne. He has subsequently served as Deputy Vice-Chancellor (Education) of the University of Western Australia (2007-2009), and Warden of Rhodes House, Oxford (2009-2012). He spoke at the State Memorial Service for Sir John Kerr in 1991, and the State Funeral for Sir Zelman Cowen in 2011. Dr Markwell is now Senior Adviser to the Attorney-General of Australia and Leader of the Government in the Australian Senate.

BY THE SAME AUTHOR

"Instincts to lead": on leadership, peace, and education (2013)

State of the Nation: aspects of Australian public policy

(edited with Rachael Thompson & Julian Leeser, 2013)

"A large and liberal education": higher education for the 21st century (2007)

John Maynard Keynes and International Relations: Economic Paths to War and Peace (2006)

Liberals face the future: essays on Australian liberalism

(edited with George Brandis & Tom Harley, 1984)

*

Also extensive involvement in the preparation of

A Public Life: The Memoirs of Zelman Cowen (2006)

CONSTITUTIONAL CONVENTIONS AND THE HEADSHIP OF STATE: AUSTRALIAN EXPERIENCE

Donald Markwell

CONNOR COURT PUBLISHING

Connor Court Publishing Pty Ltd
PO Box 7257
Redland Bay QLD 4165
Australia

sales@connorcourt.com
www.connorcourt.com

Phone 0497-900-685

ISBN: 978-1-925501-15-5

Cover design: Maria Giordano

Front cover photo: Governor-General Sir Zelman Cowen and Lady Cowen, with Prime Minister Malcolm Fraser and Mrs Fraser, welcome the Queen and Prince Philip to Fairbairn Air Force Base, Canberra, May 1980.

Printed in Australia

For Anna Cowen

and dedicated to the memory of

two great scholars of constitutional conventions –

Sir Kenneth Wheare

(26 March 1907 – 7 September 1979)

and

Dr Eugene Forsey

(29 May 1904 – 20 February 1991)

Contents

ACKNOWLEDGEMENTS

Very many people have helped in diverse ways with the papers, written over recent decades, which are brought together in this collection relating to constitutional conventions and the headship of state in Australia, and especially the office of Governor-General.

To acknowledge everyone who has contributed in some way to these papers over the decades would be impossible, but I would especially like to acknowledge with gratitude the following for support and help in various ways (including the stimulus of disagreement): H.W. Arndt, Kathryn Baldock, Sir Garfield Barwick, Stephanie and Rex Bashford, Andrew Bell, Vernon Bogdanor, Geoffrey Bolton, Peter Boyce, Stephen Brady, Troy Bramston, George Brandis, Liam Brennan, Geoffrey Browne, Dame Quentin Bryce, Sir David Butler, Laurie Claus, Guy Coughlan, Sir Zelman and Lady Cowen, Michael Crommelin, Lyn Curtis, Fr. Graham Eglington, Gareth Evans, J.M. Finnis, Eugene Forsey, Mark Fraser, Josh Frydenberg, Brian Galligan, Stewart and Jill Garrett, Kenneth Gee, Pat Hall, Tom Harley, Sir Paul Hasluck, Sir William and Lady Heseltine, Rt Revd Dr Peter Hollingworth, W.J. Hudson, Paul Kelly, Justice Susan Kenny and Ross Jones, Sir John and Lady Kerr, Yvonne McComb King and Malcolm King, Judith Kirby, Richard Krygier, Bruce Lehrmann, Anthony Low, Dorothy Markwell, Geoff Markwell, Arla Marshall, Geoffrey Marshall, Alex May, Janet McCredie, Derek McDougall, T.B. Millar, Pamela O'Brien, Robert O'Neill, Esther Pahoff, J.B. Paul, Timothy Potts, John Poynter, Jonathan Ritchie, Winsome Roberts, Jarlath Ronayne, Cheryl Saunders, Honorina Sihin, Steven and Lousje Skala, Justice Melanie Sloss, Sir David Smith, Malcolm Smith, Ben Thomas, Jim and Lynne Thomson, Anne Twomey, Daniel Ward, George Winterton, and Adolf Wood. Many of these people have "gone to their reward", and I honour their memory.

As well as thanking the various institutions at which I have studied and worked while preparing papers in this collection, I express gratitude to the Australian Research Council (ARC) for making possible a research grant which supported some of this work, and anonymous ARC reviewers who made useful comments on my work. I am indebted to many libraries and archives, and particularly thank the staff of the National Library of Australia, Canberra; the State Libraries of Queensland and New South Wales; the libraries of the Universities of Queensland, Western Australia, and Melbourne, and Victoria University, Melbourne; the Bodleian Library, Oxford; the Rhodes House Library, Oxford (as it then was); the British Library; the Public Record Office, now the National Archives, London; Cambridge University Library; the Library of Churchill College, Cambridge; the Library of Congress, Washington, D.C.; and the Firestone Library, Princeton.

Many of these papers have been published previously, and I thank those connected with their original publication and those who have given permission for their reappearance in this volume. Two pieces were co-authored, and I thank their principal authors, Geoffrey Browne and Jon Ritchie respectively, for agreeing to their reappearance here. My entry on "constitutional conventions" is reproduced by permission of Oxford University Press Australia from *The Oxford Companion to Australian Politics* edited by Brian Galligan and Winsome Roberts, 2007 © Oxford University Press, www.oup.com.au; extracts from "The Conventions of Ministerial Resignations: The Queensland Coalition Crisis of 1983", in D.A. Low (ed.), *Constitutional Heads and Political Crises: Commonwealth Episodes, 1945-85*, Macmillan, 1988, are reproduced with permission of Palgrave Macmillan; and "Griffith, Barton and the Early Governor-Generals: Aspects of Australia's Constitutional Development", *Public Law Review*, vol. 10, December 1999, is reproduced with permission of Thomson Reuters (Professional) Australia Limited, www.thomsonreuters. com.au. I also thank: *The Times* for agreeing to republication of my letter which appeared as "Royal Prerogative" in *The Times*, 9 April 1992; *The Times Literary Supplement* for permission to republish "Masters of dissolution", *The Times Literary Supplement*, 12 April 1985 (review of Christopher Cunneen, *Kings' Men: Australia's Governors-General from Hopetoun to Isaacs*, George Allen & Unwin, 1983), and "By reference to the voters", *The Times Literary Supplement*, 20 April 1984 (review of Sir Garfield Barwick, *Sir John Did His Duty*, Serendip Publications, 1983); Oxford University Press for permission to republish the entry on Sir Paul Hasluck, co-authored with Geoffrey Browne, published in *Oxford Dictionary of National Biography*, 2004 © Oxford University Press 2004-16; Guardian News & Media Ltd for permission to reprint my obituary of Sir John Kerr which was published under the title "The sacking of Gough Whitlam's government" in *The Guardian*, 26 March 1991 (and reprinted in *The Guardian Weekly*); *The Independent* for permission to reprint my supplementary obituary, "Sir John Kerr", *The Independent*, 30 March 1991; Taylor & Francis Australasia for agreeing to republication of "Sir John Kerr: a Reflection" (my "reflection" from his State Memorial Service), which appeared in *The Australian Journal of Forensic Sciences*, June-December 1991; Taylor & Francis for agreeing to republication of "Sir Zelman Cowen: Educational Leader and Healing Governor-General" (my tribute at his State Memorial Service), which appeared in *The Round Table: The Commonwealth Journal of International Affairs*, February 2012, "Australian and Commonwealth Republicanism" (with Jonathan Ritchie), which appeared in *The Round Table*, October 2006, and "Canada's Best" (review of Eugene Forsey, *A Life on the Fringe*, Oxford University Press, 1990), which appeared in *The Round Table*, October 1991; *The Sydney Morning Herald* for agreeing to republication of my letter published as "Nothing improper in advice to Kerr" on 7 January 1994; *The Weekend Australian* for permission to reprint my article "The Case for Kerr" from *The Weekend Australian*, 11-12 November 1995; Melbourne University Law Review Association, which first published "The Office of Governor-General" (2015) 38(3) *Melbourne University Law Review*; and the Menzies Centre for Australian Studies at King's College London for permission to reproduce extracts on Sir Kenneth Wheare from my paper "British Social Science and Humanities", first published in T.B. Millar (ed.), *The Australian Contribution to Britain*, Australian Studies Centre, University of London, 1988.

This book would not have come into being but for the dedicated and skilled editorial assistance and warm encouragement of Emma Yabsley, and the strong support of Dr Anthony Cappello at Connor Court. To both of them, I especially express my warm appreciation.

1

INTRODUCTION

This volume brings together a selection of papers written over recent decades that relate to constitutional conventions and the headship of state in Australia, with particular reference to the office of Governor-General of Australia.

Constitutional conventions are essentially unwritten rules based on principle and precedent, which are considered binding although usually not legally enforceable.[1] Constitutional systems frequently depend upon conventions to guide their operation, including regarding the role of the head of state. The Queen (whom Australia shares with the U.K. and several other Commonwealth countries) is Australia's head of state, with her Australian federal representative, the Governor-General, serving in day-to-day practice as a de facto head of state. She is also represented by Governors at the state level. Papers in this volume discuss conventions and other practice relating to the Crown, especially the Governor-General, in Australia's Westminster-style system of government responsible to parliament. Papers consider the "Australianisation" of the Crown since federation in 1901, the evolution of a modern Australian office of Governor-General, and the continuing debate on an Australian republic.

Controversies analysed include the exercise of the "reserve powers" by Governor-General Sir John Kerr to resolve the 1975 constitutional crisis, the long but now controversial practice of Governors-General consulting High Court judges on the exercise of their constitutional discretions, and the sometimes-contested conventions that relate to "hung parliaments" and to ministerial resignations. These studies highlight the need for careful consideration of constitutional principles and precedents to an understanding of conventions and the office of Governor-General of Australia.

Australia is both a constitutional monarchy and a federal parliamentary democracy. Although most commonly described as a "Westminster" system, Australia's constitutional system is also sometimes described as "Washminster"

[1] See ch. 2.

– a hybrid of Washington and Westminster systems. The 1890s drafters of the Australian Constitution imported aspects of Washington (a written constitution, a federal system, a powerful Senate with equal representation of the states) as well as Westminster (constitutional monarchy, government responsible to parliament). Like the constitutions ("written" or "unwritten") of other Westminster-derived systems, its written Constitution, which came into effect in 1901, can only be understood by reference to unwritten conventions. The core constitutional conventions are largely those of the Westminster-style system of "responsible government" (government responsible to parliament) that Australia has adopted and adapted from Britain.

Unlike Britain, Australia is a federation comprising six states and two mainland territories. At the federal or national level, it is a bicameral parliamentary system with a House of Representatives and a Senate of near-equal powers. The government is ordinarily formed on the basis of who (in practice, which party leader) is best able to command the confidence of the House of Representatives as Prime Minister, usually with a majority but sometimes from a minority position. One of the key messages of this book is that there are various forms of responsible government under different constitutions, and the Australian Constitution embodies a particular form of responsible government that is similar, but not identical, to that in the U.K. and some other countries. The Constitution is upheld by the highest court, the High Court of Australia (though certain discretionary decisions of the Crown have traditionally been regarded as not being subject to judicial review[2]).

In any constitutional system, the head of state is the person who occupies (or, more rarely, the people who occupy) the position at the apex of a country's constitutional system, or formal system of governmental authority. Typically the head of state will be either a monarch or a president, though there are many variations. The duties of the head of state vary greatly. It may be that the monarch has major, some, or no political or governmental function. The head of state is in some cases also head of government, but the two roles – head of state and head of government – are separated in many systems.[3]

In Australia, there is no doubt that the head of state is distinct from the

---

[2] The nature of, and limits to, the justiciability of vice-regal decisions is one of the topics that relate to the theme of this book which are not substantially discussed here.

[3] The separation between head of state and head of government is not necessarily clear-cut or stable. E.g., in the French 5th Republic, the President is head of state but may be thought to share the role of head of government with the Prime Minister to degrees varying over time, esp. between when the President does and does not have majority support in the National Assembly.

head of government (the Prime Minister). But Australia is in the unusual position that there is disagreement about who *is* the head of state as well as about who *should be* the head of state. Some say that the Queen is head of state, and some that it is the Governor-General. Many Australians would like the head of state to be an Australian president rather than either the Queen or the Governor-General.

In reality, Australia has two people at the federal level in the space that might ordinarily be thought to be occupied by a head of state. These are the Queen *and* the Governor-General. The traditional view is that the Queen is the head of state, and this is formally correct. But the Governor-General, as her representative at the federal level in Australia, has always performed almost all of the constitutional functions of the head of state. State Governors do the same at the state level. So it has been argued by some that the Governor-General "acts as head of state".[4] Indeed, it was proposed by some during the Australian republican debate of the 1990s that the Governor-General should be recognised as head of state,[5] and some have come to argue that the Governor-General *is* the head of state.[6] As suggested above, a reasonable view is to say that the Queen is Australia's head of state de jure but that, as the Governor-General fulfils almost all constitutional functions of the head of state and the Governor-Generalship has grown into a mature role of national leadership, it is appropriate to regard the Governor-General as being the day-to-day de facto head of state. Another way of saying this is to say that the functions of the head of state are shared in reality between the Queen and the Governor-General.

The fact that the Queen is the formal head of state of Australia is not unimportant. She visits Australia as its head of state. She appoints (on the Australian Prime Minister's advice) her federal representative in Australia, who reports regularly to her, and she appoints (on the advice of state Premiers) her representative in each state. The Constitution allows for legislation to be reserved for her to give her assent personally, though this is in practice essentially a dead letter. The Queen has herself opened sessions of parliament in Canberra. She also commands personal loyalty and affection from very

---

[4] E.g., Sir David Smith in George Winterton (ed.), *We, the people: Australian republican government*, Allen & Unwin, 1994, p. 157.

[5] E.g., Tony Abbott, as cited in Nick Cater & Helen Baxendale (eds), *A Better Class of Sunset: Collected Works of Christopher Pearson*, Connor Court, 2014, pp. 213-5.

[6] E.g., Sir David Smith, *Head of State: The Governor-General, the Monarchy, the Republic and the Dismissal*, Macleay Press, Sydney, 2005.

many Australians.

Australia, like Britain and other countries who share its monarch, thus has a politically neutral head of state rather than a political head of state. Unlike in many presidential systems, where the head of state has a substantive policy role, the core functions of the de jure and de facto heads of state in Australia are to contribute to the formal process of governing, including ensuring there *is* a government, and giving formal effect to government decisions, but not to have a substantive policy role. As a result either of convention or constitutional provision, the formal powers of the head of state are in almost all cases exercised on the advice of ministers (above all, of course, the Prime Minister). The head of state has so-called "Bagehot rights" – "the right to be consulted, the right to encourage, the right to warn"[7] – and also a very limited range of so-called "reserve powers", where the head of state can exercise an independent discretion. These powers, while rarely exercised, necessarily attract significant attention, as is reflected throughout this book.

Heads of state, like heads of government, have roles of leadership. In a presidential system where the head of state is also head of government, it is natural to look to the president for a significant degree of national leadership. When the headship of state is separate from the headship of government, the role of national leadership is shared, and there will be varying understandings of what aspects are expected of the head of state and which of the head of government. In such states, the head of state will typically be expected to play a unifying role – and in Westminster systems, one that is "above politics". Just what this role is expected to be may be contested and may change over time. This has certainly been the case with the evolution of the ceremonial and symbolic, and community leadership, roles of the Governor-General of Australia – most obviously with the evolution of the Governor-General from being an expression of Imperial bonds to "interpreting" an independent Australian nation "to itself". The centrality of speechmaking to the leadership given by Governors-General is one of the recurring themes of this book.

The office of Governor-General of Australia was created under the Australian Constitution, which came into effect on the federation of the Australian colonies into the Commonwealth of Australia in 1901. The significant and continuing evolution of the role of Governor-General since then, as part of a broader "Australianisation" of the Crown, is reflected throughout this

---

[7] Walter Bagehot, *The English Constitution* (1867), quoted from Oxford University Press 1955 edition, p. 67.

book. This evolution has, inter alia, been shaped by and has helped to shape the evolution of the British Empire into the modern Commonwealth. The evolution of the role has both reflected and helped to shape the growth of Australian nationhood – from a Dominion within the British Empire to a proudly independent nation – and the growth of Australian national identity. The debate about whether Australia should become a republic is perhaps more than anything else a debate about whether Australia's national identity, as it has evolved and is evolving, requires an Australian to be unambiguously clearly Australia's head of state.

The evolution of the office of Governor-General and the distinctive attributes which individual Governors-General have brought to that role are themselves part of the modern Australian story. As well as discussing the evolution of the position of Governor-General, this book contains accounts of a number of the individuals who have held that office. These are in the form of short biographical accounts of or personal reflections on them.

Moreover, to a degree that is infrequently acknowledged, Governors-General have been central to historic events. Because the Governor-General exercises the executive power of the Commonwealth of Australia, Governors-General of Australia have necessarily been involved in very many of the key events in Australian history since 1901. In many cases, this is a formal rather than substantive involvement: the Governor-General, acting on ministerial advice, has given formal effect to the substantive decisions of the government. However, because the Governor-General also has certain real and important discretions, there have also been a number of occasions on which the Governor-General has been substantively as well as formally the decision-maker, or central to the real decision-making process. The most obvious case is the dismissal of the Whitlam government by Governor-General Sir John Kerr in 1975. But as the chapter on the early Governors-General and the consultation of High Court judges shows, this is far from an isolated case. It is thus my hope that this volume might make some contribution to the understanding of aspects of Australian history which have tended to be neglected.

The Governor-General, like the Queen, plays his or her role in accord with constitutional conventions. The single most important of these is that, as part of the system of government responsible to parliament, the Governor-General exercises almost all powers on and only on the advice of ministers who are responsible to parliament, and ultimately to the public, for their advice and for the executive action flowing from it. Conventions also guide when and how the Governor-General may exercise any independent discretion. The next chapter contains discussions of the nature and content of some core Australian constitutional conventions, and sets out an array of fundamental questions (to many of which this book cannot itself provide full answers). The conventions relating to independent discretions are illustrated with particular reference to conventions relating to how the Queen in Britain or Governor-General in Australia should respond to government formation and requests for dissolution of parliament leading to an election in the case of a "hung parliament" – one in which no party or pre-existing coalition has a majority. It also examines conventions relating to ministerial resignations.

It is likely that Westminster systems such as Australia's place greater reliance on conventions that shape the nature and role of the head of state than is the case in most other constitutional systems, especially presidential systems operating under relatively comprehensive written constitutions. One of the issues for Australia, and comparable systems, is whether it would be better to codify constitutional conventions in binding form. One of the papers in this book gives several (contestable) reasons for preferring not to do so, at least in the case of key conventions related to the reserve powers of the Crown.

There have in fact been a number of attempts by Constitutional Conventions (i.e. meetings of elected or appointed officials to discuss constitutional issues) from the 1970s to the 1990s to discuss and set out desired constitutional conventions. Such Convention statements are reproduced helpfully in the appendices to the Republic Advisory Committee's 1993 report.[8] It must, however, be remembered that these Constitutional Conventions have no status under the Australian Constitution. It follows that the constitutional conventions they recommended have no formal constitutional status. These statements of conventions may be taken as evidence towards claims of the existence of conventions,[9] but do not themselves create or define conventions. Moreover, those conventions, as stated and recommended at these Conventions, have weaknesses as well as strengths.

Constitutional rules will often be contested. Often, the highest judicial authority in the state (e.g., a supreme or high or constitutional court) will determine what they are, including determining finely contested nuances

---

[8] Republic Advisory Committee, *An Australian Republic: The options,* AGPS, Canberra, 1993, vol. 3.

[9] This was done, for example, in Attorney-General George Brandis's paper on "The Practice and Precedents of Recall of Parliament Following Prorogation" given to the Governor-General on 21 March 2016.

of universally agreed words. Sometimes the legislature or the executive will decide what the rules are. Lawyers, constitutional scholars and others will argue about what the rules are, including the meaning of words in a written constitution and what the unwritten constitutional conventions are. Aspects of this book draw attention to areas where there is disagreement about what the constitutional conventions are, or about how generally agreed conventions should be applied in practice. Most particularly, the papers in the sections on conventions related to ministerial resignations and on Australia's 1975 constitutional crisis show the scope for disagreement about what the applicable conventions are.

Examination here of such constitutional controversies reflects the fact that discussion of conventions often involves assertions made in ignorance of constitutional provisions and of constitutional history. One of the key messages of this book is the need for care in seeking to determine what conventions are, and in discussing how they are appropriately applied. This requires close attention both to precedent – the often little-known history that is relevant – as well as to the constitutional principles in play.

In understanding what constitutional conventions are, the works of constitutional scholars are of great importance. Scholars of constitutional conventions need to understand the practice of various countries; it is generally understood that Australia's constitutional conventions can only be understood by reference to practice in other Westminster systems, especially now the U.K., Canada and New Zealand. This volume concludes with reflections on two of the most distinguished 20th century scholars of constitutional conventions in Westminster systems, Sir Kenneth Wheare (1907-1979), an Australian who became an Oxford don, and Dr (and for some years Senator) Eugene Forsey (1904-1991), a Canadian labour activist and constitutionalist. Both had deep understanding of the conventions of responsible government in various Commonwealth countries. It is sometimes the case that claims as to what constitutional conventions are will be influenced by partisanship. Careful scholarly analysis of constitutional principles and practice, putting aside one's own political views, is the ideal to which those making claims about conventions should aspire. Sir Kenneth Wheare and Dr Forsey seem to me to have achieved this.

Similarly, of course, it is essential that the exercise of the role of Governor-General be undertaken in a non-partisan and impartial way. Experience shows that people of prior partisan political alignment can achieve this impartiality.

The most conspicuous case is sometimes considered to be the granting to Prime Minister Menzies in 1951 of a double dissolution, against the wishes of the Labor Party, by a Governor-General who had previously been a Labor Premier, Mr (later Sir) William McKell. I am unable to think of any case of partisanship or partiality determining the conduct of a Governor-General of Australia.

The impartial analysis of principle and practice will sometimes point to a clear convention that requires action of a specific kind – e.g., that the Governor-General must under certain circumstances agree to a Prime Minister's request to dissolve the House of Representatives. In other cases, the conventions or past practice may point to an area where the Governor-General must exercise their judgment, and there are a number of courses of action which might be consistent with the Constitution and its conventions. It is this which Sir John Kerr had in mind, I think, when he called his autobiography and explanation of his action in 1975 *Matters for Judgment*.

*

The next chapter (chapter 2) considers the nature and content of constitutional conventions in Australia, with particular attention to conventions related to hung parliaments and to ministerial resignations. Chapter 3 provides an overview of "The Crown and Australia" in the form of a 1987 public lecture given at the University of London. Chapter 4 considers the early Governors-General of Australia who were, until 1931, all British aristocrats.[10] It pays particular attention to their frequent consultation of High Court judges, in particular the first Chief Justice, Sir Samuel Griffith, and his fellow judge, Sir Edmund Barton, who had been the first Prime Minister of Australia. This history of consultation of High Court judges by Governors-General is important to remember in the continuing controversy on the legitimate sources of informal advice to a Governor-General when considering the possible exercise of an independent discretion.

Chapter 5 provides biographical studies and personal reflections on three significant Governors-General – a former senior minister who became an impeccably impartial Governor-General, Sir Paul Hasluck (Governor-General, 1969-1974); a distinguished lawyer most commonly remembered for resolving the 1975 constitutional crisis by the controversial dismissal of Prime Minister Whitlam, Sir John Kerr (Governor-General, 1974-1977); and the academic

---

[10] They and later Governors-General, monarchs, Chief Justices, and Prime Ministers are listed in appendix 1.

leader and lawyer who brought "a touch of healing" after that intense controversy, Sir Zelman Cowen (Governor-General, 1977-1982). As a friend to both, I spoke at the State Memorial Service for Sir John Kerr in 1991 and at the State Funeral for Sir Zelman Cowen in 2011, and my addresses at these services are included in this chapter. Two of the recurring themes concerning these and other Governors-General discussed in this book are a sense of duty and a capacity for friendship.

Chapter 6 contains various materials considering the 1975 constitutional crisis and the conventions of responsible government, arguing that the Governor-General's action was consistent both with the terms of the Constitution and its conventions.

Chapter 7 contains a discussion from 1997 of the issues at stake in the debate on Australia's becoming a republic, and a later analysis of republicanism in Australia and elsewhere in the Commonwealth that, inter alia, considers why the proposal for an Australian republic was defeated at a referendum in 1999.

Chapter 8 comprises a 2014 paper on "The Office of Governor-General" which considers the good shape in which the modern office of Governor-General was handed on by Dame Quentin Bryce to Sir Peter Cosgrove, and refers to some of the continuing issues confronting the office.

The first appendix provides a list of the monarchs, Governors-General, Chief Justices of the High Court, and Prime Ministers since 1901. The second comprises short snippets from speeches at events involving two modern Governors-General, Dr Peter Hollingworth and Dame Quentin Bryce. These pieces are included to illustrate the backgrounds of some recent Governors-General, and aspects of how modern Governors-General fulfil their role, including with non-partisan national leadership on issues of contemporary importance. As already mentioned, the final appendix comprises biographic material on two of the most important scholars of constitutional conventions, Sir Kenneth Wheare and Dr Eugene Forsey.

*

The papers in this book were written at different times and for different purposes from the mid-1980s to 2014. The date and occasion is indicated at the start of each paper. Most of the papers in this book have been published previously, and I reiterate the thanks expressed in the Acknowledgements in this book. The papers are generally presented here as they were originally published or written, with relatively minor editing (for example, to minimise repetition, and for brevity, clarity, and consistency of style). Subsequently added material is shown in square brackets.

Having been written over a period of over 30 years, the papers reflect changing circumstances and controversies, and the evolution of thinking – on the part of the author and of others – on various issues. For example, "The Crown and Australia" (1987) reflected the widespread belief at that time that Australia did not need to become a republic, and that such a change was likely to be many years away. Later pieces reflect the rapid development in the 1990s of a strong republican movement in Australia, and a much increased receptiveness on the part of many Australians to such a change.

Similarly, the discussions of the sources of informal advice appropriately available to the Governor-General on the exercise of a constitutional discretion reflect the long and very extensive history of consultation of High Court judges by Governors-General, which it was important to refer to following ill-informed criticism of such consultation during the 1975 constitutional crisis. They also reflect the later general acceptance that, given the controversy aroused by the 1975 consultations, such consultation is unlikely to be undertaken in future, and that alternative appropriate sources of advice should be considered.

More generally, the materials on the 1975 constitutional crisis reflect the intense and evolving controversy on the events of 1975 that was sustained throughout the 1980s and into the 1990s, and that still re-emerges from time to time (for example, around the 40th anniversary of the dismissal in 2015[11]). My review (reproduced here) of Sir Garfield Barwick's book *Sir John Did His Duty* (1983) sparked a sustained debate in *The Times Literary Supplement* and then in *Quadrant*. This debate is to some extent reflected in my foreword to Sir John Kerr's unpublished book *The Triumph of the Constitution*. This foreword, completed in 1992 after the death of Sir John Kerr in 1991, is published for the first time here.

Because this book is a selection of diverse pieces written in various contexts, it does not present a comprehensive picture of all aspects of its topic. Many questions are identified but not answered, or not in depth. Although the book covers several key aspects of the history of the Governor-Generalship of Australia, it does not provide a comprehensive history (for example, it says little about the Governor-Generalship between the 1920s and the 1970s). Many issues and developments need and deserve fuller attention. For example, the 2014 paper on "The Office of Governor-General" alluded to various recent

---

[11] E.g., Paul Kelly & Troy Bramston, *The Dismissal: In the Queen's Name*, Melbourne University Publishing, 2015.

developments which merit further examination.

One of these is that there appears to be in some quarters a mistaken view that the Solicitor-General, a lawyer chosen by a government to advise and serve the government itself, should be treated also as some sort of independent legal adviser to the Governor-General. There is no constitutional or statutory basis for this view, it is contrary to most of Australia's federal constitutional practice, and it risks creating the untenable position of the Governor-General having conflicting advice from the Attorney-General and the Solicitor-General (the first and second Law Officers of the Commonwealth, respectively). With perhaps the rarest of exceptions, the views of the Solicitor-General should only be sought with the prior agreement of the Attorney-General,[12] and even then sparingly. While the Solicitor-General will often be an outstanding lawyer, it should not be assumed that he or she will be a good, let alone the best or most appropriate, source of legal advice when it may reasonably be thought by the Governor-General to be needed.

"The Office of Governor-General" alludes to the growth of the office of Official Secretary to the Governor-General since the days when Sir Paul Hasluck said that the Official Secretary was not, and should not be, any sort of constitutional adviser to the Governor-General. The growth of the office of Official Secretary has been part of a necessary process of increasing support for Governors-General in fulfilling their extensive and demanding roles. However, any attempt on the part of a future Official Secretary to act in an interventionist way, as a de facto constitutional adviser to the Governor-General free to challenge ministerial advice, especially on matters on which ministerial advice is binding and precedent is clear, would be undesirable.

Of course, the deeper the Governor-General's own understanding of constitutional principles and precedents, the less likely he or she is to seek non-ministerial advice on constitutional issues that arise. Such understanding on the part of Governors-General should, as Sir Paul Hasluck suggested, be an important criterion in the selection of distinguished Australians to serve in the country's highest constitutional office.

The practice is now well established that documents relating to the Governor-General's exercise of constitutional and related discretions are made public quickly. This reflects an appropriate level of transparency around the office of Governor-General. It is, however, noteworthy that, perhaps concomitant with the growth of the office of Official Secretary to the Governor-General,

[12] See *Law Officers Act* 1964, section 12.

there has also been growth in scrutiny of the Official Secretary by senators in the regular "Senate Estimates" committee hearing processes. Some of this questioning is aggressive and appears based on an implicit notion that the Governor-General is accountable to the Senate, which is constitutionally mistaken. The current process may have unintended consequences, and merits further consideration.

*

In March 2016, the Prime Minister of Australia, Malcolm Turnbull, advised the Governor-General, Sir Peter Cosgrove, to act under section 5 of the Constitution to recall the parliament after proroguing it.[13] This was to enable the further consideration by the Senate of blocked employment legislation which the government regarded as being of high importance. With an election due in 2016, Senate consideration of that legislation would determine if the Prime Minister later advised a "double dissolution" (dissolution of both houses of the parliament, followed by an election for all members of both houses) or a dissolution of the House of Representatives only. The latter would have seen the election of the new House of Representatives combined with an election for only half the Senate.

The Prime Minister's advice to prorogue and recall the parliament was supported by a letter from the Attorney-General and a detailed paper on "The Practice and Precedents of Recall of Parliament Following Prorogation" which showed that, although not used recently, the section 5 powers to prorogue and recall parliament had been used on 28 previous occasions, and were always exercised on ministerial advice. This advice from the Prime Minister and action by the Governor-General took most of the "commentariat" by surprise, and was widely greeted as a significant positive move on the Prime Minister's behalf.

While not disputing that the Governor-General had no discretion to reject advice from a Prime Minister with a majority in the House of Representatives to prorogue the parliament to recall it, some scholars (citing a Canadian controversy in 2008-2009) argued that it could be justified for a Governor-General to reject advice from a Prime Minister who had lost his or her majority to prorogue parliament for the purpose of avoiding its sitting (a very different case from the 2016 instance on which Prime Minister Turnbull gave advice,

---

[13] For the sake of transparency, I should acknowledge that I served as Senior Adviser to the Attorney-General and Leader of the Government in the Senate throughout the 2016 events mentioned here.

supported by Attorney-General Brandis).

The prorogation brought one session of the parliament to a close, and, as is established practice, the Governor-General opened the new session of the parliament with a speech prepared by the government outlining why the parliament had been called together. The Senate quickly again rejected the key employment legislation which the government put before it. After the parliament had voted interim Supply to fund the administration of government through the election period, and the government had brought down its 2016-2017 Budget, the Prime Minister advised the Governor-General to dissolve both houses of parliament under the provisions of the Constitution (section 57) for resolving deadlocks between the houses. His advice was supported by detailed confirmation by the Attorney-General that the relevant bills had been twice rejected by the Senate within the terms of section 57. The Governor-General naturally accepted the Prime Minister's advice. Both houses of parliament were dissolved simultaneously on 9 May 2016. This was the seventh "double dissolution" in Australian history, the earlier ones being in 1914, 1951, 1974, 1975, 1983, and 1987. After some risk of a hung parliament, Mr Turnbull won the 2 July election, but faces another complex Senate.

The events of 2016 again reflect the constitutional role of the Governor-General, and the conventions by which that role is fulfilled – and, far from the first time, how often that role and those conventions and their history are little known. I hope that this book makes some contribution to filling that gap.

2

CONSTITUTIONAL CONVENTIONS AND RESPONSIBLE GOVERNMENT

"Constitutional conventions"
in Brian Galligan & Winsome Roberts (eds)
The Oxford Companion to Australian Politics
Oxford University Press, 2007

The term "constitutional conventions" is used in two different senses: a gathering at which constitutional issues are discussed, and a constitutional rule based on practice. Constitutional conventions of the latter kind are generally understood to be rules of the Constitution, not found in the written Constitution, which are accepted as binding but are not legally enforceable. For example, the rules of ministerial responsibility to parliament – including the principle that who governs is ordinarily determined by who in the judgment of the Governor-General can best command the confidence of the lower house of parliament – are not explicitly spelt out in the Commonwealth Constitution.[1] Constitutional conventions are central to the operation of the Commonwealth and state constitutions and to the Australian system of government.

When the Commonwealth Constitution was framed in the 1890s, important provisions derived from the British system of parliamentary government were, as in the United Kingdom and in the Australian colonial constitutions, left uncodified. It was understood that the Constitution would be read in the light of conventions, without which it could not function. This also gave scope for the conventions to evolve further in practice. The conventions about the relationship of the Australian Commonwealth and states with the British government, and also the relationship between the Queen and her vice-regal representatives and governments in Australia, are of great historical

---

[1] [That is, the Constitution of the Commonwealth of Australia.]

importance, and have changed very significantly since federation as part of the evolution of Australian independence: for example, the appointment of the Governor-General (and, much later, state Governors) being made on Australian rather than British ministerial advice.

In the early decades after federation, a succession of British Governors-General sought the advice of Australian High Court judges on how to exercise their powers consistent with the law and conventions of the Constitution. The appropriate source of such advice has been a matter of controversy since the 1975 constitutional crisis.

The most fundamental constitutional conventions relate to the role of the Crown, including the dissolution of parliament, the appointment and removal of ministers, and acceptance of advice on other matters, and the collective and individual responsibilities of ministers to parliament. However, conventions relate also to other areas: for example, what powers the Senate will not exercise; how parliament will transact its business; the notion of caretaker governments; the independence of the judiciary from the executive and legislative branches; and the relations between public servants, government, and parliament. These conventions relate largely to the form and rules of political accountability.

The identification of conventions is based on precedent and practice and other evidence that a constitutional practice based on a clear constitutional principle is generally accepted as being binding. It may be that the stronger the principle and the clearer the agreement of the actors, the less the need for precedent. The recognition of conventions is itself a matter of convention or practice. While it is possible to state a number of conventions that are uncontentious, from time to time political controversies highlight the uncertainty surrounding conventions: how to identify whether or not a convention exists and in what form, the specific application and limit of a general rule, how conventions may be created (for example, by agreement, without precedent), how conventions may change, the effect of a breach of convention, and their legal standing. Conventions belong in the territory between legal rules, moral principles, and political practices. They vary greatly in strength.

Constitutional conventions were especially important in the constitutional crisis of 1975, debate about which showed much disagreement concerning the existence of conventions and their application. Was there or was there not a convention that a state parliament replace a senator who left office during his or her term – i.e., fill a casual vacancy – with a member of, arguably the nominee of, the political party from which the departing senator had come?

In 1975 the parliament of New South Wales replaced a Labor senator, Lionel Murphy, who resigned to go the High Court, with an Independent, and the Queensland parliament replaced a deceased Labor senator with a person who was [hitherto] a member of the Labor Party but hostile to the federal Labor government. The convention was said to be based on an agreement between state Premiers and the Prime Minister in 1951 that Senate vacancies would be filled from the same party, and invariable practice following the introduction of proportional representation in Senate elections in 1949. To the contrary, it was said that, however frequent the practice, this did not create a binding convention, and, by some, that exceptional circumstances in 1975 warranted the action taken.

It was argued that there was a convention, operative since federation, that the Senate not deny Supply – refuse to pass bills appropriating money – and that to do so undermined the principle that the government with a majority in the lower house be able to govern. Against this, it was asserted that the Constitution gave the Senate such power, that non-exercise of a power does not create a convention that it may not be exercised, and that it was intended by the framers of the Constitution that the Senate be able to force governments to an election through the exercise of such a power. This power was said to have been recognised by many constitutional writers and politicians, including Gough Whitlam, when the Labor opposition sought to force the Gorton government to an election in 1970, and in 1974, when the Senate did force an election by delaying the passage of appropriation bills.

Another matter of dispute was the existence or otherwise of a convention that a government unable to secure Supply from the parliament – whether by vote of the lower or upper house – should resign or go to an election. This convention was said to have been established in a succession of struggles between governments and parliament over centuries, to have been understood by the drafters of the Constitution, and to have been reflected in subsequent writings and parliamentary debates. The convention was claimed to be essential to uphold the accountability of government to the parliament, through the parliament's capacity to deny the government the money needed to govern. The counter-argument was that allowing an upper house to force a government to an election by denying it Supply would undermine the practice, or convention, that who governs is determined by who has the confidence of the lower – not the upper – house of parliament.

It was variously argued that the dismissal by the Governor-General, Sir

John Kerr, of the Prime Minister, Gough Whitlam, because of his refusal to advise an election for the House of Representatives after the Senate had maintained its denial of Supply, was consistent with and required by − or conversely, contrary to − constitutional conventions. Supporters of Sir John Kerr's action argued that, although by convention the Governor-General ordinarily acts only on the advice of ministers, both the text and conventions of the Constitution recognise the existence of certain "reserve powers" of the Crown, including a reserve power to dismiss the Prime Minister if this was required to uphold the Constitution. Opponents argued the primacy of the convention that the Governor-General act only on ministerial advice and that there were no reserve powers, or that there were reserve powers but that the action of the Governor-General in this case exceeded their boundaries, or was unwarranted or unwise.

When the House of Representatives expressed lack of confidence in the government led by the new Prime Minister, Malcolm Fraser, it was said that convention required him to resign as Prime Minister. Against this, it was claimed that the convention recognises advising an election as an appropriate response to defeat in the lower house, and that Mr Fraser had, in these exceptional circumstances, already given such advice. It was generally agreed that there was a convention that the Governor-General could not dissolve parliament and call an election other than on ministerial advice; he accepted the advice of Mr Fraser to do this.

Debate about constitutional conventions in the light of the events of 1975 raged for many years afterwards, with particular emphasis on the conventions of responsible government (a government responsible to parliament), and the reserve powers of the Crown. The claimed convention on casual Senate vacancies was codified in a constitutional amendment, approved by referendum, in 1977.

Advocates of codification of conventions argue that this will give greater certainty to all actors about the rules governing their behaviour; that some of the matters now subject to convention are too important to be left uncodified; and that codification will reduce the extent of controversy about alleged breaches of convention. Opponents of codification argue that codification will diminish the flexibility for conventions to evolve as circumstances change; will highlight rather than reduce areas of disagreement; and cannot cover all contingencies.

The scholarly study of constitutional conventions remains underdeveloped in Australia. To it must be brought the skills of the political scientist, the lawyer, the philosopher, and the historian.

~

Conventions of the Australian Constitution: questions on their nature and content
1998

Debate in the 1990s on proposed changes to the Australian Constitution, most especially the republic/monarchy debate, has (like the 1975 crisis before it) brought attention to the fact that so much of the operation of the Australian constitutional system depends on conventions rather than, or as well as, the actual text of the Constitution itself. The principles that who governs is determined by who commands the confidence of the House of Representatives, that the Governor-General must (at least almost always) act on the advice of ministers, that there are nonetheless certain limited "reserve powers", and even the existence of the office of Prime Minister, all essentially depend on conventions, and not principally on the text of the Constitution. As is well known, the Constitution itself does not even mention the Prime Minister. Present debate on constitutional change, at a crucial time in Australia's constitutional history, makes it all the more important that the conventions in these and other areas are widely understood.

For example, Mr Keating's 1995 proposal for a republic was that "the reserve powers currently possessed by the Governor-General would remain with the President, and the Constitution would provide that the constitutional conventions governing the exercise of these powers would continue, but the conventions would not be spelt out". In other words, this proposal is simply to adopt in a republican constitution the conventions relating to the reserve powers of the Governor-General as they have hitherto been. But what are these conventions? There is disagreement about this, both as to major issues of principle and as to details (e.g., under what circumstance, if any, a Governor-General would be entitled and right to reject a Prime Minister's advice to dissolve the House of Representatives). It is in part because there is such controversy about what the conventions are, as well as to what they should be, that it is proposed not to codify the powers of a President. The deliberations of the 1998 Constitutional Convention reflected uncertainty about what the conventions are, and widespread desire for some clarification and perhaps some degree of codification, but awareness also of the difficulty of this, especially on the reserve powers.

Given the importance of conventions to the working of the Australian Constitution, it is a surprising and significant omission that – although there has been valuable writing on certain aspects – there is no authoritative volume or standard reference work in existence on the conventions of the Australian Constitution. Such a rigorous and thorough study of the conventions of the Australian Constitution would clearly be of great value, both to scholarly study and to public debate, and for the future operation of the Australian Constitution.[2]

As Geoffrey Marshall has written, the idea of "conventions" has "a tangled history", and it is a "difficult" idea "whose general character has been, and still is, in dispute".[3] Marshall also identified important "cases in which it cannot be clearly stated what the conventions are, or cases in which the relevant conventions are conflicting or controversial".[4] Australian writings and public debate, especially since 1975, also reflect the fact that both the *nature* of constitutional conventions and their *content* are in dispute.

Sir Kenneth Wheare defined a "constitutional convention" as "a binding rule, a rule of behaviour accepted as obligatory by those concerned in the working of the constitution".[5] It is customary to distinguish conventions, which are usually said to be unenforceable in the courts, from law. Conventions generally arise from sustained practice – precedent – underpinned by constitutional principle. They do not arise from legislative or judicial action. They develop – harden – over time, developing from being merely current practice into being in some sense a rule of the Constitution. So, for example, the rule that (with the exception of "reserve powers") the Crown acts on, and only on, the advice of incumbent ministers hardened during the second half of the 19th century and the early 20th century into a "convention". Constitutional conventions are commonly said to be necessary to the working of constitutions; to amend, limit, or even prevent the exercise by their legal holders of powers created by law; to be often uncertain in content; to change over time; and to have a

---

[2] [Subsequent work by writers such as Brian Galligan, Anne Twomey, and Ian Killey has made useful contributions. See, e.g., Brian Galligan & Scott Brenton (eds), *Constitutional Conventions in Westminster Systems*, Cambridge University Press, 2015.]

[3] Geoffrey Marshall, *Constitutional Conventions: The Rules and Forms of Political Accountability*, Oxford University Press, 1984, Preface.

[4] Ibid., pp. 3-4.

[5] Kenneth Wheare, *Modern Constitutions*, Oxford University Press, London, 1951, p. 179.

hierarchy of importance, some being fundamental and others not.

In considering *the nature of conventions*, it is necessary to consider such questions as these:

- What is a "constitutional convention"? What is the distinction between "usage", "convention", and "law"?

- Perhaps most importantly, what are the criteria by which we can determine whether a constitutional convention exists, and what the convention actually is?

- Closely related to that: how do conventions come into existence? What extent of precedent, of behaviour showing acceptance of the binding nature of a norm, or of "authoritative" statements declaring it so, is necessary for a usage to become a convention?

- How, if at all, can conventions come into existence with immediate effect through the agreement of constitutional players? What degree of agreement, amongst what players, is necessary? Is it necessary that an agreement be supported by precedents before a convention can be said to have been created?

- Why is there so much controversy about the existence, or terms, of so many conventions?

- How do conventions change? Opponents of codifying conventions often point to the benefits of allowing conventions to evolve to meet changing circumstances. Is this what conventions do? How great is the benefit of this flexibility?

- What is it that makes conventions, which are not law and are not usually enforceable in the courts, nonetheless "binding"? What do we mean when we describe them as "binding"? What sanctions do, or can, or should, flow from a convention being breached?

- Why do people obey conventions? Why do they break them?

- What is the legitimacy of conventions which (as many do) alter or even nullify the operation of a provision of a constitution which may (as in the Australian case) have the legitimacy of popular endorsement?

- Is it really the case, as some authors claim, that the fundamental purpose of conventions is to give effect to the will of the people?

- What are the effects on conventions themselves of being breached? Does the breaching of a convention destroy it as a convention, or amend it, meaning that the convention may be regarded as still existing but as not applying in the particular category of circumstances in which it was breached, or does the convention still exist, broken but still binding for the future?

- If an action is contrary to a convention of the constitution, but not to the literal text, then is it to be regarded as "constitutional" or as "unconstitutional"? What do we mean by describing actions in those terms? Do we need the distinction used by, for example, the Supreme Court of Canada in the 1982 patriation case, between actions which are "unconstitutional in the conventional sense" and those which are unconstitutional in the legal sense?

- What is the effect on a convention of being recognised or declared (as some have been) by courts? Does this make them (as Wheare suggested) in some sense "law", or even in some way "enforceable"? Does it increase the obligation on parties to observe the convention?

- Under what circumstances should courts recognise or declare constitutional conventions?

- Some broader questions also arise: What is the importance of conventions to the Constitution, and to the political process generally? What are the arguments for, and against, codification of conventions, and how persuasive are they?

Geoffrey Sawer contended that "it may not be possible to develop any general theory of 'conventions'",[6] and this may be true. But it is surely possible to give more sustained and rigorous attention to such question than they have, for the most part, hitherto had. Moreover, much of the most influential writing on conventions is in the British tradition of analysis of constitutional conventions, derived from Freeman and Dicey in the late 19th century, and developed through the work of, for example, Anson, Jennings, Wheare (an Australian working in Britain), Marshall and Moodie, and most recently Bogdanor. In considering basic questions on the nature of conventions, it is necessary to consider the extent to which the British tradition of analysis needs to be modified to take account of the different Australian context. To what extent is Dicey's doctrine of constitutional conventions, contrasted sharply with constitutional law, still appropriate (if it ever was) in understanding the Australian Constitution? Given that key parts of the text of the Australian

---

[6] Geoffrey Sawer, *Federation Under Strain*, Melbourne University Press, Melbourne, 1977, p. 178.

Constitution, for example provisions relating to the Executive Council and to the powers of the Governor-General, can only be understood by reference to constitutional conventions, can a clear distinction in fact be sustained between "law" and "conventions"? Or, on the other hand, is it the case (as Sawer suggested[7]) that in practice the notion of "constitutionality" is broader in Britain than in Australia – that in Australia, "constitutionality" is really only measured by law, and that here, unlike in Britain, a matter contrary to constitutional convention but not to actual written text will commonly not be regarded as "unconstitutional"?

In considering *the content (or meaning) of the conventions of the Australian constitution*, it is necessary to consider such topics as these:

- The fact that the authors of the Australian Constitution deliberately wrote it as a document codified in many respects – e.g., in setting out the federal system – but leaving another fundamental principle, responsible government, very incompletely codified and to a considerable degree a matter of convention.

- Very importantly, but controversially, it is necessary to determine the *form* of responsible government which the conventions of the Australian Constitution (together with its text) created. This involves setting out:

- The key conventions of the *collective* responsibility of a government to parliament. This includes such questions – interconnected with the reserve powers – as, for example, how long a Prime Minister who may have lost the confidence of the House of Representatives can avoid testing that, and whether such a Prime Minister is entitled to a dissolution.

- The key conventions of the *individual* responsibility of ministers to parliament. For example, what, if anything, does convention require of a minister who is censured by one or other house of parliament? Is it possible to discern clear conventions as to when a minister must resign if major errors are made by his or her department, or his or her office, or him or herself?

- In making government responsible to parliament, how the conventions deal with the power of the Senate to deny Supply to a government with a majority in the House of Representatives. Does such denial have no effect on the right of such a government to govern, or does a government unable to get Supply through

[7] Ibid., pp. 177-8.

the Senate have an obligation to resign or call an election for the House of Representatives?

- Whether there was in, or before, 1974-1975 a convention that the Senate not deny Supply to a government holding the confidence of the House of Representatives; and if there was, what the effect was on that convention of the Senate's action in 1974-1975. What convention, if any, exists now?

- What are the matters on which the Governor-General must act on, and neither without nor contrary to, ministerial advice?

- Are there "reserve powers", matters on which the Governor-General must exercise his or her discretion, and may act contrary to or without ministerial advice?

- If there are reserve powers, and if they are as commonly stated, then under what circumstances the Governor-General may or should refuse advice to dissolve the House of Representatives (as in 1904, 1905, and 1909) or, under section 57, both houses; or dismiss a Prime Minister. By what conventions should a Governor-General be guided in commissioning a Prime Minister, say, in a hung parliament, or after the death in office of a Prime Minister (as in 1939, 1945, and 1967)?

- Under what circumstances may the Governor-General require demonstration that the Prime Minister commands the confidence of the House of Representatives, or that advice tendered to him represents the view of the cabinet?

- The circumstances under which the exercise of a power by a Governor-General can be subject to judicial review. Does the traditional principle that exercise of the reserve powers is non-justiciable still hold?

- The conventions regulating the appointment and removal of a Governor-General.

- Whether there was in, or before, 1975 a convention that a casual vacancy in the Senate be filled by a member of the same party as the deceased or resigning senator.[8] If there was such a convention, what effect was there on it of its being breached, twice, in 1975? This issue was resolved by a constitutional amendment in 1977.

- The role of changing conventions in the evolution of Australian independence. This can be seen, for example, in changing

---

[8] Sawer and Cooray, e.g., say there was; Lumb, e.g., that there was not.

conventions within the (British) Commonwealth on the monarch's disallowance of legislation, and on the roles, powers, and appointment of Governors-General.

There are, of course, other aspects of the Australian political process in which conventions are important. For example, there are conventions on the role of the Speaker in the House of Representatives and the President of the Senate, or governing the conduct of public servants called to give evidence to parliamentary committees, or concerning appointments to public authorities. There are, or are claimed to be, conventions relating to the calling of half-Senate elections, and to the reservation and disallowance of legislation; and much else besides.

Conventions need to be analysed through a thorough study of precedents, and of discussions of these issues by political actors and authorities, at least from the time of the federation convention debates of the 1890s, and, as appropriate, earlier. The key question – what are the present conventions? – usually needs to be answered by reference to how the conventions stood at federation, how they evolved since, how they may be evolving now, and (as appropriate) how it would be good to see them develop in future.

It is necessary to consider Australian constitutional conventions in international comparative perspective – most importantly, comparing Australia's conventions with those of other "Westminster" systems, such as the U.K., Canada, and New Zealand, whose own conventions and constitutional experience are at times a guide to Australia's conventions. It can also be helpful to compare Australian conventions with practice in some other countries – for example, how deadlock between the U.S. Congress and President over a budget ("closing down the federal government") compares in constitutional significance and effect with deadlock on Supply between the Australian Senate and House of Representatives. Just as there are conventions on the exercise of executive power in the Australian Constitution, so in the U.S. there are conventions on this which, in the words of William Howard Taft, President and later Chief Justice, seem "almost to amend the Constitution".[9] In considering the role of the Governor-General in a hung parliament (e.g., on whom to commission as Prime Minister, or how to react to a request for an election), the conventions established in various western European countries, monarchies and republics alike, with long experience of minority or coalition

[9] Quoted from Louis Fisher, *Constitutional Conflicts between Congress and the President*, Princeton University Press, 1985, p. 24.

governments can provide relevant comparisons.

There has been an increasing amount written on the conventions of the Australian Constitution, especially since the 1975 crisis. Some of this valuable work has been in the context of discussion of proposed constitutional reforms.[10] To take an important aspect, the literature on the reserve powers still "reveals", as George Winterton wrote, "considerable disagreement concerning their scope and the merits or demerits of particular regal or viceregal actions or threatened actions".[11] A disappointing amount of what has been written about various conventions, or supposed conventions, has not been based on a close and detailed reading of the full range of past precedents and authorities, or on clear, precise conceptual analysis. Much discussion of conventions is in passing, in the midst of discussion of other issues. Through sustained analysis, conceptual rigour, and thoroughness of historical research, it may be possible for scholars in future to settle some questions conclusively, and to identify with clarity the grounds for disagreement on other questions.

Identifying with clarity what the conventions of the Australian Constitution are, or even calmly identifying what the lines of controversy are, surely contributes to public debate on Australia's constitutional future at a crucial time in our history. It also helps political and constitutional actors know what conduct is, and what is not, required by or consistent with the conventions of the Constitution. This is an issue which is of critical importance as Australia debates the question of the powers appropriate to an Australian president, and the extent to which (if at all) those powers should be codified. Authoritative discussion of this could be especially helpful in the midst of any future constitutional crises. Simply to reduce what the Republic Advisory Committee called the "significant degree of uncertainty at the edges"[12] would be a valuable advance.

---

[10] See, e.g., Republic Advisory Committee, *An Australian Republic: The Options*, AGPS, Canberra, 1993, vol. 2, appendices 5-7.

[11] George Winterton, *Parliament, the Executive and the Governor-General*, Melbourne University Press, Melbourne, 1983, p. 150.

[12] Republic Advisory Committee, *An Australian Republic: The Options*, AGPS, Canberra, 1993, vol. 1, p. 28.

Conventions of responsible government: a hung parliament

The conventions of responsible government include conventions governing whom the Queen in Britain or the Governor-General in Australia commissions to be Prime Minister in a parliament in which no party or pre-existing coalition has a majority, and how the Queen or Governor-General should respond to requests for dissolution of a hung parliament. These issues have arisen for time to time in Australia since federation and were very much under discussion in Britain in the 1980s and 1990s when hung parliaments were frequently anticipated (but never eventuated in those decades). In 2010, elections in both Britain and Australia produced hung parliaments, resolved in Britain by formation of a coalition government and in Australia by a minority government governing with the support of the Green and Independent members. The two short pieces below – a letter to *The Times* during misplaced anticipation of a hung parliament coming out of the 1992 British elections, and an effort in 1986 to list conventions or principles related to the formation of a government in a hung parliament – were discussions of these issues in the British context in the 1980s and 1990s. The basic points also apply in Australia.

~

Letter to the Editor, The Times
9 April 1992

Sir, It was surprising that Lord St John of Fawsley should end his otherwise excellent article (April 8) on the Queen's role in a hung parliament by envisaging no circumstance in which she should refuse an incumbent Prime Minister's request to dissolve the House of Commons.

On the contrary, if the Prime Minister had clearly lost the confidence of the Commons, for example in a vote on some vital issue, and it were clear beyond reasonable doubt (e.g., through a cast iron agreement between parties making up a majority) that someone else could command its confidence, then the Queen would be acting in accordance with constitutional principle and precedent to refuse a request for dissolution from the incumbent Prime Minister and, upon his resignation (which would naturally follow), to ask the leader who clearly had the confidence of the Commons to form a government.

A Prime Minister without the confidence of the Commons has no right to a dissolution (indeed, strictly speaking, no Prime Minister has a right to a dissolution); and a workable parliament that has rejected one Prime Minister but will clearly support, say, the leader of the Opposition, is entitled to continue.

Leaving aside the delayed dissolution of November 1910, the power of refusal of dissolution has not been exercised in Britain this century because the circumstances have not arisen where it should. They have arisen in some Commonwealth countries, where representatives of the Crown have, quite properly, exercised this power. For example, this has happened three times at the national level in Australia (1904, 1905, and 1909) before its then three-party system developed into (in effect) a two-party system.

For the Queen to refuse a dissolution in the circumstance described would not be partisan. No fair-minded person would imagine that it was. The earlier in a new parliament this situation arose, and the clearer the wish of the Commons to continue with a new Prime Minister, the stronger the case for refusing a dissolution would seem.

Nonetheless, whether the Queen granted or refused a request for dissolution in such circumstances, the risk of her being dragged into controversy would be unavoidable. When it is clear that another leader could command the confidence of the Commons, it would be better for a Prime Minister who had lost its confidence to resign rather than request a dissolution.

~

Some principles or conventions applicable to formation of a government in a hung parliament, 16 July 1986

1. The object is to find the leader best able to command the confidence of the House; but the means must ensure that the appearance and reality of the Crown's impartiality is not tarnished.
2. A Prime Minister losing her majority at an election may stay on to face the parliament unless another leader clearly has a majority, in which case the Prime Minister should resign and the other leader form a government.
3. The Prime Minister is entitled to seek to form a coalition or obtain sufficient parliamentary support to remain in office.
4. When a Prime Minister resigns, she offers the Queen no advice as to her successor. The Queen might choose to ask her opinion, but is not

bound by it. [Australian practice on this is more complex.]

5. When a Prime Minister resigns on defeat (either at the polls or in the House), the Queen may ask the leader of the largest party (or, where the Prime Minister's party is the largest party, the next largest party) to *try* and form a government, or *if* he can do so. Implicit in this is that such a government may be able to carry on with the confidence of the House for a reasonable period.

6. Alternatively, the Queen might *immediately* appoint the leader of the largest (or next largest) party as Prime Minister.

7. No leader assumes office if it is clear that he cannot command the confidence of the House and that someone else can. The Queen might discuss this with him.

8. Because every parliament must be given the chance to work, if it is clear at the outset of the new parliament that the Prime Minister does not have the confidence of the House but that an alternative government with the confidence of the House can be formed, a request for a dissolution from that Prime Minister should be rejected, and, upon the Prime Minister's resignation, the leader who can command the confidence of the House appointed.

9. This last principle also applies when a government that has been sustained by the House subsequently loses the confidence of the House and it is clear that an alternative government with the confidence of the House can be formed; however, after considering such factors as the duration of the present parliament and government, the Queen might grant such a request.

10. The Queen would be entitled to make clear to the person she is inviting to form a government that a dissolution request will not be granted.[13]

11. A new dissolution should only be granted at the outset of a new parliament if it is impossible to find a government that can command the confidence of the House (e.g., Newfoundland, 1972).

12. The Queen, directly or through her Private Secretary, may consult anyone she chooses as to how to proceed.

13. In the exercise of her "Bagehot rights", the Queen would be entitled to seek to dissuade a Prime Minister either from resigning at a particular moment or (more likely) pressing on the Queen a request for dissolution.

14. The Queen would be entitled, but not obliged, to call a conference of party leaders (and others) to resolve the question of who can command the confidence of the House.

---

[13] Precedents: U.K. 1916, Bonar Law; Australia 1918, Sir Harrison Moore's advice. On Bonar Law case, see Robert Blake, *The Unknown Prime Minister*, Eyre & Spottiswoode, London, 1955, pp. 334, 336.

Conventions of responsible government: ministerial resignations

The conventions and other practices relating to ministerial resignations are an important part of the workings of responsible government in a Westminster-style system. They relate to the individual and collective responsibility of ministers to parliament. Several of these conventions were discussed in a paper discussing ministerial resignations during the Queensland coalition crisis of 1983.[14] Following a split between the National and Liberal parties in the governing coalition, the Liberal ministers resigned, the National Party Premier (Joh Bjelke-Petersen) advised the Governor to reject their resignations, and the Governor accepted this advice. Some days later, the Liberal ministers resigned again, and their resignations were accepted. These events brought into focus, inter alia, the conventions relating to ministerial resignations, and specifically the relationship between ministers, the Premier, and the Crown in this context.[15]

From "The Politics of Ministerial Resignations: The Queensland Coalition Crisis of 1983"
D.A. Low (ed.), Constitutional Heads and Political Crises:
Commonwealth Episodes, 1945-85
Macmillan, 1988

Queensland inherited from Britain the institutions of the Crown and of responsible government. The Queen is Queen of Queensland, as well as of Australia. She is represented in Brisbane by the state Governor, who (prior to the *Australia Acts* of 1986) was appointed, and could only be dismissed, by the Queen on the advice of the British government. Normally, of course,

---

[14] For the sake of transparency, I should mention that I served as Research Assistant to the Leader of the Parliamentary Liberal Party in Queensland throughout these events.

[15] Also of interest may be "The Politics of Ministerial Resignations", Patrick Weller & Dean Jaensch (eds), *Responsible Government in Australia*, APSA/Drummond, 1980. Referring to the initially unexplained resignation of Eric Robinson as Minister for Finance in the Fraser government in 1979, and his reinstatement three days later, it demonstrates (contrary to claims widely made at the time) that neither precedent nor principle requires a minister to make a public explanation of their resignation; many ministers have resigned without a public explanation. It also shows that the announcement of many resignations has been delayed, and resignations have quite often been combined with appointment to another post, or been followed by later reinstatement to the ministry. It further shows the importance of careful study of history and principle in making claims about conventions.

this advice was really that of the Queensland Premier. However, in 1976, the British government declined to advise the Queen to re-appoint Sir Colin Hannah because in 1975 he had made partisan public remarks. Instead, the late Sir James Ramsay was appointed to be the new state Governor and he was in office during the 1983 crisis.[16]

There is little dispute that, after the coalition split, it was proper for the Governor to allow Mr Bjelke-Petersen to remain as Premier, at the head of a minority government, pending elections. Constitutionally, the most controversial aspect of this crisis was the Premier's advice to the Governor to reject the Liberal ministers' resignations. This can best be understood in the light of the following conventions, which are evident in the past practice of ministerial resignations in Britain, Australia, Canada, and comparable countries, and are reflected (though rarely made explicit) in writings on the Westminster system.

1. Formally, ministers are appointed by the Crown. The exact nature of this varies, of course, but in Queensland ministers are appointed by the Governor both as members of the Executive Council and as ministers. They hold office at the pleasure of the Crown, and so remain in office (legally bound to fulfil their ministerial responsibilities) until the "pleasure of the Governor" is that they should no longer hold office. That is, a resignation is not effective until it is accepted by the Governor. This is the formal, legal situation.[17] However, as in so many other contexts, the legal powers are, and should be, exercised in accordance with the conventions that have emerged from past practice. The following principles summarise some of these conventions.

2. Just as ministers are chosen by the Premier, so they resign by offering their resignation to the Premier;[18] this may be couched in terms of *offering* to resign or as actually doing so. This is reflected in all the cases listed under point 3. This principle was very clearly demonstrated in Canada in 1896 when seven members of Sir Mackenzie Bowell's cabinet tried to resign direct to the Governor-General, who replied that he could only receive such resignations through the Prime Minister.[19]

---

[16] [See also Anne Twomey, *The Chameleon Crown: The Queen and Her Australian Governors*, Federation Press, 2006.]

[17] See e.g., Sir Ivor Jennings, *Cabinet Government*, Cambridge University Press, 3rd ed., 1969, pp. 83, 88, 207. *Halsbury's Laws of England*, 4th ed., vol. 8, Butterworths, London, 1974, pp. 599-600. *Marks v. The Commonwealth* (1964) 111 CLR 549.

[18] A. Berriedale Keith, *The British Cabinet System*, Stevens, London, 1952, p. 83.

[19] J.R. Mallory, *The Structure of Canadian Government*, Macmillan, Toronto, 1971, p. 80; see also p. 85.

3. The Premier will either accept the resignation immediately (usually with a modicum of regret) or delay accepting it, perhaps while trying to persuade the minister not to go, or, as an element of that persuasion, telling the minister that the resignation is not accepted and that he should remain. British instances of such delay before acceptance of a resignation include – Lord Randolph Churchill's resignation, 1886; Joseph Chamberlain, 1903; and Augustine Birrell, 1916.[20] Instances of attempts at dissuasion, successful or not, include – the Duke of Devonshire, 1903 (temporarily successful); Beauchamp and Simon (successful), Burns and Morley (unsuccessful), 1914; Lloyd George, 1913, November 1915, April 1916 (all successful); Arthur Henderson, January and August 1916 (successful); Sir Oswald Mosley, 1930 (unsuccessful); Snowden, Samuel, and other Free Traders, January 1932 (successful); two junior ministers (Mr Dick Nugent and Lord Carrington) over the Crichel Down affair, 1954 (successful); Lord Carrington (unsuccessful), (Sir) John Nott (successful), 1982; and Leon Brittan, 1986 (unsuccessful). In 1946, Sir Ben Smith delayed his resignation for almost two months "in deference to the Prime Minister's wishes".[21] It has been widely suggested that Attlee should have rejected Dalton's resignation in 1947. It seems that several of George Brown's resignations in the 1960s were ignored by Harold Wilson, at least one was withdrawn after talks, and the last (unexpectedly) accepted.

In Canada in 1942, Mackenzie King sought to dissuade Ralston from resigning, and Ralston did not press his resignation. However, when King wished to expedite Ralston's departure from the government in 1944, he seems to have regarded Ralston's 1942 letter of resignation as not having been withdrawn and so open to acceptance by the Prime Minister at any time. King also believed that he had a right "not [to] accept some of the resignations of Ministers" (at least for a time).[22]

In 1902, the Premier of Victoria, Alexander Peacock, refused to accept the

---

[20] The reader can readily check these and other cases by referring to the biographies or autobiographies of the ministers and Prime Ministers involved, diaries (e.g., Lord Riddell, Richard Crossman), histories, and Hansards and newspapers of the time. See also: R.K. Alderman and J.A. Cross, *The Tactics of Resignations: a Study in British Cabinet Government*, Routledge and Kegan Paul, London, 1967. S.E. Finer, "The Individual Responsibility of Ministers", *Public Administration*, vol. 34, 1956. P.J. Madgwick, "Resignations", *Parliamentary Affairs*, vol. 20, 1966-1967. Don Markwell, "The Politics of Ministerial Resignations", in Patrick Weller & Dean Jaensch (eds), *Responsible Government in Australia*, Drummond, Melbourne, 1980.

[21] Finer, op. cit., p. 392.

[22] J.L. Granatstein, *Canada's War: The Politics of Mackenzie King's Government, 1939-1945*, Oxford University Press, Toronto, 1975, pp. 236-41, 353-6.

resignation of several of his ministers. In the same year but at the federal level, Alfred Deakin withdrew his resignation after concessions and a personal plea from Barton. When in 1903, C.C. Kingston wrote to Barton to resign, Barton asked him to reconsider; when Kingston insisted on resigning, Barton said, "I must reluctantly consent to your action".[23] When the Cabinet (to whom Prime Minister Harold Holt had referred it) decided in 1967 that Howson's resignation should be rejected, it was universally accepted that (in Sir Paul Hasluck's words) it was the Prime Minister "in whose hands these matters finally lie".[24] In October 1970, when he learnt that his then wife had appeared in an advertisement for Sheridan-brand sheets, Andrew Peacock offered his resignation to the Prime Minister, Mr (now Sir John) Gorton. Russell Schneider records:[25]

> Gorton, a knockabout chap at the best of times, laughed at the situation and when Peacock pressed the resignation called him a "bloody fool". But that night Peacock, enraged over the affair, humiliated and determined to quit the ministry, drafted his resignation and went back to his hotel for a near sleepless night. At 10am the next day, 21 October, Peacock handed a brief letter of resignation to Gorton and remained in his office discussing the situation for almost an hour. Gorton, amused and bemused, steadfastly refused to accept. Finally, after thrice offering to leave the ministry, Peacock agreed to withdraw his resignation.

4. The decision as to how to react to a minister's resignation is a *political* decision; for the composition of the government is a political matter for decision by the Premier. He might *consult* cabinet colleagues, and perhaps the Crown, but the decision as to how to react is his. The Crown has, in this as in all other matters, the rights Bagehot made famous – to be consulted, to encourage, and to warn. The Crown and the Premier might well discuss, at the initiative of either, the composition of the government and whether it would be desirable to discourage the resignation of a minister. It would not be improper for the Crown to discuss with a minister his intentions, and perhaps to discourage him from resigning. (When Malcolm Fraser resigned from the Australian cabinet in 1971, he spent an hour with the Governor-General, Sir Paul Hasluck, on the day of his resignation; it was reported that on the following day both the Prime Minister and Deputy Prime Minister tried unsuccessfully to have him withdraw his resignation.[26]) Discussions with

---

[23] *Commonwealth Parliamentary Debates: House of Representatives*, 24 July 1903, pp. 2590-1.
[24] Ibid., 8 November 1967, p. 2839.
[25] Russell Schneider, *The Colt from Kooyong*, Angus & Robertson, Sydney, 1981, pp. 48-9.
[26] *Sydney Morning Herald*, 9 & 10 March 1971.

the Crown affect neither the minister's right to proceed with and even insist on his resignation, nor the fact that it is for the Premier to decide whether or not to accept the resignation. The wishes of the Crown are not binding in character, and there is no disrespect to the Crown in a minister proceeding with a resignation the Crown has discouraged: for example, Lloyd George still intended to resign from Asquith's cabinet in April 1916 despite efforts of Lord Stamfordham, the King's Private Secretary, to persuade him to stay (he remained in the cabinet only after concessions were made).[27]

5. It is taken for granted in all discussions of ministerial responsibility and related matters that ministers have a *right* to resign; no one imagines that members of parliament can be required – conscripted – to be ministers against their will. Prime Ministers may seek to dissuade them from going, and as part of that might initially refuse to accept their resignations, but if the minister insists on resigning, Prime Ministers accept that. This is evident in some of the exchanges referred to in this chapter. Sir George Grey in 1866,[28] Joseph Chamberlain in 1903,[29] Lloyd George in 1915[30] and, it seems, many other ministers have believed that they were entitled to *insist* on resigning. Lord Derby wrote to Lloyd George in 1918:[31]

> A man in office is not only entitled, but it is his duty, to resign if he thinks that the Government to which he belongs is doing something which he disapproves and which in his opinion is detrimental to the best interests of the Nation.

Lord Salisbury put the convention of collective responsibility thus:[32]

> For all that passes in Cabinet each member of it *who does not resign* is absolutely and irretrievably responsible, and has no right afterwards to say that he agreed in one case to a compromise, while in another he was persuaded by his colleagues.

Without a *right* to resign, this convention is unworkable. Dr Eugene Forsey, the great Canadian constitutionalist, has written that in the Canadian crisis of 1944, Mackenzie King propounded the "highly original" theory that "no minister is entitled to resign from the Cabinet 'in circumstances where

[27] See, esp., *Lord Riddell's War Diary 1914-1918*, Ivor Nicholson & Watson, London, 1933, pp. 174-5.

[28] *Letters of Queen Victoria 1837-1861*, vol. 3, John Murray, London, 1907, pp. 94-5.

[29] Julian Amery, *The Life of Joseph Chamberlain*, vol. 5, Macmillan, London, 1969, p. 403.

[30] *Lord Riddell's War Diary*, op. cit., p. 136.

[31] Quoted from Lord Beaverbrook, *Men and Power 1917-1918*, Collins, London, 1956, p. 374.

[32] Quoted from Madgwick, op. cit., pp. 59-60; emphasis added.

as a consequence of [his] action the whole structure is almost certain to collapse,' unless he is prepared to accept the premiership himself." Dr Forsey continued:[33]

> Colonel Ralston's comment was: 'That is the strangest doctrine I have ever heard enunciated in this House. If I were not respectful of the Prime Minister, I would call it just plain nonsense.' Nonsense it is. Did anyone ever hear of this theory when Stanley and Buccleuch resigned in 1846, or Russell in 1855, or Cranborne in 1867, or Chamberlain and Trevelyan in March 1886, or Churchill in December 1886, or Chamberlain, Ritchie, Hamilton, and Devonshire in 1903, or Mr Bevan a few months ago [1951]? If any British Prime Minister had talked in this vein, people would have thought he had taken leave of his senses.

Windeyer J in *Marks v The Commonwealth*[34] concluded from his analysis of offices held "at the pleasure of the Crown" that "although at common law the resignation of an office was only complete in law when it was by acceptance assented to, yet in practice acceptance of a surrender or resignation in whatever form it was made was a formality that was sometimes deferred but not refused". As Windeyer also said, the "principle ... that a man must remain at his post until relieved ... is not incompatible with a right to be relieved".[35]

6. If the Prime Minister wishes not to accept a resignation, he does not place the minister's resignation before the Crown; that is, he gives the Crown no advice at all, because it is not for the Crown, but for the Prime Minister, to decide whether or not to accept a resignation.

7. These conventions apply as fully in the case of ministers resigning on the withdrawal of their party from a coalition government as on any other occasion. Resignations have been accepted in the past on the break-up of a coalition: for example, in the 1932 British case already mentioned; when "at the end of the First World War ... the Labour Party instructed its members to withdraw from the Coalition Government" in Britain;[36] when the Country Party under Earle Page refused to serve under Menzies in Canberra in 1939; when the Victorian coalition broke on the withdrawal of Country Party ministers in 1935; and so on.

8. The conventions are, of course, somewhat different when it is the Prime Minister himself or herself resigning. Whereas the resignations of other ministers are resignations of individuals from the Prime Minister's

[33] Eugene Forsey, *Freedom and Order*, The Carleton Library, Toronto, 1974, p. 90.

[34] *Marks v The Commonwealth* (1964) 111 CLR 549 at 590.

[35] At 579.

[36] Alderman & Cross, op. cit., p. 38.

government, the resignation of the Prime Minister is the resignation of the entire government. Where other ministers tender their resignations to the Prime Minister, the Prime Minister submits his resignation to the Crown. Like the Prime Minister with individual ministers, the Crown might well ask the Prime Minister to delay his resignation or even not to resign at all (but either stay in office or advise dissolution of the House depending on the circumstances). If the Prime Minister insists on resigning the Crown accepts this. There is no suggestion that insisting on such a resignation, contrary to the wishes of the monarch or her representative, is disrespectful to the Crown. For instance – in 1855, Lord Aberdeen's government withdrew its resignation at Queen Victoria's request; in 1886, Lord Russell's government left office despite the Queen's wish that they stay; in 1905, Balfour resigned against the King's wish; in 1908, Campbell-Bannerman (on his deathbed) resigned earlier than the King wished; after the December 1923 election, Baldwin complied with the King's request that he not resign immediately but face the new parliament (Vernon Bogdanor has rightly deprecated the suggestion that the King might have *rejected* such a resignation);[37] in August 1931, the King three times dissuaded Ramsay MacDonald from resigning, though, as Kenneth Rose writes, "had MacDonald persisted in his wish to resign, the King could not have prevented him".[38]

---

[37] Vernon Bogdanor, *Multi-party politics and the Constitution*, Cambridge University Press, Cambridge, 1983, p. 97.

[38] Kenneth Rose, *King George V*, Weidenfeld & Nicolson, London, 1983, p. 378.

3

THE CROWN AND AUSTRALIA (1987)

Trevor Reese Memorial Lecture
Australian Studies Centre, Institute of Commonwealth Studies
University of London
20 January 1987[1]

In the mid-1960s, the Commonwealth of Nations seemed to many to be lurching from crisis to crisis, mainly – then as now – over Southern Africa. It was in this climate of crisis as usual that in 1965, Trevor Reese wrote an article entitled "Keeping Calm about the Commonwealth".[2] He spoke of the gradual but spontaneous evolution of the Commonwealth and of its contemporary value, and argued that reports of its death, like Mark Twain's, were premature; but that, because it "functions ... as a flexible and informal system of co-operation between States", little, if anything, was to be gained from artificial schemes to bolster it. We should, in short, keep calm about the Commonwealth.

The theme of this lecture in tribute to Trevor Reese is very similar. The link between the Crown and Australia – which plays some part in the bonds of Commonwealth – has evolved over time, adjusting to Australia's changing circumstances, and developing in this 20th century an increasingly Australian identity as Australia has developed as a nation. The monarchy – a constitutional monarchy – plays a valuable role in the Australian constitutional system. It is likely to be with us for many years to come. And I shall argue that, with Australia's Constitution currently being reviewed, there are some changes that could sensibly be made to the constitutional provisions relating to the Crown, but these are neither many nor especially important. In short, I shall

---

[1] Published as *The Crown and Australia (The Trevor Reese Memorial Lecture, 1987)*, University of London, 1987.

[2] Trevor Reese, "Keeping Calm About the Commonwealth", *International Affairs*, vol. 41, no. 3, 1965.

suggest that Australians should keep calm about the Crown and calm about their Constitution.

Having said something more of Trevor Reese, I should like, first, to give some overview of the evolution of the links between the Crown and Australia, making some reference to republicanism; secondly, to touch on the present constitutional role of the Crown in Australia; and, thirdly, to say something of how it might – and should – develop.

I do not assume that Trevor Reese would necessarily agree with all that I shall argue. But I hope, at least, that he would think some discussion of these issues worth undertaking. Trevor Reese lived in Australia for what he called "six happy years", 1956-1962.[3] In 1964, his short but masterly political history of *Australia in the Twentieth Century* was published. It is an incisive, concise, measured account, beautifully written, and marked by the dry wit that sparkles in so much of Trevor Reese's writings.

I cannot speak with first-hand knowledge of the quiet, warm-hearted, considerate man to whom others have paid such warm tributes at other times. But anyone who reads Trevor Reese's writings will see that he had "that vital intangible, a scholar's instinct", as his mentor, Professor Gerald Graham, put it in his tribute in the *Journal of Imperial and Commonwealth History*,[4] of which Trevor Reese was founder-editor. He applied this scholar's instinct to the close and thorough study of a number of aspects of Commonwealth history – British imperial policy in the 18th century in the American colony of Georgia; the 19th and 20th century evolution of the Empire and Commonwealth as reflected in the history of the Royal Commonwealth Society; and Australia in the 20th century, including what Robert O'Neill[5] has called a "classic" study of Australia's and New Zealand's relations with the United States of America as they developed from the Second World War.

Australia's links with the British Crown began with Captain Cook. Trevor Reese wrote that during Cook's journey of discovery, "the English colours were displayed ashore and on a tree an inscription carved to signify formal annexation, consent to which the natives were assumed to have granted by

---

[3] Trevor Reese, *Australia in the Twentieth Century: A Short Political Guide*, Pall Mall Press, London, 1964, p. 9.

[4] Gerald Graham, *Journal of Imperial and Commonwealth History*, vol. 5, no. 1, 1976, p. 3.

[5] R.J. O'Neill, *Australia, Britain, and International Security: Retrospect and Prospect (The Trevor Reese Memorial Lecture, 1985)*, University of London, 1985, p. 2.

their absence".[6] And the historian of colonial Georgia elsewhere noted that "the principal social motive" for the foundation both of Georgia in 1732 and of the penal settlement in New South Wales in 1788 "was clearly one of convenience in enabling the mother-country to rid herself of persons she did not want".[7]

It is from these humble origins that the history of the Crown and Australia begins. It is a story of the development of penal colonies governed by all-powerful Governors into the increasingly self-governing colonies of the mid-19th century; the federation in 1901 of these colonies into a Commonwealth of Australia "under the Crown", with the monarch represented in that Commonwealth by a Governor-General, while retaining the six state Governors; and the evolution of the office of Governor-General to one much more distinctly Australian.

The government of the first British settlement "was vested entirely in the governor, subject to the final, though distant, control of a minister in the English government in London". "The main problem was to keep the convicts, soldiers and officials alive" and, later, sober.[8] It was not all smooth going, and not just because so many of the inhabitants were somewhat reluctant to be there. The efforts of Governor Bligh "to suppress the use of spirits as the only acceptable medium of exchange ... eventually led", on the twentieth anniversary of settlement, 26 January 1808, to the *coup d'état* we remember as the "Rum Rebellion".[9] One — admittedly partisan — witness recorded that when the little army from the New South Wales Corps marched to Government House to depose the Governor, "his unfortunate Excellency (the representative of Majesty) was found beneath a bed upstairs, to which he had flown for refuge".[10] (This point has, however, been much disputed.)

Bligh's chief adversary, John Macarthur, assailed him as a "tyrant", and many of the early Governors, including the great Macquarie, were, rightly or wrongly, so assailed. This had much to do with the sides the Governors took on local issues, not least the rights of ex-convicts. From 1823, a nominated

---

[6] Trevor Reese, *The History of the Royal Commonwealth Society, 1868-1968*, Oxford University Press, London, 1968, p. 4.

[7] Trevor Reese, *Colonial Georgia: A Study in British Imperial Policy in the Eighteenth Century*, University of Georgia Press, Athens, Georgia, 1963, pp. 133-4.

[8] Gordon Greenwood (ed.), *Australia: A Social and Political History*, Angus & Robertson, Sydney, 1955, pp. 7, 1.

[9] Ibid., p. 8.

[10] Quoted from Alan Birch & David Macmillan, *The Sydney Scene 1788-1960*, Melbourne University Press, 1962, p. 43.

legislative council shared responsibility with the Governor for legislation. But it did not control the Executive Council, which comprised senior government officials appointed by the Governor and the British Colonial Secretary. Little by little the powers of the Governor were reduced. In 1842, the N.S.W. Legislative Council gained elected members, though with a high franchise qualification.

The clamour for more representative institutions, for self-government, and for the executive government to be responsible to the legislature, became louder and louder, culminating in 1850 in the grant of self-government to the four eastern colonies of N.S.W., Victoria, South Australia and Van Diemen's Land. The legislative council of each was free to frame its own constitution. The 1850s saw the framing of such constitutions based on, though not fully introducing, the doctrine of responsible government, which underlies Australia's – and Britain's – political institutions to this day.

The doctrine of responsible government has been expressed this way:[11]

1) That the Executive is subject to control by Parliament and holds office by the sanction of Parliament.
2) That the powers vested in the Governor by the various Constitution Acts are, with certain exceptions, not exercisable by him personally but on the advice of and through the ministers responsible to Parliament.

The establishment of responsible government meant that for the first time in Australia the executive was subject to control by parliament. Trevor Reese's *History of the Royal Commonwealth Society* tells us that the Australian colonies were following a path recently beaten in Canada.[12] But responsible government was not completely achieved in the 19th century. It applied to matters local to the colony, in which the Governor was comparable to a constitutional monarch; but in matters "touching the interests of the mother country" – such as navigation, immigration and protection – the Governor retained the right as an agent of the Imperial – or British – government to, for instance, reserve bills for the royal assent.[13] In local matters, the Governor would almost always act on and only on the advice of ministers supported by the legislature; but he also retained – as Governors-General and state Governors do to this day – a very narrow area of independent discretion, over the appointment and

---

[11] R.D. Lumb, *The Constitutions of the Australian States*, 2nd ed., University of Queensland Press, Brisbane, 1965, p. 66.

[12] Reese, *History of the R.C.S.*, op. cit., pp. 8-10.

[13] John Quick & Robert Garran, *The Annotated Constitution of the Australian Commonwealth*, Angus & Robertson, Sydney, 1901, p. 388. See also, e.g., H.V. Evatt, *The King and His Dominion Governors*, Oxford University Press, London, 1936, chs 2 & 3.

dismissal of ministries and requests for dissolution of parliament to bring on elections.

The campaigns of the 1840s and early 1850s in N.S.W. for self-government, extension of the franchise and against renewed transportation of convicts revealed, though not for the first time, a streak of republican sentiment that has emerged from time to time in Australian public debate ever since. But as the other objectives of the campaigners were met, their "red republicanism" subsided. Indeed, some of those threatening a republic, such as the young Henry Parkes, later Premier of N.S.W. and a "father of federation", went on to become staunch defenders of the Crown.

The most prominent republican of this time was Dr John Dunmore Lang, whom Trevor Reese described as "a fiery, heavily built Presbyterian minister".[14] In 1851, believing the gold rushes would help bring forth the republic he sought, he "published a little fantasy about Australia in 1871, twenty years on", in which he envisaged Australia as a federal republic like the United States of America.[15] It may well be that such radical proposals retarded the cause of Australian federation. Republicanism certainly gained some support on the gold fields; but it was not, for instance, central to the protest at Eureka.

The 1880s were another period of some republican fervour in the Australian colonies, as they were in Britain. Queen Victoria's golden jubilee year, 1887, exactly a century ago, drew from Australia great profusions of loyalty to Britain and enthusiasm for the Queen; Henry Parkes, who had threatened a republic in 1849, spoke of the Queen "in language little short of idolatry".[16] But there were loud notes of dissent. Two loyalist public meetings in Sydney to mark the jubilee were disrupted by republicans, leading the organisers to arrange a third meeting which was, according to Manning Clark, policed by "foot-ballers, larrikin undergraduates and prize-fighters". The meeting was a great success. But it so angered the young Henry Lawson that he wrote the first of his poems to be published: "A Song of the Republic" appeared in *The Bulletin* in 1887. The "signs of the times" foretold, said Lawson, that the day of the republic was near.[17]

Lawson was part of a Sydney republican circle, partly political, partly literary, impressed by the American example, allied to if not part of the

[14] Reese, *History of the R.C.S.*, op. cit., p. 51.

[15] Eric Fry (ed.), *Rebels and Radicals*, George Allen & Unwin, Sydney, 1983, p. 101.

[16] C.M.H. Clark, *A History of Australia*, vol. 4, *The Earth Abideth for Ever, 1851-1888*, Melbourne University Press, 1978, p. 397.

[17] Ibid.

"growing Radical-Labour movement",[18] opposed to honours and aristocracy, and combining its assertively Australian hostility to Britain with a strong commitment to a white Australia.

The choice presented by radical Australian nationalists was between an Australian identity and an Australia ruling itself, on the one hand, and, on the other, an Australia both politically and culturally subordinate to Britain. This is the dichotomy that today gives the work of that Old Testament prophet turned Church historian, Manning Clark, its scorching fire. But it was and is a false dichotomy. As A.G.L. Shaw tells us of the 1880s: "Of course many Australians managed to combine an intense local patriotism with allegiance to Britain". And Trevor Reese wrote of the same phenomenon.[19] Sir Henry Parkes, the artist Tom Roberts, and the author of the well-known Australian novel *Robbery under Arms*, "Rolf Boldrewood", are just a few instances. Interestingly, Trevor Reese placed some stress on the anti-republican Boldrewood's "appreciation of the individuality of the Australian peoples and their way of life".[20] And Lawson himself ended up a supporter of the British Empire.

This is, I think, an important point: though republicanism has been evident in both political and literary expressions of Australian nationalism for at least 140 years, Australian nationalism can be strong and proud without being republican and, as more than a century of Australian nationalism has shown, without Australia being a republic.

Indeed, the 1890s were the period when, more than ever before, the citizens of the Australian colonies came to think of themselves as Australians, and the movement towards federation triumphed. Yet it was in 1896 that *The Bulletin* "dropped its republicanism" because "European rivalries and Japanese militarism" made British defence seem more valuable.[21] And there were few republican voices heard in the long debates on federation.

Quick and Garran, in their commentary on the Australian Constitution, published in 1901, explained how the words "under the Crown" in the preamble to the Constitution reflected "loyalty to the Queen as the visible central authority uniting the British Empire".[22] They went on:

> Some years ago a few ardent but irresponsible advocates of Australian federation indulged in predictions that the time would inevitably come when Australia would separate from the mother country and become

---

[18] A.G.L. Shaw, *The Story of Australia*, 5th ed., Faber & Faber, London, 1983, p. 160.

[19] Ibid. Reese, *Australia in the Twentieth Century*, op. cit., pp. 85-6.

[20] Ibid., p. 12.

[21] Sydney Labour History Group, *What Rough Beast? The State and Social Order in Australian History*, George Allen & Unwin, Sydney, 1982, p. 78.

[22] Quick & Garran, op. cit., pp. 294-5.

an independent Republic. Those ill-considered utterances caused, at the time, strong expressions of disapproval throughout the colonies, which effectively prevented the repetition of such suggestions, as being beyond the arena of serious contemplation and debate.

The development of the Crown and Commonwealth in the 20th century now means that Australia can be fully independent, as it is today, without being a republic. But a century ago, and well into the 20th century, loyalty to the Crown and loyalty to the Empire were inseparable. Australians overwhelmingly thought of themselves as "Australian Britons"; they looked to Britain for defence; and, in any event, the Empire did not impinge on Australia's domestic affairs. J.D.B. Miller made this point in his contribution to a volume of essays about Anglo-Australian relations dedicated to Trevor Reese;[23] he made it by quoting a passage from a short story by Rudyard Kipling. An Englishman says to an Australian: "Have you started that Republic of yours down under yet?" The Australian replies: "No. But we're goin' to. Then you'll see".

"Carry on. No one's hindering", says the Englishman.

The Australian scowls. "No. We know they ain't. And — and — that's what makes us all so crazy angry with you ... What can you do with an Empire that — that don't care what you do?"

The Constitution, drafted by Australians and approved at referendum by the people of Australia, came into effect on 1 January 1901. It provided for a Governor-General to be "Her Majesty's representative in the Commonwealth" (section 2); but it also left intact the constitutions of the states, so that the Queen continued to be represented also by six state Governors. Attempts to make the state Governors subordinate to the Governor-General came to nought. The Constitution was based on the Westminster doctrine of responsible government, combined with the American model of a strong federal Senate. The Governor-General was given various powers, but either the letter of the Constitution or constitutional conventions required that these would, with rare exceptions, be exercised only on ministerial advice. I shall return to this constitutional role of the Governor-General later.

It is sometimes said, dismissively, that Australia's Constitution is "archaic, horse and buggy, anachronistic". But as Sir Daryl Dawson, a Justice of the Australian High Court, has said, this view fails to recognise both that "the Australian Constitution works" and that it is, in practice, "not the same as it was in 1901" but has evolved.[24] This has included evolution of the position of the Crown. This point was well made at the first Constitutional Convention

---

[23] A.F. Madden & W.H. Morris-Jones (eds.), *Australia and Britain: Studies in a Changing Relationship*, Frank Cass, London, 1980, p. 97. See Rudyard Kipling, *Debits and Credits*, Macmillan, London, 1965, p. 307.

[24] Sir Daryl Dawson, "The Constitution — Major Overhaul or Simple Tune-up?" (The Southey Memorial Lecture, 1983), *Melbourne University Law Review*, vol. 14, 1984, p. 354.

– a gathering of state and federal politicians to discuss constitutional reform – in 1973. The Prime Minister, Mr Whitlam, moved a vote of thanks to the Governor-General, Sir Paul Hasluck, for opening the Convention. Mr Whitlam said of the Governor-General:[25]

> He holds a great office; he represents the Head of State of our nation. In this century how much that office has grown. The first Governor-General swore fealty to the Queen of the United Kingdom of Great Britain and Ireland. Henceforth the Governor-General will swear fealty to the Queen of Australia and her other Realms and Territories, Head of the Commonwealth. In this office and in those titles is shown the development of our nation.

There are, I think, four major ways in which Mr Whitlam's thesis – that the Crown has changed in line with Australia's development as a nation – can be demonstrated. They amount to what might be described as a very considerable "Australianisation" of the Crown. This development has not always been smooth – the first appointment of an Australian as Governor-General is testimony to that – and in the case of the Australian states it has been especially slow, though the *Australia Acts* last year has rectified that. In speaking of this and, later, the constitutional role of the Crown, I will refer in most cases only to the position at the federal level, relating to the Governor-General.

The first development to note was the gradual but relatively early abandonment of the role of the Governor-General as an agent of the Imperial government. For example, the early Governors-General, like the colonial Governors, reported back to the Colonial Secretary in London; the Governor-General was the formal channel of communication between the British and Australian governments. Though the abandonment of this Imperial role occurred over many years, the clear marker to it was the Imperial Conference of 1926. The conference – in a declaration Trevor Reese likened to the Athanasian Creed[26] – held it to be "an essential consequence" of the "equality of status" of Great Britain and the Dominions, of which Australia was one, that "the Governor-General of a Dominion is the representative of the Crown, holding in all essential respects the same position in relation to the administration of public affairs in the Dominion as is held by His Majesty the King in Great Britain, and that he is not the representative or agent of

---

[25] *Proceedings of the Australian Constitutional Convention*, Sydney, 3-7 September 1973, p. 7.

[26] Reese, *Australia in the Twentieth Century*, op. cit., p. 86. The text of the declaration is in, e.g., A. Berriedale Keith (ed.), *Speeches and Documents on the British Dominions 1918-1931*, Oxford University Press, London, 1938, p. 161ff.

His Majesty's Government or of any Department of that Government". The "official channel of communication" would "be, in future, between Government and Government direct". The Governor-General would be constitutional monarch within Australia, but no longer have an Imperial role.

But who was now to advise the King on whom to appoint as Governor-General? This is the second area of development to which it is necessary to refer. The first Governors-General were appointed by the monarch on the nomination of the Colonial Secretary, that is, the British government. The first eight Governors-General – from 1901 to 1931 – were British aristocrats, generally men of ordinary ability with undistinguished political careers at Westminster. Though some were excellent, not all were well suited to facing the isolation, expense and hostility from some radical, including republican, elements that the job involved. Correspondence in the British Library shows that in 1908, Lord Elgin, the Colonial Secretary, and Sir Henry Campbell-Bannerman, the Prime Minister, had in desperation to sound out several peers before the young Lord Dudley took the job.[27] He was not a great success.

In 1930, difficulties in the appointment of a Governor-General arose in a quite different way. The Australian cabinet asserted a right to give the King binding advice on who the Governor-General should be, and proposed Sir Isaac Isaacs, a High Court judge, of whom our Chairman, Sir Zelman Cowen, is, of course, biographer. The King objected. One of his reasons was that a local nominee "must have local political predilections" and his impartiality would be open to doubt.[28] The King looked forward to the day when "a citizen of one Dominion [was] appointed Governor or Governor-General of another part of the British Commonwealth"; but that idea, though gaining occasional support in some quarters, never reached fruition, and its day has clearly passed.

In the event, Prime Minister Scullin insisted on Isaacs, and the King agreed. This was not before the Imperial Conference of 1930 had declared certain principles as flowing "naturally from the new position of the Governor-General as representative of His Majesty only": the King made his appointment on the advice of his ministers in the Dominion concerned, and "the ministers concerned [would] tender their formal advice after informal consultations

---

[27] See: Ripon Papers 43552 ff. 44-51; 43518 ff. 158-163. Campbell-Bannerman Papers 41225 ff. 230-240. Additional MS. 43552 fol. 46. Also interesting are: Iddesleigh Papers Add. MS. 50033 ff. 95-96. British Library, London.

[28] Christopher Cunneen, *Kings' Men: Australia's Governors-General from Hopetoun to Isaacs*, George Allen & Unwin, Sydney, 1983, p. 177.

with His Majesty".[29] This has been the practice since, though usually − and, I think, rightly − the advice to the Queen is that of the Australian Prime Minister alone and has generally not been discussed in cabinet. Apparently not all Prime Ministers have been as scrupulous as Sir Robert Menzies was in the instance of Sir William Slim's appointment to ensure that the "informal consultations" are early and open enough to give the Queen some effective say in who her representative will be.

Until the *Australia Acts* of 1986, appointment of state Governors continued to be on the advice of the British government, not of the state government. Generally, but by no means invariably, the British government gave the Queen the advice the state government wished given. Now, however, this advice "shall be tendered by the Premier of the State" direct.[30]

Sir Isaac Isaacs was the first Australian to become Governor-General. The arguments against such an appointment − that a "local man" could not be impartial, that appointment of an Australian weakened the link with Britain − were met by the arguments that British peers could not be assumed impartial either, and that Australia should assert its nationhood. But it was not until the appointment of Lord Casey, an Australian, on the advice of Sir Robert Menzies in the mid-1960s that it was generally accepted that, Royalty perhaps excepted, the Governor-General would be an Australian. In at least one state, it has been much more recently still that this has come to be accepted.

Although it was on the advice of an Australian Labor government that the Duke of Gloucester became Governor-General in 1945, it is clear from the opposition of Mr Hayden (when leader of the Labor Party)[31] to the appointment of Prince Charles as Governor-General that many in the Labor Party today believe that the Governor-General should always be an Australian. Many other Australians thought the idea unwise because of the danger of the heir to the throne becoming embroiled in acute controversy, as Australia's 1975 crisis shows is all too possible.

The process whereby the Governor-Generalship of Australia has come to be "Australianised" has been paralleled by an "Australianisation" of the Queen. Whereas, for instance, King George V was King "of the United Kingdom of Great Britain and Ireland and of the British Dominions beyond

[29] Keith, op. cit., p. 222.

[30] *Australia Acts* 1986, section 7(5).

[31] [W.G. Hayden was a minister in the Whitlam government, Labor Opposition Leader, Foreign Minister, and Governor-General of Australia (1989-1996).]

the Seas", King George VI's Coronation Oath in 1937 expressly named each of the Dominions, including Australia. The Canadian Prime Minister, W.L. Mackenzie King, stressed the point that "for the first time, in this great ceremony, it was recognized that the relationship between the King and [the] people of [the Dominions] is direct and immediate".[32]

Australia's *Royal Style and Titles Act* of 1953 declared the Queen to be "Elizabeth the Second, by the grace of God, of the United Kingdom, Australia and her other Realms and Territories Queen, Head of the Commonwealth, Defender of the Faith". Thus when the Queen visited Australia in 1954 she came as Queen of Australia. Sir Robert Garran, who over fifty years before had co-authored the great Quick and Garran *Annotated Constitution of the Australian Commonwealth*, wrote at the time:[33]

> Our Queen comes to us, not as Queen of a far-off country, representing authority exercised over us from the other side of the world, but as one of ourselves: as our own Queen of Australia, who reigns here, not in accord with her despotic will, but by and with the advice of her Australian Ministers.

In 1973, an Australian Act removed the reference to the United Kingdom in the Queen's title in Australia, thus bringing into even clearer light her status as "Queen of Australia". It also removed reference to her as "Defender of the Faith".

It has been argued in Australia that the removal of other constitutional links between Britain and Australia – such as the ending of all appeals to the Privy Council, and termination of the power of the United Kingdom parliament to legislate for Australia – through removing any suggestion of Australian dependence on the U.K., strengthens the Queen's position as Queen of Australia. It does this by highlighting the fact that her relationship with her people there is direct and immediate and not part of some broader pattern of British dominance. It should be noted that almost all the practices in the states which Mr Whitlam identified in his book, *The Whitlam Government*, as detracting from the "Australian identity of the monarchy" have been rectified by the *Australia Acts* proclaimed last year.[34]

The Australian Hawke Labor government believes, I think, that the 1984 revision of the Letters Patent and the revoking of the Royal Instructions relating

---

[32] W.L. Mackenzie King, *Crown and Commonwealth*, Canadian Broadcasting Corporation, Ottawa, 1937, p. 2.

[33] Sir Robert Garran, *Prosper the Commonwealth*, Angus & Robertson, Sydney, 1958, p. 336.

[34] E.G. Whitlam, *The Whitlam Government*, Penguin, 1985, p. 132.

to the office of Governor-General are further steps in making provisions to do with the Crown reflect as much as possible Australia's development as a nation. But some more conservative Australians believe that some aspects of these changes – such as the removal of reference to the Governor-General as "Commander in Chief" – reflect a desire, not to modernise the monarchy, but to achieve a "republic by stealth". Some point to the elimination of the official use of "God Save the Queen" except when a member of the Royal Family is present; some allege the removal from public view of portraits of the Queen in some public buildings, though the government denies there has been any government decision to do so; some were relieved that nothing came of the government's attempt to end the requirement that people seeking naturalisation must swear allegiance to the Queen. Strengthening the Australian identity of the Crown does not, such critics think, require removal of the manifestations of it from Australian life.

The Australianisation of the Crown was, I think, promoted by the decline of the idea, once so important, that loyalty to the Crown was equivalent to loyalty to the British Empire; this helped a shared Crown to be seen increasingly in Australia as an Australian one. This change came gradually, of course. Even when it was widely accepted that for legal purposes and for purposes of declaration of war the Crown was not one and indivisible, it was still thought fundamental that the British Empire and Commonwealth was "united by a common allegiance to the Crown". But this latter view was officially abandoned in 1949 when the newly independent India was allowed to remain within the Commonwealth while becoming a republic. India continued to accept the King as "the symbol of the free association of [the Commonwealth's] independent member nations, and, as such, Head of the Commonwealth".[35] Some of the newspaper hysteria last summer about the Queen, Mrs Thatcher and the Commonwealth might have been diminished had it been remembered that that title – "Head of the Commonwealth" – is symbolic and carries with it no powers or rights.

Trevor Reese records that "Chifley and Evatt represented Australia at the [1949] Commonwealth Conference in London and were not happy with the compromise formula for Indian membership, declaring that the Australian government believed the personal relationship of the sovereign to the Commonwealth to be of supreme importance".[36] Chifley regretted that

---

[35] S.A. de Smith, *Constitutional and Administrative Law*, 3rd ed., Penguin, 1978, p. 653.
[36] Reese, *Australia in the Twentieth Century*, op. cit., p. 143.

India had become a republic; Menzies argued that "common allegiance to the Crown" was the basis of the unity on which the Commonwealth depended, though he later said that he learned to live with the formula allowing India and later many other countries to remain in the Commonwealth as republics.

I have so far touched on four major developments in the Crown in Australia in the 20th century – the abandonment of any Imperial role for the Governor-General; the appointment of the Governor-General on the advice of the Australian Prime Minister; the appointment of Australians as Governor-General; and the "Australianisation" of the Queen. But we have barely touched on the constitutional role of the Governor-General. This is an area of some controversy, and the five propositions I wish to put would not all command universal agreement.

First of all, the Governor-General acts in almost all cases on and only on the advice of ministers. This, of course, is fundamental to responsible government.

The second point is that, like the Queen, the Governor-General has the rights that Walter Bagehot made famous – "the right to be consulted, ... to encourage, [and] ... to warn".[37] These can be exercised both in formal meetings of the Executive Council and in informal discussions with ministers, especially the Prime Minister.

My third proposition is that there have always been and remain some matters on which the Crown has an independent discretion. These are often called the "reserve powers" of the Crown; they relate to the appointment and dismissal of ministries, and requests for dissolution of parliament to bring on elections. It was established very soon after federation that – with only the most bizarre exceptions possible – the reserve powers did not include the right to withhold the royal assent from legislation. If legislation is unconstitutional, it can be declared so by the High Court.

The Governor-General's independent discretions come into play only on rare occasions; they are exercised as part of the Crown's role to ensure the maintenance of constitutional government, and generally give the Governor-General no power other than to send the matter back either to parliament or the people.

There are various instances in Australia's federal history and in the

---

[37] Walter Bagehot, *The English Constitution* (1867), quoted from 1963 edition, Fontana/Collins, p. 111. For the Australian application, see Sir Paul Hasluck, *The Office of Governor-General*, Melbourne University Press, 1979, pp. 17-20.

experience of the states of the exercise of these independent discretions. Take appointment first. Usually it is clear which leader can command a majority in the House of Representatives and therefore become Prime Minister. But not always. It is an old-established convention that an outgoing Prime Minister has no right to name his or her successor; his or her opinion, if it is sought by the Governor-General, is not binding. Instead, convention gives the Governor-General an independent discretion; *he or she* must choose. If he or she commissions someone who is defeated in parliament, there must either be a new government or a new election.

Australia has had some instances of the appointment of Prime Ministers which have had no parallel in Britain in the 20th century. The first Governor-General, Lord Hopetoun, had to commission a Prime Minister before the first federal parliament had been elected, and his botching of it is remembered as "the Hopetoun blunder". Whereas no British Prime Minister in the 20th century has died in office, this has happened on three occasions in Australia – in 1939, 1945, and 1967 – and the Governor-General has had to appoint a short-term Prime Minister pending the election by the deceased Prime Minister's party of a new leader. As in Britain, so in Australia, a "hung parliament" might involve the Crown in assessing the parliamentary situation to decide whom to commission as Prime Minister.

Just as Governors-General have had to exercise their discretion on the appointment of ministries, so Australia provides examples of the dismissal of ministries. In N.S.W. in 1932, the Governor, Sir Philip Game, dismissed Jack Lang as Premier after Lang's government persisted in breach of federal legislation over the payment of interest on loans and was "unable to carry on essential services without breaking the law".[38] At the federal level in 1975, the Governor-General, Sir John Kerr, dismissed the Prime Minister, Mr Gough Whitlam, because the latter was unable to secure passage of money bills through the Senate to finance the carrying on of government services and refused to advise a dissolution of parliament and the holding of elections, which would have unblocked Supply. In both 1932 and 1975, the opposition leader – in a minority in the lower house – was appointed Premier or Prime Minister – in 1975 on an explicitly caretaker basis – until elections could be held, and in both cases the dismissed leader was defeated overwhelmingly at the polls. Both dismissals generated enormous controversy, though the degree

---

[38] Evatt, op. cit., p. 164.

of bitterness evident since the 1975 dismissal has far exceeded that after the 1932 dismissal, and, regrettably, continues to overshadow much discussion of constitutional reform in Australia.

Australia has also seen the exercise of another reserve power, the refusal of advice to dissolve parliament. Where a Prime Minister clearly commands a majority in the lower house, it seems to be clear that – except perhaps in the most bizarre circumstances – any advice from him to dissolve the House cannot be refused. However, on three occasions at the federal level in Australia – in 1904, 1905, and 1909 – Governors-General have refused advice to dissolve. These three instances were in the days "of shifting party alliances before Australia's two-party mould was set".[39] In each case, the government was defeated in the House of Representatives. As it was clear that another leader could form a government commanding majority support there, the Governor-General refused the request of the defeated Prime Minister for a dissolution and he resigned; the leader who could command a majority was commissioned as Prime Minister.

On those occasions where Prime Ministers have advised the dissolution of the whole of both Houses under the special constitutional provisions for resolving deadlock between the houses – in 1914, 1951, 1974, 1975 (under most unusual circumstances, of course) and 1983 [and later in 1987, and 2016] – the Governor-General has sought to assure himself that the constitutional requirements for a double dissolution have been met, and in each case they have. Some authorities take the view that the Governor-General must be convinced, not only that the technical conditions are met, but that parliament is unworkable; but other authorities disagree. [There is no such requirement in the Constitution.]

The proposition that the Governor-General must always and invariably act on and only on the advice of the incumbent ministers – that is, that there are no reserve powers – is heard from time to time. But the wording of the Constitution, the practice before and since federation, and the writings of major constitutional authorities – such as Dr H.V. Evatt and Dr Eugene Forsey – all support the existence of reserve powers. These powers must, of course, be exercised in accordance with constitutional conventions; the exact nature of these conventions is usually but not always clear.

The fourth proposition I wish to put is that, in the exercise of his various

---

[39] Don Markwell, "Masters of Dissolution", *The Times Literary Supplement*, 12 April 1985 [reprinted in ch. 4 of this book].

functions, the Governor-General is free to consult whomever he or she believes it prudent to consult. A discretion to act without or against ministerial advice must surely carry with it a discretion to seek such wise counsel about the matter as the Governor-General thinks he needs. There has been a very considerable history of consultation of High Court judges by Governors-General. At least three Chief Justices of Australia (Sir Samuel Griffith, Sir Owen Dixon, and Sir Garfield Barwick), a number of other High Court judges, and at least eight Governors-General (Lords Northcote, Dudley and Denman, Sir Ronald Munro Ferguson, Lords De L'Isle and Casey, Sir Paul Hasluck, and Sir John Kerr) have considered that it is proper for a representative of the Queen, in seeking the best legal advice in a crisis, to consult the Chief Justice of Australia and for the Chief Justice to give him his advice, at least on non-justiciable matters.[40] The exercise of the reserve powers has traditionally been held to be non-justiciable — that is, not subject to review by a court — and recent developments in administrative law seem to me not to have changed this. Some commentators have suggested further or alternative means of providing Governors-General and state Governors with impartial advice (e.g., through panels of eminent constitutional authorities); but nothing has yet come of these proposals.

The fifth and final proposition I wish to put is that the Queen has no part in the constitutional functions of the Governor-General. The Constitution provides that the Governor-General will do such things as appoint ministers and dissolve parliament. His decisions cannot be overturned by the Queen. It seems now to be well-established that, though a representative of the Queen will report regularly to her, he will not risk embroiling the Queen in controversy by seeking from her prior approval for his action. This was the principle on which, for instance, Sir John Kerr acted in 1975 and Sir Paul Scoon in Grenada in 1983, and to it has been added the authority of our Chairman, Sir Zelman Cowen.

Thus, with rare and minor exceptions, the Queen's only action under the Australian Constitution is the appointment of the Governor-General on the advice of the Australian Prime Minister. The *Australia Acts* of 1986 means

---

[40] See J.B. Paul, "The Dismissal: History Justifies Barwick's Advice", *The Bulletin*, 1 March 1983. Richard Lucy, *The Australian Form of Government*, Macmillan, 1985, pp. 247-50 (& Lucy's letter, *Quadrant*, Sept. 1986). Don Markwell, "On Advice from the Chief Justice", *Quadrant*, July 1985, & letters to *Quadrant*, Oct. 1985 & April 1986. [See chs. 4 & 6 of this book, incl. re future Chief Justices Sir Harry Gibbs and Murray Gleeson and future Justice Sir Keith Aickin supporting this view.]

that, except when she is in a state, the only power the Queen can exercise in state affairs is the appointment of the Governor on the state Premier's advice. There is very considerable authority for the proposition that the Queen, however reluctantly, would also remove a Governor-General or Governor from office on the advice of the relevant Prime Minister or Premier to do so. The belief that such advice might be given and that the Queen would then be embroiled in the Australian crisis was a major factor in shaping Sir John Kerr's handling of the 1975 crisis. There is a strong case for some greater security of tenure for representatives of the Queen; this has been provided for in the Letters Patent relating to the Governorship of at least one State.

What can we say of the future of the Crown and Australia? There are, I think, three key questions to consider about this. First, should Australia become a republic? Secondly, will it become a republic? Thirdly, what other changes, constitutional or otherwise, might sensibly be made?

The central arguments advanced for Australia's becoming a republic are basically twofold. First, it is argued that a truly Australian national identity is incompatible with sharing a monarchy which is, first and foremost, that of another country. Secondly, it is argued that the monarchy is incompatible with truly democratic political institutions in Australia, or that a republic will at least be more democratic.

Neither of these propositions is especially compelling. I have earlier suggested that it was possible in the 19th century for what Trevor Reese called "a distinctive Australian tradition"[41] to develop while Australia was a monarchy and with only some Australian nationalists favouring a republic. There is, I think, little evidence, if any, to suggest that the development of Australia's sense of its own identity or its image abroad is being stunted by the Crown. As I have mentioned, Mr Whitlam's concerns about this have almost all been met, and others could be met without Australia becoming a republic.

Nor is it at all apparent that Australia's parliamentary democracy and constitutional monarchy give less effective expression to the will of the people than the institutions of any other country, or that in those ways in which they might be thought to do so – such as electoral boundaries in some states – the matter has anything to do with the Crown.

In the Australian and British systems, the monarch is not seen as partisan or political. But perhaps the greatest advantage of the present system is that it works. We can have no certainty that any alternative system would work better

[41] Reese, *Australia in the Twentieth Century*, op. cit., p. 12.

than the present, and there is every possibility that it would not work so well. As Professor Geoffrey Bolton has argued, any attempt to make Australia a republic might split the federation; quite simply, some of the states might not remain within a republican Australia.[42]

It may be that the shared monarchy contributes something to the warmth of regard held for Australia in Britain, and in a world of tension such links are an asset. The Queen is "the sole symbolic link uniting all" nations of the Commonwealth.[43] Although the Commonwealth includes many republics, the position of the Queen and her successors as a unifying force in it would be, I think, gradually weakened by the abandonment of the monarchy by countries such as Australia.

What are the prospects of Australia's becoming a republic? Such a change would need to be approved at referendum by a majority of Australian voters in a majority of states. Opinion polls fairly consistently show strong majorities – around 60% – in favour of retaining the monarchy, with around 30% favouring a republic and the rest undecided. Few people doubt the message of the opinion polls that any such proposal in the foreseeable future would be soundly defeated.

In 1981, the national conference of the Australian Labor Party included republicanism in its party platform; but Labor's Senator Gareth Evans has described this decision as virtually "accidental", and it was made by a small margin.[44] Partly because it would be defeated, and partly because it would be extremely divisive, Labor politicians who support a republic as a long-term goal do not favour pushing the issue now; it is very low down on Australia's political agenda.

Nonetheless, many people would probably agree with the premise of a recent book by Professor George Winterton that "an Australian republic is inevitable".[45] It is said by some that the tide of events – of Australia's constitutional development and of the diminution of its links with Britain – leads inexorably to a republic; that there has been a gradual shift of public opinion in favour of a republic; that the 1975 constitutional crisis significantly encouraged this; that so has non-British immigration; and that republican

---

[42] Evidence to the Executive Advisory Committee of the Constitutional Commission, Perth, 1986.

[43] *A Year Book of the Commonwealth 1973*, H.M.S.O., London, 1973, p. 2.

[44] George Winterton, *Monarchy to Republic: Australian Republican Government*, Oxford University Press, Melbourne, 1986, p. 14.

[45] Ibid., p. ix.

sentiment is strongest among the young and will therefore grow over time.

There is a certain plausibility to most of these propositions. Yet, when critically examined, most of them are at best uncertain. It seems to me that the logic of what I have called the "Australianisation" of the Crown is not necessarily that it will end in a republic, but that the Crown will continue to adjust gradually in line with Australia's changing circumstances; this has been the story of the last two centuries, and it has produced what most Australians seem to believe is a constitutional monarchy appropriate to the circumstances of modern Australia.

As we have seen, some republicans in Australia in the 1850s and 1880s believed that Australia would inevitably – indeed, soon – become a republic; what seemed to them the tide of history has, like natural tides, ebbed and flowed ever since. Maybe the economist Keynes was right when he said that "the inevitable never happens. It is the unexpected always".[46]

Professor Winterton's book brings together the evidence of over 20 opinion polls in Australia on the question of "monarchy versus republic". Only one of the polls was before 1966. As Professor Winterton says, these polls must be read with caution. But the clearest message of them is that, while there have been some fluctuations in sentiment over the last 20 years, there has been very little decline in support for the monarchy or growth in republican sentiment over that time. For instance, confronted in July 1966 with the false dichotomy of retaining existing links with Britain or becoming an entirely separate republic, 63% of respondents favoured present links and 28% favoured a republic; in February 1986, asked the same question, the percentage favouring existing links was identical, at 63%, and the republican vote had risen a staggering 2% – from 28% to 30% – in 20 years. Where in such minor shifts an "inevitable" republic is to be found, I do not know.

Both Professor Winterton and Senator Evans have acknowledged, in Winterton's words of last year, "the absence of any appreciable growth in republican sentiment during the last decade". So much for the alleged impact of the 1975 crisis. Indeed, Winterton writes that "an outstanding feature of the opinion polls over the last decade is the remarkable consistency of the pro-monarchy vote". Interestingly, the opinion polls suggest that republican sentiment may well have been stronger during the "early euphoria" of the Whitlam Government than at or after its end.[47] While the 1975 crisis clearly

---

[46] *The Collected Writings of John Maynard Keynes*, vol. 28, p. 117.
[47] Winterton, op. cit., pp. 12-3, 154.

converted some Australians to republicanism – Mr Whitlam being the most important – its greater effect seems to have been to activate existing republicans and to give acute emotional intensity to some advocates of a republic.

Between the Anglophobes and the Anglophiles in Australia today, there is a large body of Australians whose attitude to the Crown is, I think, largely one of sympathetic indifference. For many people in Australia, as in Britain, the real interest is not arcane constitutional matters, but the family soap opera – the regular pictures of the Princess of Wales in the *Australian Women's Weekly*, frequent Royal Tours, including their "walkabouts" – the term, if not the idea, must be an Australian contribution – and the occasional Royal Wedding. A survey suggested that 83% of television sets in Sydney were tuned into the wedding of the Prince and Princess of Wales in July 1981.[48]

Opinion polls show much stronger support for a republic amongst non-British immigrants than amongst immigrants from the U.K. and people born in Australia. But it cannot be assumed that this republicanism is transmitted to the Australian-born descendants of non-British migrants. Neither should too much be made of the greater inclination to republicanism among the young than among their elders; there is ample evidence from Australia's history of young republicans growing into older monarchists. It is not, I think, altogether irrelevant to the future that, in the words of one Australian journalist, "Prince Charles ... enjoys a transcendental warmth among Australians that no one can deny, having visited the country eight times and spent some of his schooldays here".[49]

So my answer to the question, "will Australia become a republic?", is that it well might one day, but that that day is probably far off, and that it cannot be assumed to be "inevitable".

I have suggested that Australia's monarchy has evolved in line with Australia's changing circumstances. What changes are appropriate now? This is a question that the Constitutional Commission currently reviewing Australia's Constitution will also be asking.[50]

It would be good to see a more satisfactory provision for resolving deadlocks between the two houses of parliament on Supply. The provision I

[48] *Sydney Morning Herald*, 6 August 1981, p. 9.

[49] Red Harrison, "Was the Royal Tour worth all the trouble and expense? The Prince and Princess in Australia", *The Listener*, 21 April 1983, p. 6.

[50] [A Constitutional Commission was appointed in 1985 to propose reforms to the Australian Constitution in time for the Australian "bicentenary" of British settlement in 1988. Referendum proposals arising from it were all defeated.]

would favour is making a double dissolution automatic if the Senate failed to pass the Supply bills after a set number of days. There is little chance that any proposal to remove the Senate's power to block Supply would be passed in the three outlying states, even if it passed elsewhere.

Apart from such changes, perhaps the single most important question is whether it would be wise to codify in legal form the conventions – either as they are or as we would like them to be – relating to the reserve powers. The Australian Constitutional Convention (politicians from the state and federal parliaments), meeting in Brisbane in 1985, in fact adopted a set of "18 principles" relating to some aspects of the Crown's independent discretion. But these "18 principles" were silent on important questions, inconsistent in major respects with well-established conventions, and liable in some instances to cause uncertainty and controversy rather than prevent it. The status of these "principles" is problematic: they cannot bind either politicians or Governors-General, and they will have no force in a court of law.

Some countries have detailed constitutional provisions setting out procedures relating to the appointment and removal of ministries and the calling of elections – matters which in Australia, as in Britain, are left largely as a matter of constitutional convention. The arguments for such codification are that it would make the constitutional position more certain; by so doing would reduce or eliminate the instances where the Crown, through exercising an independent discretion, is drawn into damaging controversy; and would enable issues of, say, appointment and dismissal of ministries to come before the courts and so be settled finally on legal grounds. Against this it is argued that codification would not necessarily eliminate uncertainty, as there might then be debate about the meaning of the words, just as there is uncertainty and debate about the meaning of words in the existing Constitution; that to leave such matters to the adjudication of the courts is to invite delay where speed is sometimes of the essence, and to risk damaging respect for the courts whenever they have to make controversial decisions about political matters; that questions such as who is to be the government are best decided by remitting them to parliament or the people, which is all the Crown can do, rather than to the courts; that if the Governor-General makes a mistake, the parliament or the electorate will correct it, and there is thus no need or place for the courts; that codification would make the principles inflexible and incapable of evolution; that they could not possibly cover all the diverse and unique circumstances in which the Crown might have to exercise an independent discretion; and that codification would change the spirit of politics from one where there is some realisation, however slight, of the need to play fairly and not embroil the "umpire" to one where you play the rules as hard as possible. If there were a greater realisation by politicians in Australia of the need to observe the conventions of the Constitution and not to embroil the Crown needlessly in controversy, I would myself think the case against codification to be overwhelming. Even so, it seems to me convincing.

It would not, I think, be inappropriate to write into the Constitution some explicit recognition there that the Queen is Queen of Australia. But this is certainly not necessary, and it may raise other difficulties that it is, perhaps, best to avoid. There has in the past been all but universal agreement that certain outdated provisions to do with the Crown should be removed from the Constitution.[51] The provision in section 3 that "the salary of the Governor-General shall not be altered during his continuance in office" seems inappropriate in times of continuing inflation. As I have said, I would myself hope that the Constitutional Commission would recommend some means of ensuring greater security of tenure for the Governor-General.

Such changes, modest as they are, would fit in well with the gradual development of the Crown throughout this century. As this lecture has argued, the Crown has been developing an Australian identity in line with the growth of Australia as a nation, on which Trevor Reese's study of *Australia in the Twentieth Century* placed much stress. This "Australianisation" of the Crown has added to its strength and durability.

Just as Trevor Reese argued that the Commonwealth could not be bolstered by grand artificial schemes, so I would argue that far more important than changing words in the Constitution is that the office of Governor-General and the state Governorships should continue to be occupied by men – and, in future, women – of the highest quality. And it is essential for politicians to remember that, as much as possible, they should seek to avoid confronting the Crown with necessarily controversial decisions. In the words of one former Governor-General, "no constitution can work smoothly if politicians play too rough".[52]

---

[51] See, e.g., Gareth Evans, "The 'Machinery of Government' Constitutional Referendum Bills", *Australian Law Journal*, vol. 57, 1983, pp. 699-700.

[52] "Whitlam and Kerr, The P.M.'s Cataclysmic Errors" (interview with Sir John Kerr), *The Bulletin*, 17 September 1985, p. 68.

4

THE EARLY GOVERNORS-GENERAL AND THE CONSULTATION OF HIGH COURT JUDGES

Review of Kings' Men: Australia's Governors-General
from Hopetoun to Isaacs
by Christopher Cunneen (1983)
Published as "Masters of Dissolution"
The Times Literary Supplement
12 April 1985

As with the United Kingdom and several other Commonwealth countries, the apex of Australia's system of government is the Crown. In practice this means the Governor-General, the representative in Canberra of the Queen. Christopher Cunneen's account of the early Governors-General extends from the federation of six colonies into the Commonwealth of Australia in 1901, with a British peer as representative of Queen Victoria, through to the term of office of the first Australian-born Governor-General, Sir Isaac Isaacs.

The role of the early Governors-General was a dual one: first, as representative of the monarch, fulfilling responsibilities (such as appointing Prime Ministers) under Australia's written Constitution; second, as agent of the British government in Australia. The second role ceased, in one sense, with the 1926 Imperial Conference; more broadly, it diminished over a period of years, including the decline of the role of the Governor-General as conduit of Australia's external relations, which were then conducted through the British Empire. Cunneen traces the evolution of the post to one solely as representative of the monarch, appointed on the advice of the Australian Prime Minister. This evolution was not entirely smooth; the greatest controversy was in 1930 over the insistence of the Australian Prime Minister on the appointment of Isaacs, a septuagenarian Australian lawyer-politician personally unknown to the

King, who had not been consulted. It was not until the 1960s that it came to be a matter of course that, Royalty perhaps excepted, the Governor-General would be an Australian. Isaacs succeeded a string of eight British aristocrats. One was the second Lord Tennyson; another, Lord Stonehaven, became Chairman of Baldwin's Conservative Party. Cunneen regards the most successful as Sir Ronald Munro Ferguson (later Lord Novar), a Scotsman whose term (1914-1920) spanned the First World War and its traumas in Australia. The Governors-General were generally men of ordinary ability with undistinguished political careers, usually on the Conservative side, at Westminster. Some found themselves unsuited to this lonely, thankless job in one of the sparsest regions of the Empire.

The post involved its early occupants in much personal expense, isolation from their homes, hostility from some radical elements in Australia, and a tricky position in the jealousies between the governments and Governors of the states and the newly emerging Commonwealth of Australia. It is not surprising therefore that in 1908 Lord Elgin, the Secretary of State for the Colonies, and Sir Henry Campbell-Bannerman had to sound out several peers before the young Lord Dudley took the job. In 1912, Lord Denman was evicted from Government House in Sydney by the New South Wales government (though the Governor-General retained his more important residence in Melbourne); one irreverent Australian cartoonist depicted the Sydney eviction as "the second expulsion from Paradise". In the 1920s, Lord Stonehaven became the first Governor-General to occupy the homestead which became Government House in that sheep-farm turned capital, Canberra.

To tell this story requires the skills of the historian and the insight and discipline of the constitutional lawyer. Despite Cunneen's considerable talents as a biographer and historian, *Kings' Men* has some serious deficiencies. First, although the author describes the book as "a study of the role of Governor-General", it betrays his lack of any consistent notion of the role under the Australian Constitution. On some occasions he refers favourably to, or at least recognises, the Governor-General's role as "umpire" in some difficult situations; yet elsewhere he adopts the doctrine, which has no foundation in Australian constitutional law or practice, that a Governor-General should always follow the advice of the incumbent ministers, even when, for example, they advise an election when an alternative government could carry on governing with majority support in the House of Representatives.

The second major flaw is that there is much material relevant to Cunneen's subject which he does not include. For example, in at least two of the three cases of refused requests for dissolutions (1904 and 1909), the Governor-General acted after consulting the Chief Justice of the High Court of Australia (Sir Samuel Griffith), and Sir Ronald Munro Ferguson consulted both Griffith and another High Court judge, the former Prime Minister, Sir Edmund Barton, on many occasions. These consultations were so central to the work of the early Governors-General, especially Munro Ferguson, that no account of that work could be complete without extensive reference to Griffith and Barton. Yet Cunneen gives precious little indication of this.

Cunneen also does not mention that in 1908 the Australian Prime Minister, Alfred Deakin, tried to get Lord Elgin to persuade Lord Northcote to stay on longer as Governor-General. Describing Northcote as "a prominent 'diehard' in the controversy over reform of the House of Lords", he fails to mention that Northcote opposed the Tory decision to block the Finance Bill of 1909.

Kings' Men contains many simple errors. For example, the office of the Governor-General is not a "department" (just as Mrs Thatcher's office is not a "department"). Cunneen wrongly implies that Sir Robert Menzies, then Opposition Leader, opposed the appointment of Sir William McKell as Governor-General in 1947 principally because McKell was an Australian: rather, Menzies's main concern was that McKell was appointed straight from partisan Australian politics (he was the Labor Premier of New South Wales). This detracts from what is otherwise a valuable work, especially important given how little has been written on the Governors-General of Australia. It is a readable contribution to a neglected field, of interest to students of the British Empire and of Australian constitutional history alike.

"Griffith, Barton and the early Governors-General:
Aspects of Australia's constitutional development"
Public Law Review
December 1999

During the first two decades of the Commonwealth of Australia, Governors-General consulted frequently with two judges of the High Court, Chief Justice Sir Samuel Griffith and Sir Edmund Barton. These consultations included aspects of the "reserve powers" of the Crown. The extent of the consultations was not known until the 1980s. Since those early decades there has been a gradual if uneven movement towards the "Australianisation" of the Crown. At a time when Australia is debating changes to its headship of state, the question of what informal sources of advice may be open to a future President or Governor-General deserves careful consideration.

In November 1916, the Governor-General of Australia, Sir Ronald Munro Ferguson, wrote to the King's Private Secretary, Lord Stamfordham, on the defeat of the Hughes government's first conscription referendum. Sir Ronald defended the calling of such a referendum, not envisaged in the Constitution, by saying that: "The two most notable and experienced men in Australia – Griffith and Barton – were of [the] opinion" that Hughes was right in seeking a referendum, and the Governor-General was right to agree to this.[1]

This article examines the way in which Sir Samuel Griffith, first Chief Justice of Australia from 1903 to 1919, and Sir Edmund Barton, a judge of the High Court from 1903 until his death in 1920, were consulted extensively by a succession of Governors-General on constitutional and other matters, and developed very close relationships with at least one Governor-General, Sir Ronald Munro Ferguson. Surprisingly, although snippets of this history had been touched upon in various works – such as J.A. La Nauze's biography of Deakin,[2] and in Christopher Cunneen's study of the early Governors-General[3] – the full extent of the relationships and consultations was not known until the mid-1980s.[4] The research which brought it to light has attracted particular interest from writers on the 1975 constitutional crisis – such as Sir Garfield

---

[1] Novar papers, MS 696, fol 10454, National Library of Australia.
[2] J.A. La Nauze, *Alfred Deakin: a biography*, vol. 2, Melbourne University Press, 1965, p. 570.
[3] Christopher Cunneen, *Kings' Men: Australia's Governors-General from Hopetoun to Isaacs*, George Allen & Unwin, Sydney, 1983, pp. 81-2, 112-6.
[4] See Don Markwell, "On Advice from the Chief Justice", *Quadrant*, July 1985.

Barwick[5] and Mr Bill Hayden,[6] both writing in their autobiographies. But, in elaborating on previously published research in this field, the focus here will not be on 1975, on which perhaps too much has been written, but on the first two decades of the Commonwealth of Australia, on which, undoubtedly, too little has been written.

Griffith and Barton, those "two most notable and experienced men in Australia", are today too little remembered. A detailed biography of Griffith has been written, by Roger Joyce,[7] but it is a disappointing book. It is very pleasing that Geoffrey Bolton, a distinguished historian, is soon to publish what promises to be the definitive biography of Barton.[8] Even now, as we approach the centenary of federation, the fresh attention paid to Barton as Australia's first Prime Minister does not extend to his subsequent 16 years of service on the High Court.

This article, first, gives some background to the story of these years; secondly, sets out in some detail the consultations of Griffith and Barton by successive Governors-General; thirdly, tells the sad story of Barton's disappointment on being passed over as Chief Justice on Griffith's retirement in 1919; and finally, considers briefly how this story reflects aspects of Australia's constitutional development.

Background

Griffith and Barton were both major pioneers of federation. Griffith was twice Premier of Queensland in the 1880s and early 1890s, principal author of the 1891 draft Constitution for Australia, and Chief Justice of Queensland from 1893 until his appointment as Chief Justice of the High Court of Australia in 1903. Barton was also a barrister and colonial politician. He became the leading advocate of federation in New South Wales after the death of Sir Henry Parkes in 1896. At federation, Barton was commissioned as the first Prime Minister of Australia. He left the Prime Ministership in 1903 to serve under Griffith and alongside R.E. O'Connor on the High Court.

In the period we are considering − from 1903 to 1919 − the membership of the Court grew, first of all with the addition of two judges, Isaac Isaacs and H.B. Higgins, in October 1906. O'Connor died in November 1912, and two

[5] Sir Garfield Barwick, *A Radical Tory*, Federation Press, Leichhardt, 1995, pp. 289-91, 298.

[6] W.G. Hayden, *Hayden: an autobiography*, Angus & Robertson, Sydney, 1996, pp. 291-2.

[7] R.B. Joyce, *Samuel Walker Griffith*, University of Queensland Press, 1984.

[8] [Geoffrey Bolton, *Edmund Barton: The One Man For The Job*, Allen & Unwin, 2000.]

further positions on the Court were created. The three vacancies were filled in early 1913 by Frank Gavan Duffy, Charles Powers, and George Edward Rich. There were no further changes to the Court until Griffith retired in October 1919, and Adrian Knox was appointed to succeed him.

Until 1931, the Governors-General of Australia were all British aristocrats or politicians. The Governor-Generalship was no sinecure. In its first three years, the Commonwealth went through two Governors-General. In the period we are concerned with, there were four: Lord Northcote, from January 1904 to 1908, an experienced politician whom Cunneen describes as "conscientious, virtuous but dull";[9] Lord Dudley, from 1908 until 1911, a man generally regarded as the least adequate Governor-General Australia has had; Lord Denman, from 1911 to 1914, whose performance was regarded as sound, but whose tenure was marked by the decision of the N.S.W. Labor government to deny the Governor-General use of Government House, Sydney, and whose suitability as Governor-General of Australia was perhaps diminished by his allergy to wattle; and from 1914 to 1920, Sir Ronald Munro Ferguson, later Lord Novar, an independent-minded Liberal MP from Scotland, who was arguably the most successful of the Governors-General before Isaacs became the first Australian to be appointed in 1931. Munro Ferguson was certainly one of the most vigorous Governors-General – too much so for some.

The early Governors-General had dual roles. First, they represented the monarch and fulfilled that role under the Constitution – that executive power vested in the Governor-General – which the Governor-General still fulfils today. Secondly, in theory until the Imperial Conference of 1926 and in practice probably until some time later, the Governors-General were agents of the British government in Australia and thus guardians of the Imperial connection. Some of the consultations of High Court judges were on Imperial matters; many were on matters within the Governor-General's role as de facto constitutional monarch.

This constitutional role also had, and has, a dual aspect. On the one hand, there are those matters, such as government policy, where, though the Governor-General can express opinions to the Prime Minister or other ministers, he or she must ultimately accept their decision. In such matters, the Governor-General's power is confined to Bagehot's famous 1867 aphorism, "the right to be consulted, the right to encourage, the right to warn".[10] On the

[9] Cunneen, op. cit., p. 48.
[10] Walter Bagehot, *The English Constitution* (1867), quoted from Oxford University Press 1955 edition, p. 67.

other hand, there are certain matters where there is a real discretionary power – where the Governor-General must make the decision, and where, if in his or her judgment the extraordinary circumstances demand it, the advice of ministers can be rejected or, in some cases (such as appointing or dismissing a Prime Minister), he or she may act without advice from incumbent ministers. This is the realm of the so-called "reserve powers" of the Crown, and these relate principally to the Governor-General's right to reject advice to dissolve parliament, and the power to appoint and dismiss Prime Ministers. This is a complex and controversial area, and although it will touch on consultations outside this area, much of this article relates to Governors-General seeking help on the exercise of their reserve powers. These powers were exercised in the early decades of federation much more than subsequently since the unsettled nature of the party system at that time created more circumstances than later requiring vice-regal decision.

A distinction must be drawn between two uses of the word "advice". In the formal sense of the word, a Governor-General can only receive "advice" from his ministers; this includes binding advice, and advice – for example, that parliament be dissolved – which the Governor-General is not bound to accept. In a non-formal sense, the word "advice" can be used to cover the opinions and information from all sources which the Governor-General may obtain in helping to determine how to exercise his or her powers.

This article will show that the early Governors-General felt themselves to be in need of assistance in understanding their constitutional powers, the conventions by which they must be exercised, and how those powers and conventions related to the particular circumstances they faced. Governors-General regarded themselves as entitled to seek advice from High Court judges and from other individuals on the exercise of their discretions. They thought themselves entitled to seek advice without seeking the approval of the Prime Minister. In return, the High Court judges who were consulted – Griffith and Barton – regarded themselves as entitled to offer advice, both when it was sought by the Governor-General and when it was not. Though both were jealous of the independence of the High Court and of its reputation, they did not regard these as being compromised by such consultations. Political leaders were generally (though not necessarily always) aware of these consultations, including successive Prime Ministers, and did not disapprove of them. So far as can be ascertained, all involved thought that if the Governor-General's discretion were to be a real discretion, he must be able to decide himself whom he would consult. It was not considered that the standing of the Court was threatened by judges being consulted. Though most understandable in the exercise of the reserve powers, which were, and are, generally regarded as not subject to judicial review, this view appears also, surprisingly, to have prevailed in cases which might well have ended up – and, in at least one case, did end up – before the Court.

The party situation in the first two decades of federation was unsettled. In 1901, there were two large groupings – Protectionists and Free-traders – and a smaller Labor Party. With Labor strengthening its position, the parliament elected in 1903 saw three near-equal parties or, in Deakin's cricket analogy, "three elevens",[11] and, during that parliament, each of them had a turn in government, Watson and Reid sandwiched between Deakin's first and second terms. After the 1906 election, Labor supported Deakin's remaining in power, but withdrew support in November 1908, and the Labor leader, Fisher, became Prime Minister. However, in May 1909, the non-Labor forces "fused", driving Labor from power and effectively laying the basis for Australia's two-party system. Labor emerged from the 1910 election with a clear majority over the Fusion (later the Liberal Party), and was to remain in government for seven years, with only the brief interruption of Cook's slim Liberal majority in 1913-1914, which he lost in the double dissolution of 1914. After the first conscription referendum of 1916, the Labor Party split, Prime Minister Hughes staying in power with the support of his breakaway National Labor grouping and the Liberals. These groups joined as the Nationalist Party in January 1917, and won a handsome victory over Labor in the election of May 1917. After the election of December 1919, in which the new Country Party gained ten seats, Hughes clung to power with a slender majority.

It was in this context of shifting alliances between parties, of fusions and splits, that the Governors-General had cause to exercise their discretionary powers. For example, on three occasions – in 1904, 1905, and 1909 – when governments were defeated in the House of Representatives and requested dissolution, the Governor-General refused the request and, on the subsequent resignation of the government, appointed someone else, who could command majority support in the House, to be Prime Minister. This survey of the consultations of Griffith and Barton will begin by looking at those cases.

---

[11] La Nauze, op. cit., p. 363.

Consultations of Griffith and Barton by Governors-General

1904 (and possibly 1905)

In August 1904, the Watson government – the first federal Labor government – was defeated in the House of Representatives on its Arbitration Bill. Watson requested a dissolution of the House, but the Governor-General, Lord Northcote, refused the request. Watson resigned, and Reid became Prime Minister. Lord Northcote and Griffith had discussed at the end of May the likelihood of Watson's being defeated, something Griffith predicted.[12] On 12 August 1904, the day the Watson government was defeated in the House, Lord Northcote telegrammed asking Griffith to see him the next day. Griffith wrote that Northcote "consulted me about the political position".[13]

On the Monday, 15 August, Northcote wrote to his friend, Lord Selborne, in South Africa:[14]

> Watson has sent me a formal request for a Dissolution but he knows I shall refuse it, and is coming for lunch and resignation today. He has admitted to me privately that he feels no surprise at my refusal, and that he and his colleagues have full confidence in my fairness towards them.

That day Northcote refused Watson's request, and Watson subsequently resigned.

It is possible that Griffith was consulted again in 1905 in anticipation of, or immediately after, the defeat of Reid's government. But important source materials for this period do not exist.

1909

The decision on 1 June 1909 of the Governor-General, Lord Dudley, to refuse the request of Andrew Fisher for a dissolution after his defeat in the House of Representatives by the Fusion, has been much misrepresented by historians. Some accounts do not mention that the Governor-General consulted Griffith; others present the Governor-General as blindly following Griffith's advice, without even reading the government's memorandum, which argued for a dissolution, or portray Dudley as refusing the dissolution request without giving his reasons.

In fact, the Governor-General presented Fisher with a detailed and cogent six and a half page response to the government's memorandum. It

---

[12] MS Selborne, dep 197 fol 114, Bodleian Library, Oxford. Chandos 2/27, Northcote letter of 29 and 31 May 1904, Churchill College Archives, Cambridge.

[13] Griffith papers, ML MSS 363/44 fol 92, Mitchell Library, Sydney.

[14] MS Selbourne, dep 197 fol 125, Bodleian Library, Oxford.

began: "The Governor-General has carefully considered the Prime Minister's memorandum of 31st May in which he advises a dissolution of the House of Representatives."[15] Dudley sent a copy of the government memorandum and his response to the Colonial Office with what an official there described as "another excellent and lucid despatch"[16] on the crisis. In the Mitchell Library, Sydney, and the National Library, Canberra, are drafts, prepared by Griffith, of the Governor-General's response.[17] Griffith's diary records that on 31 May he "lunched with Lord Dudley" and "Wrote Notes for him re proposed dissolution".[18] The memorandum Dudley actually gave Fisher is longer – about one and a half times longer – than Griffith's draft, and makes more specific reference to the arguments of Fisher's memorandum to the Governor-General. While Dudley's memo was clearly based in large part on the Griffith draft, much was added and much changed. It is not clear who did the adding and adapting.

It may have been influenced by Deakin, who was again to follow Fisher as Prime Minister. Deakin's diary records that on 1 June, the day Fisher resigned, Deakin received an "SWG memo" and suggests that he, Deakin, wrote "Notes" on it, but for what purpose is not recorded.[19] Later the same day, Deakin "accepted responsibility"[20] for forming a new government.

All in all, Dudley seems to have handled the matter well. However, questions remain concerning the precise role of Deakin, and whether Dudley may have shown partiality towards him.

1914 double dissolution

The Cook Liberal government, elected in 1913, had a one-seat majority in the House of Representatives, but was in a clear minority in the Senate. Cook set about creating the preconditions for a double dissolution – that the Senate reject pieces of government legislation twice, with an interval of three months between the first Senate rejection and the House passing the legislation again.

In May 1914, as Cook's request for a double dissolution was getting nearer,

[15] CO 418/71 fol 48-54, Public Record Office (P.R.O.), London.
[16] Ibid., fol 31.
[17] Griffith papers, ML MSS 363/8X fol 36-44 (handwritten), 45-47 (typed), Mitchell Library, Sydney. Novar papers, MS 696 fols 3790-3793, National Library, Canberra.
[18] MS Q197, Griffith diary entry for 30 May 1909, Dixson Library, Sydney.
[19] Deakin papers, MS 1540/2/29, Deakin diary entry for 1 June 1909, National Library, Canberra.
[20] Ibid.

a new Governor-General, Sir Ronald Munro Ferguson, arrived to replace Lord Denman. Denman gave Munro Ferguson a letter containing advice on various aspects of the Governor-Generalship. He included comments on the possible sources of help on how to handle the expected request:[21]

> I suppose Griffith and Barton are the most reliable authorities, should you want advice. Isaacs is a judge who I believe is thought well of by the Labour Party (it is sad how everyone in this country, even the judges, are supposed to have partisan leanings), but perhaps Griffith and Barton might hardly like a third opinion being sought. There is a very good authority here on constitutional law Professor Harrison Moore, who is considered both able and impartial; his opinion might be worth asking quite privately, – but Barton particularly should be sound, as he has political as well as legal knowledge.

This last comment also fitted Griffith, Isaacs, Higgins, and Powers.

Denman did not suggest Munro Ferguson should seek Cook's permission to consult such authorities, and Munro Ferguson's various letters show he did not think he needed such permission.

When, on 2 June, Cook asked for a dissolution, the new Governor-General asked Cook "whether it would be in conformity with precedent and constitutionally correct for me to see Mr Fisher or anyone named by him" and "Whether I could consult say the Chief Justice".[22] Cook opposed the Governor-General's seeing Fisher, but "was very willing that I should see the Chief Justice".[23] Munro Ferguson saw Griffith the next day, and found that Griffith agreed with him on "the full discretionary powers [the Constitution] gives to the Governor-General to decide for or against a double dissolution irrespective of the advice tendered by his Ministers".[24] The government had argued that the Governor-General was bound to follow the Prime Minister's advice. The Governor-General made clear to Cook his dissent from this doctrine. However, because no alternative government could command a majority in the House, he agreed to a double dissolution.

Munro Ferguson expressed himself delighted with the assistance he had received from Griffith.[25] He did not see the Opposition Leader, Fisher, although, contrary to the view of Cook and of Griffith, he regarded himself

[21] Novar papers, MS 696 fol 7399, National Library, Canberra.

[22] Ibid, fol 10283-10284. MS Harcourt, dep 479 fol 21-22, Bodleian Library, Oxford.

[23] Ibid.

[24] CO 418/123 fol 39-40, P.R.O. Novar papers, MS 696 fol 4618, National Library, Canberra (very slightly different from P.R.O. text).

[25] MS Q191, Griffith papers, vol. VII, fol 926, Dixson Library, Sydney.

as free to do so should he believe it necessary. He was supported in this view by the Colonial Secretary, Lewis Harcourt.[26]

When the Fisher Labor government came to power after the elections of September 1914, it became clear that the government would publish the correspondence between the Governor-General and Cook over the double dissolution request. Being concerned to assert his discretion as to whether or not to grant the double dissolution request, the Governor-General asked Griffith for a memorandum setting out his earlier advice,[27] and Griffith wrote one.[28] Over subsequent years, Munro Ferguson took other opportunities, with the further help of Griffith, Barton and Sir Harrison Moore, to stress to the Colonial Office, and thus to posterity, that he had granted the double dissolution "upon a review of the political situation".[29] Some of this material was set out in an article by Dr H.V. Evatt, then a High Court judge, in 1940. Evatt wrote: [30]

> The fact that [Munro Ferguson] called in aid two 'outside', though very distinguished, authorities on constitutional practice [Griffith and Harrison Moore] illustrates the difficulties confronting a King's representative who is not himself expert in a very difficult topic. Because of the lack of certainty in these matters, Dominion Governors have frequently felt themselves at liberty to adopt a similar course.

In 1914, the parliament was dissolved at the end of July in preparation for elections in early September. However, World War I broke out between the dissolution of the old parliament and the election of the new. This raised a problem. As the Governor-General wrote, "Parliament voted sufficient money to last under normal conditions until October".[31] But mobilisation for war represented a major additional "drain on the Treasury". The Governor-General and Chief Justice simultaneously tried to contact each other. Griffith referred to a suggestion "that some means should be devised for resuscitating

[26] MS Harcourt, dep 479 fol 54-55, Bodleian Library, Oxford.

[27] Griffith papers, ML MSS 363/7X fol 24-26, Mitchell Library, Sydney. Novar papers, MS 696 fol 4637, National Library, Canberra. CO 418/123 fol 354, P.R.O.

[28] Griffith papers, ML MSS 363/8X fol 49-50, Mitchell Library, Sydney. Novar papers, MS 696 fols 4495-4498, 10290-10291, National Library, Canberra. CO 418/123 fol 352-353, P.R.O.

[29] Novar papers, MS 696 fols 4363, 4437, 4502, 4620-4623, 4635, 4703-4705, 4707, 4709-4712, 8560, 8956-8958, 10442, National Library, Canberra. Griffith papers, ML MSS 363/7X fol 38-39, ML MSS 363/8X fol 83-90, Mitchell Library, Sydney. CO 418/123 fol 335, CO 418/133 fol 349, CO 418/145 fol 415-420, CO 418/186 fol 195-197, P.R.O.

[30] H.V. Evatt, "The Discretionary Authority of Dominion Governors", *Canadian Bar Review*, January 1940, p. 9.

[31] CO 418/123 fol 185, P.R.O.

Parliament or otherwise" postponing the election.[32] This suggestion was being pressed especially by Hughes, but opposed by the government and privately by Fisher. Griffith suggested that Munro Ferguson recommend that the Colonial Secretary "should ask the self-governing Dominions and States whether" they would object to the Imperial parliament legislating to provide that, if the Empire went to war when a parliament was dissolved, the Governor-General or Governor could recall the old parliament. Griffith said that he made this suggestion "on my responsibility as a Privy Councillor", and that the Governor-General need not consult the government before making the suggestion to the Colonial Secretary.[33]

The Governor-General replied: [34]

> Yesterday morning I told Mr Cook of my intention to consult you as to how the financial situation created by the War and D.D. could best be met. He warmly approved. He had wished to see you himself and begged to have your views which he thought you might be disposed to communicate with less reserve to me.
>
> I had not long wired to you when your welcome letter arrived. ...

To cut a long story short, Griffith and Munro Ferguson exchanged several letters over subsequent days, Griffith refining his proposal[35] and then pressing the Governor-General to send it to the Colonial Secretary regardless of the Prime Minister's approach.[36] Munro Ferguson reported the Prime Minister's lack of enthusiasm for the plan. Cook preferred to proceed with the election and "negotiate with Opposition Leaders outside of Parliament to get their approval for war spending".[37] But Munro Ferguson told Griffith of his having sent off the plan to the Colonial Secretary, Harcourt, endorsing it.[38] Harcourt telegrammed: "Please thank Griffith for suggestion which however HMs

---

[32] Novar papers, MS 696 fol 3770-3774, National Library, Canberra. MS Harcourt, dep 479 fol 83-84, Bodleian Library, Oxford. Griffith papers, ML MSS 363/7X fol 1-5 (draft), Mitchell Library, Sydney.

[33] Ibid.

[34] MS Harcourt, dep 479 fol 85-86, Bodleian Library, Oxford. Griffith papers, ML MSS 363/7X fol 6-9, Mitchell Library, Sydney. Novar papers, MS 698 fol 3783-3784, National Library, Canberra (slight variation in wording).

[35] Ibid., fol 3776-3777. MS Harcourt, dep 479 fol 95, Bodleian Library, Oxford. Griffith papers, 363/7X fol 10 (draft), Mitchell Library, Sydney (SWG to RMF, 15 August 1914).

[36] Novar papers, MS 696 fol 3778-3779, National Library, Canberra. MS Harcourt, dep 479 fol 97, Bodleian Library, Oxford.

[37] Novar papers, MS 696 fol 3785-3786, National Library, Canberra. Griffith papers, ML MSS 363/7X fol 11-13, 16-18, Mitchell Library, Sydney.

[38] MS Harcourt, dep 479 fol 81, 93-96, Bodleian Library, Oxford. Novar papers, MS 696 fol 3785, 5095, National Library, Canberra. Griffith papers, ML MSS 363/7X fol 16-18, Mitchell Library, Sydney. C0418/123 fol 171-172, P.R.O.

Government do not consider practicable."[39] Thus, the election proceeded, Cook was defeated and Fisher led Labor back to power.

During the war

During the war, the Governor-General consulted both Griffith and Barton on many issues. They helped guide him through the shoals of Fisher's departure as Prime Minister in 1915, the first conscription referendum, which was defeated in October 1916, the split in the Labor Party but with Hughes staying in power at the head of a minority government, his entering into government with the Liberals and the formation of the Nationalist Party, and the second conscription referendum in December 1917, the defeat of which was followed by Hughes's resignation and recommissioning as Prime Minister.

1915

In October 1915, Fisher gave up the prime ministership to go to London as Australia's High Commissioner, a post the Governor-General regarded as no less important than the Prime Ministership. Fisher (1916-1921) followed Reid (1910-1916) and preceded Cook (1921-1927) in the post − all three of them former Prime Ministers. On Fisher's giving up the Prime Ministership, the Governor-General sought advice on the transition. It would be up to the caucus to elect a new leader, and a new ministry. Munro Ferguson was gravely concerned at what he saw as the damage the caucus system did to responsible government. Griffith wrote to him:[40]

> The political government of the Commonwealth is still in theory what is called 'responsible government', and knows nothing of Caucus. ... When [Mr Fisher] surrenders his office his recommendations [for ministers] will fall with it, which is commonly described by saying that the resignation of the Prime Minister carries that of his colleagues. Their successors will be appointed by you on the recommendation of some other person, though of course the motives which induce him to make the recommendations are not examinable. That is my view of the Constitution.

First conscription referendum

Fisher's successor as Prime Minister, Hughes, called a referendum in October 1916 to approve conscription for overseas military service. Some months earlier, Munro Ferguson had told Lord Stamfordham:[41]

---

[39] Ibid., fol 19-21.
[40] Novar papers, MS 696 fol 3753 (copy), 3754-3755 (original), National Library, Canberra.
[41] Ibid., fol 10443.

... I learnt from the Chief Justice last night, in strict confidence, that in his opinion this Government has no power to conscript for overseas service and that the point, if raised, might have to be settled by the Imperial Parliament. This must not leak out.

Perhaps this was a reference to the idea of introducing conscription by regulation under the *War Precautions Act*. In any case, we have already seen that Munro Ferguson quoted Griffith and Barton as believing that Hughes was right to call a referendum. Hughes's biographer, Fitzhardinge, thinks Griffith's attitude was important in leading Hughes to call a referendum.[42]

This was not the only occasion on which Griffith told a Governor-General what the High Court was likely to decide if a matter came before it. In 1904, he had told Northcote that "if the matter ever reached the High Court, he had no doubt the Watson [Arbitration Bill] would be declared to be unconstitutional".[43]

However, contrary to Northcote's wishes, it was this case that established that the Governor-General should not act himself as referee of the constitutionality of legislation but leave that for decision by the courts. In 1913, Lord Denman wrote that Griffith "thinks it quite likely that the High Court will reverse the decision of the NSW Tribunal" concerning Government House, Sydney.[44]

1917 election

As we have seen, Hughes lost the 1916 conscription referendum, the Labor Party split, and Hughes remained in office with the support of the Liberals. On 4 January 1917, Munro Ferguson recorded that Hughes was "'wishful' to know if he c[oul]d get a dissolution". The Governor-General said he "must consider and w[oul]d consult".[45] The Governor-General recorded the following day:[46]

Saw Sir E. Barton and consulted him under P[rivy] C[ouncillor]'s oath (that most useful prov[ision] of the Const[itutio]n). ... Sir E. was of opinion that Prime Minister w[oul]d have to make a statement in writing on wh[ich] I c[oul]d base any decision when required, on granting or refusing a Dissolution.

Barton thought a dissolution not justified, but suggested that Munro

[42] L.F. Fitzhardinge, *William Morris Hughes: a political biography*, vol. 2, *The Little Digger 1914-1952*, Angus & Robertson, Sydney, 1979, pp. 179-80.

[43] Chandos 2/27, letter of 25 April 1904, Churchill College Archives Centre, Cambridge.

[44] MS Harcourt, dep 479 fol 113, Bodleian Library, Oxford.

[45] Munro Ferguson diary entry, 4 January 1917. Copies of Munro Ferguson's diary entries during his term as Governor-General are held by Professor John Poynter of the University of Melbourne.

[46] Ibid., 5 January 1917.

Ferguson consult Griffith, without telling Griffith of Barton's opinion.[47]

Munro Ferguson recorded for the next day, 6 January 1917:[48]

> Saw Sir S. Griffith and consulted him as P[rivy] C[ouncillor]. I described
> the situation and the P[rime] M[inister]'s conversation.
>
> ... I ... showed Sir Samuel a draft of a letter [to] the P.M., requiring, as
> occasion might arise, a statement showing need for a Dissolution. Sir S
> approved of this draft with a verbal alteration.
>
> ... It was obvious that to grant a dissolution with the result uncertain
> might prove more disturbing than ought else to the Kings Service. I
> wrote my letter and sent it to the P[rime] M[inister].

However, Hughes did not press for an election at that time.[49] But, after
the formation of the Nationalist Party government soon afterwards, he did,
on 5 March, request an election, and the Governor-General assented.[50]

Second conscription referendum, and Hughes's resignation

During the 1917 election campaign, Hughes pledged that his government
would not introduce conscription without approval in a referendum. So a
second conscription referendum was held on 20 December 1917. Hughes
gave a public pledge — and one to the Governor-General — that he would
resign if the referendum were defeated.[51] Both before and after its defeat, the
Governor-General sought advice. He recorded in his diary for 7 December
1917:[52]

> Saw Chief Justice ... Sir S[amuel] concurred in the view that should the
> Referendum go 'No' it w[oul]d be for the Governor-General to exhaust
> the powers of Parl[iament] before giving a Dissolution to anybody.

Griffith's view was that the referendum had no binding force, and did not
affect the responsibility of the cabinet and parliament. He "entirely agreed"
with Munro Ferguson "that it would be against the spirit of the constitution to
enact conscription in any other way than by act of Parliament".[53]

After the defeat of the referendum, the Governor-General believed the
Prime Minister would resign to honour his pledge. Expecting this to happen,

---

[47] Ibid.
[48] Ibid., 8 January 1917.
[49] Ibid., 12 January 1917.
[50] Ibid., 5 March 1917.
[51] Ibid., 5 December 1917.
[52] Ibid., 7 December 1917.
[53] Ibid.

Munro Ferguson discussed with Barton[54] and Griffith[55] his intention to try all major political leaders to see if any could form a government which could carry on without a further election.

On Saturday, 29 December 1917, the Governor-General saw Hughes and urged him "to resign and recommend that another leading member of the Nationalist Party be sent for."[56] On New Year's Day 1918, the Governor-General wrote to the Prime Minister:[57]

> ... I have a letter from Sir E. Barton, to thank me for a bottle of wine [Munro Ferguson gave wine to Griffith and Barton at Christmas over several years], in which he expresses very the like view to that which I put forward on Saturday.

Munro Ferguson then quoted Barton's letter as urging the desirability of a resignation by Hughes, but not a "sham resignation". This was to "keep faith with the people" — a political or ethical opinion, it seems, rather than a legal one.[58]

Hughes did resign as Prime Minister on 8 January 1918. The Governor-General interviewed the major leaders of the opposition Labor Party, various Nationalist ministers, and some backbenchers. He was forced to conclude that only Hughes could lead a government commanding a majority in the House of Representatives.[59] Hughes was recommissioned with the same cabinet as before.

The Governor-General's legal advice

In 1917, Hughes had agreed that the Governor-General was entitled to "independent legal opinion" other than from the Attorney-General. Hughes was himself Attorney-General as well as Prime Minister. The Governor-General listed Sir Robert Garran (the Solicitor-General [clearly suggested ad hominem]), Sir Samuel Griffith, Sir Edmund Barton, and Sir William Irvine as possible sources of advice, and recorded:[60]

> The Prime Minister agreed. He also undertook to inform me should his view differ from that of Sir R. Garran, or of Mr Mitchell, or of any other

[54] Ibid., 22 December 1917.
[55] Ibid., 25 December 1917.
[56] Cunneen, op. cit., p. 136.
[57] Novar papers, MS 696 fol 2691, National Library, Canberra.
[58] Barton's letter is at ibid., fol 4078-4079.
[59] See ibid., fol 8961-8963. CO 418/169 fol 47-55, P.R.O.
[60] Novar papers, MS 696 fol 4763, National Library, Canberra. See also Munro Ferguson diary entries for 1 March 1917, 8 September 1917, 11 February 1918.

leading lawyer whom he might consult.

Munro Ferguson did have quite a deal of contact with Garran. Sir William Irvine, who had been Attorney-General under Cook in 1913-1914, was in 1917 a strongly pro-conscriptionist Nationalist backbencher, and from March 1918 Chief Justice of Victoria. Geoffrey Sawer described him in 1917 as "by far the most able and respected federal political leader".[61] The "Mr Mitchell" mentioned was, almost certainly, Edward Fancourt Mitchell, who was pre-eminent at the Victorian Bar. Mitchell was to be defeated by Stanley Melbourne Bruce for the Nationalist preselection for the seat of Flinders in 1918, to succeed Sir William Irvine.

Other consultations

The consultations of Griffith and Barton already mentioned were largely on questions of the reserve powers – affecting who would or should be Prime Minister. But Griffith and Barton were consulted, or gave views unsought, on other matters. One of the most striking cases occurred on 19 May 1916. Griffith wrote to the Governor-General:[62]

> I have today ascertained that the question of the validity of some of the War regulations is about to be brought before the High Court. It would be a public calamity if the Court were compelled to pull down the whole fabric.
>
> Under the circumstances, and as Parliament is sitting, I think it is consistent with my duty to the Sovereign to suggest to you that you should invite the attention of Ministers to the danger, for there is no doubt that the extent of the powers conferred by existing legislation is open to much question; which can only be solved by Parliament or the Court.
>
> Any help I can give in planning any necessary legislation is, as I told Mr Hughes before he left for England, at the service of the Government.

This letter seems extraordinary unless, perhaps even if, considered in the context of the emergency of war. Griffith was both volunteering advice to the Governor-General and the government, and offering further advice on a matter – war regulations – that clearly could, and did, come before the courts.

---

[61] Geoffrey Sawer, *Australian Federal Politics and Law, 1901-1929*, Melbourne University Press, 1956, p. 159n.

[62] Novar papers, MS 696 fols 3739-3741, National Library, Canberra. See also Joyce, op. cit., p. 352.

The Governor-General replied the next day:[63]

> I am exceedingly obliged for your letter ... I have seen the acting Prime Minister [Senator Pearce] who will be in communication with you immediately. He is anxious to see you.

Griffith's diary records for 20 May 1916, when he was in Melbourne:[64]

> In Chambers in morning. Lunched at Government House. Senator Pearce called re War Precautions Bill.

The full sequence of events is difficult to reconstruct. But in the case of *Farey v Burvett*, heard in May-June 1916, the *War Precautions Act* and price fixing orders made under it were upheld by the Court. Griffith, Barton, Isaacs, Higgins, and Powers construed the defence power so broadly as, in Professor Brian Galligan's words, "to permit near-dictatorial federal action in executing the war effort".[65] Duffy and Rich dissented. It may be that Griffith's alarm over the *War Precautions Act* arose from his fear that more judges than Duffy and Rich would take a narrow view of the defence power. Isaacs in fact gave the most expansive reading of it, and Griffith a more cautious one.

Griffith's 1916 advice had a parallel in 1939, when Sir Owen Dixon helped frame the regulations of the Central Wool Committee,[66] and arguably in 1951 when Sir John Latham advised Menzies and Earle Page on possible constitutional amendments "that would enable [the Commonwealth Government] to take action during the transitional pre-war period".[67]

Griffith and Barton were consulted on a variety of other matters. For example:

- in 1915, when prompted by the Colonial Secretary to ascertain and influence Australian opinion on a possible deal between the Empire and Japan on former German islands in the Pacific, Munro Ferguson sought the views of both Griffith and Barton,

---

[63] Novar papers, MS 696 fol 3742. Griffith papers, ML MSS 363/7X fol 37a, Mitchell Library, Sydney. Senator Pearce, Minister for Defence, was also Acting Prime Minister for nine months during 1916.

[64] Ibid., Griffith diary entry for 20 May 1916.

[65] Brian Galligan, *Politics of the High Court: a study of the judicial branch of government in Australia*, University of Queensland Press, 1987, p. 95.

[66] Latham papers, MS 1009/62/199, 200-201, National Library, Canberra. See *Commonwealth Parliamentary Debates: House of Representatives*, 19 September 1939, p. 679, per document tabled by R.G. Menzies.

[67] Latham papers, MS 1009/62/684-685, National Library, Canberra.

amongst others;[68]

- both Griffith and Barton shared Munro Ferguson's view that the Governor-General was entitled to more regular contact with the Prime Minister;[69]

- in November 1916, during a major coal strike, Griffith wrote to the Governor-General offering himself as a possible conciliator to settle the dispute: the Governor-General passed this on to Hughes, who replied that "unfortunately Sir Samuel's letter ... arrived too late to permit of his offer being availed of";[70]

- over many years, Barton and Griffith pushed – through both Munro Ferguson and Hughes – and Isaacs later pushed also, for regular Dominion representation on the Judicial Committee of the Privy Council, and perhaps creation of a single court of final appeal for the whole Empire;[71]

- in 1917 and again in 1919, Griffith sent Munro Ferguson material he had prepared advocating strong sanctions against trade unionists breaking the law – proposals the Governor-General recommended to the Prime Minister.[72]

The extent of Griffith's contact with the Governors-General can be seen by examining the entries in Griffith's diaries. These record over 200 contacts with five Governors-General over 16 years. There were in fact contacts additional to these, not recorded in his diaries.[73]

Sir Edmund Barton had an even closer relationship with Munro Ferguson than Griffith did. Just a few examples:

- in October 1914, Barton advised the Governor-General on the need for the Imperial government to take the Dominions more

---

[68] MS Harcourt, dep 468 fol 249-250, dep 479 fols 128, 237, 272-273, 330, Bodleian Library, Oxford. Munro Ferguson diary entries for 16 May 1915, 26 October 1917. CO 418/176 fol 94, P.R.O.

[69] CO 418/144 fol 304, P.R.O. See also Munro Ferguson diary entry for 8 November 1917.

[70] Joyce, op. cit., pp. 352-3.

[71] Ibid., pp. 351-2.

[72] Ibid., pp. 353, 356. Munro Ferguson diary entries for 26 September 1917, 28 April 1919. Griffith papers, ML MSS 363/1, Griffith diary entry for 8 September 1916, Mitchell Library, Sydney.

[73] For example, Griffith's letter to Munro Ferguson of 19 May 1916. See Novar papers, MS 696 fol 3739-3741, National Library, Canberra.

into its confidence;[74]

- in 1917, Munro Ferguson sought Barton's opinion on whether it was constitutionally proper for a new parliament to be opened without "a King's Speech": Barton agreed that it was not;[75]

- in 1917, at the Prime Minister's instigation,[76] Munro Ferguson sought Barton's views on whether it was proper for there to be a Royal Commission into allegations in the Senate that Hughes was corrupt: Barton advised that "no Ministry could ask for a Royal Commission into its own purity".[77]

The Irish Republican Brotherhood

However, an issue in 1918 showed that Griffith, Barton, and their High Court colleagues were conscious of the need to preserve the independence of the Court.[78] Briefly, the government wished to appoint either Griffith or another High Court judge to preside over a tribunal to decide whether the internment, already carried out, of seven alleged members of the Irish Republican Brotherhood was justified by the evidence. Griffith, however, took the view that the internment of aliens was an administrative act which under international law was at the discretion of the government of each country; that for a judge to make the decision or pronounce upon a decision would be to have him perform a ministerial function, which would not be proper; but that a judge could properly advise a minister on the minister's performance of his functions. In short, the judge could advise the minister what to do but not, in effect, do it for him. So, Griffith suggested an alternative to the government proposal:[79]

> ... A Privy Councillor, however, acting in discharge of his duty to the Sovereign, may ask another Privy Councillor for advice, which is quite a different thing.

After all, Griffith said, "I have never hesitated to offer opinion to the Governor-General as a Privy Councillor, even without being asked."[80] But Griffith insisted that ministerial functions must not be conferred on a judge.

---

[74] Ibid., fol 4040-4047.

[75] Ibid., fols 4682-4687, 8972.

[76] Munro Ferguson diary entry for 15 March 1917.

[77] Ibid. See also Novar papers, MS 696 fol 10578, National Library, Canberra.

[78] See Joyce, op. cit., pp. 354-5.

[79] Novar papers, MS 696 fol 4784, National Library, Canberra.

[80] Ibid., fol 4787.

His attitude was supported by all High Court judges,[81] the Governor-General,[82] and, seemingly, the Colonial Office.[83]

Griffith's retirement, and the deaths of Barton and Griffith

Especially after Sir Samuel Griffith's stroke in March 1917, both the Governor-General and at least some of his brother judges on the High Court, not least Barton, grew increasingly conscious of the need for a pension to be provided to enable Griffith to retire. On Christmas Day 1917, having visited Griffith, Munro Ferguson wrote in his diary: "I wish Sir S G could have Peerage and Pension. He merits both if ever man did."[84] In January 1918, Hughes agreed with Munro Ferguson's recommendation to the Colonial Secretary that Griffith and Sir John Forrest be made peers;[85] but only Forrest was in fact elevated to the peerage. By June 1918, Munro Ferguson had extracted from the Acting Prime Minister, Watt, a promise "to try to get a pension for the Chief Justice".[86] The Governor-General wrote in his diary:[87]

> Sir E[dmund] needs one also. ... He [Barton] is an old dear. There's no one in Austr[alia] I like so much. After him I like being with the CJ – who is a little alarming though I don't believe he means to be so. The Chief Justice the most intellectual personage here.

A Bill providing for a pension for the Chief Justice was finally passed in December 1918. In June 1919, Griffith submitted to the government his resignation as Chief Justice. Barton and Munro Ferguson were appalled that for over three weeks it was not even acknowledged by the Acting Attorney-General.[88]

On 25 July, a ceremony to farewell Griffith was held in the High Court sitting in Brisbane. Neither Griffith nor Barton was well enough to be there.[89] The next day, in Brisbane, the Governor-General visited Griffith, who told him that he believed the most appropriate successor as Chief Justice was the leading Sydney barrister, Adrian Knox. Munro Ferguson "promised to tell

[81] Ibid., fol 4798.
[82] Ibid., fol 4776. Munro Ferguson diary entries for 30 July 1918, 27 August 1918, 29 August 1918, 7 September 1918.
[83] CO 418/170 fol 138, P.R.O.
[84] Munro Ferguson diary entry for 25 December 1917.
[85] Ibid., 5 January 1918.
[86] Ibid., 7 June 1918.
[87] Ibid.
[88] Ibid., 21 July 1919. See also entries for 6 July and 16 October 1919.
[89] Joyce, op. cit., p. 356.

Ministers I agreed Adrian Knox was the successor to him. [Sir Samuel] was feeble but right on the spot."[90]

After Hughes returned from overseas, in early September Munro Ferguson conveyed to him Griffith's view. At least one judge, Powers, wrote to Griffith saying that he wanted Barton as Chief Justice;[91] as we shall see, it became clear that Barton desperately wished for the post. But on 16 October, the Governor-General received a letter from the Prime Minister telling him of the government's decision to appoint Knox. Their reasoning was that, with Barton's health precarious, it offered greater stability to the Court to appoint a distinguished lawyer "in the prime of life".[92] With elections impending, this decision reduced the risk of an incoming Labor government being able to appoint a new Chief Justice. Munro Ferguson wrote to London:[93]

> Mr. Hughes asked me if I would convey to Sir Edmund [Barton] the Government's very deep appreciation of his unique services to the Commonwealth, and profound regret that circumstances made it impossible to bestow this final honour upon him. My own friendship for Sir Edmund, and my knowledge of his great worth, rendered this a very painful duty, but I felt that there was much to be said for the course taken by the Government.

Munro Ferguson wrote in his diary for the day on which he received Hughes's letter:[94]

> Saw Sir E. Barton. I never felt more personal sympathy. He really felt most for Lady Barton's disappointment. I had not realized till the evening before how much he w[oul]d have liked the CJship. I said what I thought re the motive of the Govt – and this did offer some consolation. He is a dear old man and one of the ablest and most loyal of HM's servants in any part of the Empire.

Barton sent a prearranged message to his wife telling her the news, and later told the Governor-General that he "did not lie awake more than an hour" that night despite his disappointment.[95] Trying to console him, Munro Ferguson saw Barton in all four times in four days, one night taking him to dinner with Sir William Irvine, and the next day to the Caulfield Cup.[96]

On 11 November, Barton wrote to Munro Ferguson enclosing a letter from

[90] Munro Ferguson diary entry for 26 July 1919.
[91] Griffith papers, ML MSS 363/5X fol 207.
[92] Novar papers, MS 696 fol 2824, National Library, Canberra.
[93] CO 418/178 fol 438-439, P.R.O.
[94] Munro Ferguson diary entry for 16 October 1919.
[95] Ibid., 7 January 1920.
[96] Ibid., 17 and 18 October 1919.

Griffith. Barton, who also referred to his own ill health, wrote of Griffith's letter:[97]

> It shouts out − though he does not think it does − the advice he gave when consulted as to the appointment of his successor. It also shows that his dominant desire was to requite in deadly fashion the man who had injured him, & that to make this certain he did not care if he killed the man who had helped him. However, that man means to live.

What Barton appears to mean is that Griffith was so keen to ensure that Isaacs was not appointed as Chief Justice, either in 1919 or on the death of Barton if Barton were appointed Chief Justice, that he urged the appointment of a leading barrister not on the Court. Barton's own animosity to Isaacs is documented in Sir Zelman Cowen's biography of Isaacs. Sir Zelman also describes "the clash of views" and "profound temperamental incompatibility" between Griffith and Isaacs.[98] There is no firm evidence of which I am aware that Griffith had been motivated specifically to keep Isaacs out of the Chief Justiceship: but it seems highly likely.

Munro Ferguson replied to Barton's letter, describing what Griffith had written as "a hard, unsympathetic letter", but saying that he knew that "the one consideration in [Griffith's] mind was to secure at all costs the utmost measure of stability for the High Court": "I do know that Sir Samuel entertains warmer feelings towards you than towards anyone else. ..."[99]

Less than two months later, on 7 January 1920, Barton died. The Governor-General wrote in his diary:[100]

> ... Later came news of death of Sir E Barton our best friend in Australia and one of our best anywhere. He greatly admired Nellie [Lady Helen Munro Ferguson] and was always glad to talk over anything with me and he was the one man to whom we could talk without any reserve whatever.

Munro Ferguson immediately wrote a letter of great warmth to Lady Barton, saying how deeply he and Lady Helen "share in your sorrow".[101] Griffith died eight months later, in August 1920.

---

[97] Novar papers, MS 696 fol 4106-4107, National Library, Canberra. See also Joyce, op. cit., p. 357.

[98] Zelman Cowen, *Isaac Isaacs*, Oxford University Press, 1967, p. 120.

[99] Novar papers, MS 696 fol 4104-4107, National Library, Canberra.

[100] Munro Ferguson diary entry for 7 January 1920.

[101] Barton papers, MS 51/1/1647a , National Library, Canberra.

Privy Councillorship

There is an important postscript to this sad story. During the Irish Republican Brotherhood issue previously mentioned, Munro Ferguson had written:[102]

> The advantage to the Representative of the Crown of being able to consult a responsible person, such as the Chief Justice, the Prime Minister, and even the Leader of the Opposition, and others, under the oath of the Privy Council is great.

On the appointment of Adrian Knox as Chief Justice, Munro Ferguson urged Hughes and the Colonial Secretary that Knox be made a Privy Councillor. He wrote:[103]

> ... it is of the greatest importance that the Governor-General as a P[rivy] C[ouncillor] should be able to confer with, and ask the advice of, the Chief Justice in the same capacity.

An officer of the Colonial Office minuted:[104]

> The reason which the Governor-General gives for asking that the Chief Justice should be made a Privy Councillor is a somewhat curious one. Sir R.M.F. takes a stricter view of the duties and responsibility of Privy Councillors than I fear is generally held nowadays.

Knox was sworn as a Privy Councillor by the Prince of Wales in Melbourne in May 1920.

Aspects of Australia's constitutional development

If Munro Ferguson's view of the Privy Councillorship seemed old-fashioned in 1919 or 1920, how much more so it seems today, when neither the Governor-General nor the Prime Minister nor any member of the High Court is a Privy Councillor. With the development of Australia's own honours system, it is most unlikely that we will see further appointments to this body from amongst Australian public figures. In their time, Griffith and Barton were in fact the only Privy Councillors on the High Court, and it may have been formally as Privy Councillors that Munro Ferguson, like previous Governors-General, consulted them. But the reality was that, as the most senior fathers of federation and of the Constitution on the Court, and for their other qualities and experience, they were the most obvious figures not in parliament for a Governor-General

---

[102] Ibid., fol 8978. See also MS Harcourt, dep 479 fol 120b, 124-125, Bodleian Library, Oxford.
[103] C0418/178 fol 439, P.R.O.
[104] Ibid., fol 432.

to consult. As Munro Ferguson wrote in 1915:[105]

> It will make an extraordinary change when Australia loses Sir Samuel and Sir Edmund. They are extraordinarily good and very different types of Public Servants.

Among the many changes since those days has been a change in the Crown itself. There has been a gradual and uneven process of "Australianisation" of the Crown. The landmarks have included the abandonment of the Imperial role of the Governor-General in and after 1926, the move in 1930 to the Governor-General being appointed on the nomination of the Australian government, the appointment of Australians only as Governor-General, and successive changes in the Royal Style and Titles to establish the monarch specifically as King or Queen of Australia. It is not directly relevant to this article whether this process will shortly conclude with the establishment of an Australian republic or whether, for the time being, an Australian monarchy will remain. The events discussed here – most of which took place in Melbourne – were very, very early in the process of "Australianisation". These Governors-General were British, agents of Empire, appointed on the nomination of the British government by the King "of the United Kingdom of Great Britain and Ireland and of the British Dominions beyond the Seas".

Yet, in some of these events stirrings of what was to come can be glimpsed. World War I highlighted for some the potential for conflict between the Governor-General's Imperial role, in which he wished to see the greatest possible Australian contribution to the war effort, and his duty of impartiality between parties as constitutional "umpire" within Australia. Munro Ferguson's handling of Hughes during his manoeuvring to remain Prime Minister in 1916 and subsequent years appeared to many in the Labor movement to be partial, and contributed to their desire to have an Australian as Governor-General chosen by the Australian government. This was achieved in 1930-1931.

The position of High Commissioner to London was to become one of the means of communication between Australia and the Imperial government which contributed to making the Imperial role of the Governor-General redundant. The growth of direct communication between the Australian and Imperial governments through the visits of Australian ministers to London – such as Hughes's long visits in 1916 and 1918-1919 – also contributed to this.

---

[105] Munro Ferguson diary entry for 24 March 1915.

It may seem strange to us now that in the early years of Labor in power in Australia – before and during World War I – constitutional traditionalists had such difficulty in adjusting to something that is now taken for granted: that the Labor caucus will elect the leader of the Labor Party, and a Labor ministry.

It may seem equally strange, with the Statute of Westminster and the *Australia Acts* behind us, that Australians should have been as eager as Griffith was in 1914, and as Hughes was then and in 1917, for the Imperial parliament to make laws affecting Australia, including changing its constitutional arrangements, though of course they thought Australia and the other Dominions should be consulted first. Australians have long since thought that the *only* way to change the Australian Constitution was by referendum within Australia.

There have been consultations of High Court judges by Governors-General and by governments, and by state Governors, since Griffith and Barton. Sir John Latham was consulted by ministers on various matters, including on the death of Prime Minister Lyons in 1939, on what to advise the Governor-General to do.[106] Sir Owen Dixon was consulted by the government during World War II, and by the Governor of Victoria, Sir Dallas Brooks, during the 1952 Victorian constitutional imbroglio.[107] On the disappearance of Prime Minister Holt in 1967, Lord Casey consulted Sir Garfield Barwick on what to do.[108] Most famously and controversially, during the 1975 crisis, Sir John Kerr consulted both Sir Garfield Barwick and a judge who would later be seen as a major reforming Chief Justice, Sir Anthony Mason.

But known cases of consultation of High Court judges by Governors-General are fewer after the departure of Griffith and Barton than during their time. There are a number of reasons why this might be so, apart from the special positions of these two "founding fathers", and the fact that the archival records for later periods are less revealing. The Imperial role of the Governor-General officially disappeared, reducing the need for consultation. There were fewer occasions on which use of the reserve powers needed to be considered. For example, after 1909 no government defeated in the House of Representatives sought a dissolution when it was clear that there was an alternative government that could command the confidence of the House. Consultations are more likely to be necessary when the Governor-Generalship is occupied by a British aristocrat than when it is occupied by an

---

[106] Book review, *Quadrant*, vol. 7, no. 4, 1963, pp. 82-3.
[107] J.B. Paul, "The Dismissal: history justifies Barwick's advice", *The Bulletin*, 1 March 1983.
[108] See W.J. Hudson, *Casey*, Oxford University Press, 1986, p. 309.

eminent Australian with long experience in the law and/or politics. But even such Australian Governors-General have felt the need for consultation: for example, Lord Casey in 1967.

Few, if any, of us would now approve of a government or a Governor-General seeking or receiving advice from a High Court judge on a matter which of its nature was reasonably likely to come before the Court: draft regulations, or legislation, for example. Even on non-justiciable matters, such as exercises of the reserve powers, we would expect a Governor-General and judges to exercise caution and prudence. In the wake of fierce criticism of the protagonists in the 1975 crisis, it is likely that this approach will be adopted.

In 1986-1987, Sir Zelman Cowen chaired the committee which advised the Constitutional Commission on Executive Government matters. The advisory committee was split on the question of whether to say that it was inappropriate for a Governor-General, seeking expert advice on how to handle a constitutional crisis, to consult judges. A majority said it was inappropriate.[109] The majority also contended that "a pool of talent" exists – "amongst constitutional lawyers, political scientists, constitutional historians, ex-politicians, retired judges and others"[110] – which a Governor-General could draw upon. Professor Anthony Low had suggested "that a panel of independent advisers might be provided for the Governor-General".[111]

So far as can be ascertained, the current debate on changing the headship of state has bypassed the question of what sources of informal advice might be open to a future president or Governor-General if he or she faced a constitutional crisis. Whether or not Australia is to become a republic, perhaps it is time to again consider this question. Our constitutional history suggests that sooner or later it could again become a question of some importance.

---

[109] *Executive Government: Report of the Advisory Committee to the Constitutional Commission,* Canberra, 1987, p. 45.
[110] Ibid., p. 46.
[111] Ibid.

5

THREE GOVERNORS-GENERAL: HASLUCK, KERR, COWEN

Sir Paul Hasluck, Governor-General 1969-1974

> *Published as "Hasluck, Sir Paul Meernaa Caedwalla (1905-1993),*
> *diplomatist and politician"*
> *by Geoffrey Browne and D.J. Markwell*
> Oxford Dictionary of National Biography
> *Oxford University Press, 2004*

Sir Paul Meernaa Caedwalla Hasluck (1905-1993), diplomatist and politician, was born on 1 April 1905 at Perth, Western Australia, the second child of English-born parents, E'thel M.C. Hasluck and his wife, Patience Eliza Wooler. Both parents were Salvation Army officers and moved at regular intervals around the state to wherever the army required them to work. Hasluck attended various state schools. The four years spent at Collie in the south-west of Western Australia from 1913 left "a deeper imprint" on him than any other period of his life.[1] He took part in farm work, learned to ride and to love horses, and read avidly. At the boys' home his father managed, he also became acquainted with several Aboriginal boys, whom he greatly admired. In bush life Hasluck found a "sense of peace" and "intimacy with the whole of existence", which he would always "search to recapture".[2]

Hasluck won a scholarship to the Perth Modern School, which he attended from 1918 to 1922. In January 1923 he began work as a cadet journalist on *The West Australian*. Journalism gave him a "crash course of education in the ways of the world", and the chance "to meet people of

---

[1] Sir Paul Hasluck, *Mucking About*, Melbourne University Press, Melbourne, 1977, p. 52. [A recent biography is Geoffrey Bolton, *Paul Hasluck: A Life*, UWA Publishing, 2014.]
[2] Hasluck, op. cit., p. 54.

all kinds."[3] He became an active member of the Australian Journalists' Association. Through the association he became friendly with a future Prime Minister, John Curtin. In 1928 and 1929 Hasluck won the Lovekin prize for journalism, and went on to complete a diploma of journalism course at the University of Western Australia. A founding member (1926) and office-bearer of the Royal Western Australian Historical Society, Hasluck was one of the "earliest and most innovative practitioners of oral history".[4] On 14 April 1932 he married Alexandra Margaret Martin Darker (*d.* 1993), a schoolteacher whom he had met at university. They had two sons. In 1934 he commenced an arts course at the University of Western Australia. He graduated B.A. in 1937 and later completed an M.A.

From 1925 Hasluck read widely in Aboriginal anthropology. He found that "being interested in Aboriginals was unusual in those days". He was invited to accompany the 1934 Moseley Royal Commission into the social and economic condition of Western Australian Aborigines. He continued to write about the social problems of Aboriginal communities, and was highly critical of official incompetence and neglect. His M.A. thesis, on 19th-century native policy in Western Australia, was published in 1942 as *Black Australians*.

In 1939-1940 Hasluck held a temporary appointment as lecturer in history at the University of Western Australia. Early in 1941 a chance encounter with John Curtin (by then federal Opposition Leader) resulted in Hasluck accepting an offer of appointment to the Department of External Affairs in Canberra. From 1942 he worked closely with his minister, Dr H.V. Evatt, as speechwriter and adviser. He was a delegate to the San Francisco conference of June 1945, where the United Nations Charter was drawn up. He was then appointed to the executive committee of the United Nations preparatory commission, which met in London over several months in late 1945. He then became Australia's first permanent representative to the Security Council. The beginnings of the cold war saw constant conflict between the Soviet Union and other Council members, and Hasluck performed admirably under testing circumstances. His task was not made easier by Evatt's capricious personality. Hasluck resigned his

[3] Ibid., p. 120.
[4] G. Bolton, "Oral historian", T. Stannage, K. Saunders, & R. Nile (eds), *Paul Hasluck in Australian history: civic personality and public life*, University of Queensland Press, 1998, p. 37.

post in March 1947. He later accused Evatt of wishing to make the staff of External Affairs "his personal possession".

Hasluck returned to the University of Western Australia as reader in history in March 1948. He worked half-time on the political and social volume of the official history of Australia's participation in the Second World War, having in 1943 accepted an invitation to contribute two volumes. The first volume was published, to considerable acclaim, in 1952. However, by this time Hasluck had left academic life and embarked on a career in politics (the second volume did not appear until 1970). In 1948 he was invited to contest the federal seat of Curtin for the Liberal Party. Hasluck had not sought a political career. His own approach to politics was humanitarian and non-ideological, emphasising both individual respect and individual responsibility. He was pleased to hear himself described as a "nineteenth-century liberal".[5] He won the seat at the general election of December 1949, which saw the Liberals, led by Robert Menzies, returned to power. As Hasluck saw it, he did "not have to clamber and contrive" to be elected to parliament. He "was asked to do it and complied".[6]

In May 1951, after only 18 months on the backbenches, Hasluck was appointed Minister for Territories, a post he was to retain for 12 years. The newly created portfolio, which gave him responsibility for both the Northern Territory and Papua New Guinea, presented formidable difficulties. Both territories required policies for the development of Indigenous populations, were severely lacking in infrastructure and basic services, were heavily dependent on parsimonious Australian Commonwealth funding, and were further handicapped by inadequate administrative structures. Both territories were also on a path of constitutional development that would, eventually, lead to self-government. In the case of Papua New Guinea there was the further need to create a sense of nationhood. Hasluck was criticised for proceeding too cautiously along the road to independence. Yet he set an "often frenetic pace" to bring about change, securing significant funding increases for infrastructure, and for education and social welfare.[7] He succeeded in his broad goal of promoting truly national institutions. Central to his approach was his belief

---

[5] Hasluck, op. cit., pp. 282-3.

[6] Ibid., p. 286.

[7] Robert Porter, *Paul Hasluck: A political biography*, University of Western Australia Press, 1993, p. 157.

that the people of Papua New Guinea should make their own choice as to when independence should come and what form it would take.

Hasluck was a formidable administrator. He was "remarkably successful in being able to move from bold policy principles to a methodical and painstakingly close scrutiny" of policy implementation.[8] "Uncompromising in his readiness to monitor, inspect and scourge", he was, it was accurately said, determined to be both his own minister and departmental head.[9] His exacting standards and impatience for results did not make him easy to work with. Nonetheless, he retained the respect of his senior officers. His "nation building" achievements on behalf of Papua New Guinea constituted an outstanding legacy.

The territories portfolio made Hasluck de facto minister for Aboriginal affairs, a position for which he was well suited. His first major speech in parliament had called for "comprehensive national action" to improve the conditions of Aborigines.[10] In line with his belief in the primacy of local solutions, he proposed Commonwealth-state co-operation, with the Commonwealth of Australia offering new funding for state programmes rather than taking direct responsibility for Aboriginal affairs. Hasluck was disappointed and bewildered by the indifferent response from the states. He responded by working vigorously to increase provision for health, education, and welfare for Aborigines in the Northern Territory. He also sought to lead by example by abolishing racially based legislation, but the principal measure, the 1953 welfare ordinance, created new problems of racial categorisation.

Hasluck's personal ethos placed great emphasis on individual responsibility. In *Black Australians* he had noted how, over the course of the 19th century, Aborigines had gradually lost their status as British citizens, and had been reduced to the condition of dependent beings in need of protection. Accordingly, while not the originator, he became the most prominent advocate of the policy of "assimilation", which he saw as a process by which Aborigines would gradually regain full citizenship and, as he put it, come to "live in the same manner as White Australians do".[11] The cultural paternalism implicit in assimilation provided

[8] Ibid., p. 154.
[9] H. Nelson, "Papua New Guinea", in Stannage, Saunders, & Nile, op. cit., p. 158.
[10] Porter, op. cit., p. 194.
[11] Ibid., p. 197.

justification for the long-established practice of removal of half-caste children from their families. Hasluck was not an unqualified supporter of that practice, but neither did he condemn it. Although he respected Aboriginal cultural values, his historical perspective had convinced him that these values could not endure sustained contact with white society. He underestimated the resilience of Aboriginal culture, with its focus on the group rather the individual. In the context of the 1950s Hasluck's policies, based upon equality and social justice, were "innovative and idealistic", raising expectations and bringing Aboriginal issues into the mainstream of political debate.[12]

Hasluck served briefly as Minister for Defence during 1963-1964. For the next five years he held the post of Minister for External Affairs under four Prime Ministers, Menzies, Holt, McEwen, and Gorton. Vietnam was the dominant foreign policy issue, and Hasluck maintained a firm line against what he saw as Chinese-inspired aggression by communist North Vietnam. In early 1968, in the aftermath of the death by drowning of Prime Minister Holt, Hasluck was the most obvious choice as Holt's successor.[13] Hasluck "adopted a Coriolanus-like attitude" and refused to lobby his party colleagues for their votes.[14] He was defeated narrowly by John Gorton. On 10 February 1969 his parliamentary career ended, concurrently with his appointment as GCMG and the announcement that he would be Australia's next Governor-General. (He had already been sworn of the Privy Council in 1966, and was appointed GCVO in 1970.)

Hasluck's performance of his constitutional role was flawless. As Governor-General he took seriously his rights "to be consulted, ... to encourage, [and] ... to warn", and lucidly expounded the role and responsibilities of his office.[15] He was known to be discreet and could offer advice, based on years of political experience. Gough Whitlam's inexperienced ministry found Hasluck's "interest and counsel very

---

[12] P. Read, "Northern Territory", in A. McGrath (ed.), *Contested ground: Australian Aborigines under the British crown,* Allen & Unwin, 1995, p. 285.

[13] [That is, after the veto of William McMahon, by the Country Party leader, John McEwen, in December 1967.]

[14] A. Downer, quoted in H.S. Albinski, "Vietnam", in Stannage, Saunders, & Nile, op. cit., p. 180.

[15] E.g., Sir Paul Hasluck, *The Office of Governor-General,* Melbourne University Press, 1979. Hasluck, "Tangled in the harness", *Quadrant,* November 1983; reprinted in Hasluck, *Light That Time has Made,* National Library of Australia, Canberra, 1995.

valuable".[16] Whitlam offered him an extension of office, but in deference to his wife's wishes he relinquished the post at the end of his five-year term in July 1974. He was appointed KG in 1979.

Freed from the requirements of public office, Hasluck relished the opportunity to return to writing. In 1976 he published *A Time for Building*, a consideration of his stewardship of Papua New Guinea. An autobiography, *Mucking About*, appeared in 1977. *Diplomatic Witness* (1980) was an account of his time in External Affairs, and an indictment of Evatt. *Shades of Darkness* (1988) reflected on Aboriginal affairs and administration. His *Collected Poems* had been published in 1969, but two more volumes now followed. There was a steady output of book reviews and journal articles. The posthumous *The Chance of Politics* (1997), drawn from notes written during his years in parliament, contained some scathing portraits of his political contemporaries.

Hasluck's character defies easy assessment. His was a long and active life, with a remarkable variety of significant achievements. Yet in his judgments of himself and of the value of his work, there is a recurrent sense of pessimism. In *Mucking About* he describes himself as a "failure as a human being".[17] He ended *Mucking About* at the point where he was about to enter politics, saying:[18]

> From that point onward my life ceased to be my own. I was unable to do many things I would have liked to do and was required to do many things I had no personal interest in doing. Duty took charge ...
> I kept assiduously to my political career, often feeling I was the wrong driver in the wrong truck.

Some of the sense of loss may have reflected family circumstances. He became estranged from his wife, although they remained under the one roof. In 1973 one of their sons, Rollo, died suddenly of viral myocarditis. Hasluck's devotion to "duty" meant the suppression of many youthful character traits. The gregarious young man, who was also capable of a mystical sense of communion with the bush and with animals, was not easily recognised in the prim and pedantic public man, who inspired respect rather than affection. Away from official tasks, youthful exuberance could return. In New York the Minister for External Affairs was once

---

[16] E.G. Whitlam, *The Truth of the Matter*, Melbourne University Press, 1979, p. 17.

[17] Hasluck, *Mucking About*, op. cit., p. 28.

[18] Ibid., p. 287.

reported as having spent the early hours of the morning playing bongoes and snare drums at a party. Among friends he was regarded as excellent company, appreciative of good talk, wine, and food. He died in Perth on 9 January 1993. His son Nicholas,[19] a novelist and judge, survived him, as did his wife, who died five months later. Dame Alexandra Hasluck was herself a distinguished social historian. Hasluck's state funeral was held at St George's Anglican Cathedral, Perth. At his wish, eulogies were replaced by trombonists playing "When the saints go marching in".

Sir John Kerr, Governor-General 1974-1977

Obituary published as "The sacking of Gough Whitlam's government"
The Guardian
26 March 1991

Sir John Robert Kerr, born Sydney, 24 September 1914; died Sydney, 24 March 1991.
Sir John Kerr was a giant in Australian public life. His brilliant academic and legal career culminated in his appointment in 1972 as Chief Justice of New South Wales, and in 1974 as Governor-General of Australia. He was most famous for dismissing the Whitlam government to resolve the grave constitutional crisis of 1975, which made him one of Australia's most controversial figures.

Kerr also gave vigorous leadership in the fight against communism in the trade unions in the 1950s, in preparation for independence for Papua New Guinea, in administrative law and judicial reform, and in many other legal and community activities.

Born in 1914, the son of a boilermaker, Kerr decided at the age of 11 that he would follow a career at the Bar in the footsteps of a local Labor politician, Dr H.V. Evatt. Evatt (at the time a High Court judge) helped finance Kerr's university studies. Their intimate relationship lasted until the split in the Labor Party in the 1950s. By remarkable coincidence, Evatt was to write (and discuss with Kerr as he did so) *The King and His Dominion Governors* (1936), one of the most important books on the reserve powers of

---

[19] [On Nicholas Hasluck, see Donald Markwell, *"Instincts to lead": on leadership, peace, and education,* Connor Court, 2013, pp. 130-3.]

the Crown which Kerr exercised in 1975.

Kerr's university career was outstandingly successful. Called to the Bar in 1938, he quickly established himself as a "Labor lawyer". Flirting briefly with Trotskyism and always a strong anti-Stalinist, his antipathy to Soviet communism grew over the years. In 1938, he married Alison (Peggy) Worstead. Called up in 1942, Kerr became a leading figure in the Australian Army's Directorate of Research and Civil Affairs, which involved him in planning for military administration of territories liberated from the Japanese – New Guinea, Borneo, Hong Kong, and Japan itself. This led to his appointment in 1945 as Principal of the Australian School of Pacific Administration, which trained colonial administrators. To research French colonialism, Kerr appointed Nancy (Anne) Robson, a brilliant Australian scholar of French, whom he was to marry in 1975 after the death of his first wife. He returned to the Bar in 1948.

The late 1940s and 1950s saw a bitter struggle by "industrial groups" against communist dominance of Australian trade unions, and Kerr led in a succession of court cases dealing with communist ballot-rigging. He believed that the Labor Party's leaders should strongly support the "industrial groups". But Evatt (Labor's leader, 1951-1960) turned on the "groupers", and precipitated a split in the party in 1954 that was to keep it out of power until 1972. Kerr left the Labor Party, but rejected leadership in the breakaway Democratic Labor Party. Instead, he devoted himself to his legal practice, his family, and diverse activities ranging from the Industrial Relations Society to the Association for Cultural Freedom. The 1950s and 1960s were busy years for Kerr. His work on plans for the future of Papua New Guinea was enlightened and influential. It was fitting that he was present, as Governor-General, in Port Moresby in 1975 when the Australian flag was lowered for Papua New Guinea's independence.

In 1965 Kerr was made an Honorary Life Member of the Law Society of England and Wales and in 1966 became an Australian federal judge. The Kerr Report of 1971 proposed a new structure for reviewing administrative decisions in the Australian federal bureaucracy. Its major recommendations were implemented in 1977. Kerr's commitment to law reform gained further scope when he was appointed Chief Justice of New South Wales in 1972, but in 1973 he was asked by the Labor Prime Minister of Australia, Gough Whitlam, to accept nomination as Governor-General, taking office in July 1974.

In 1974-1975, the Whitlam government was facing mounting economic and political problems. Labor's support plummeted, helping precipitate the 1975 constitutional crisis. The Labor government had a majority in the lower house (House of Representatives), but the non-Labor Opposition, led by Malcolm Fraser, controlled the elected upper house (Senate). In October 1975, the Senate refused to pass the appropriation (Supply) bills until the government called a general election. It had been generally accepted (indeed by Whitlam himself in 1970 and 1974) that a Senate denial of Supply must lead to an election, since a government can only govern with Supply endorsed by parliament. But in 1975 Whitlam refused to call a general election, and sought to govern without Supply. Deadlock between the two houses continued for weeks, and money for government services was beginning to run out.

Having consulted the Chief Justice of Australia, the Governor-General acted on November 11 to resolve the crisis. He believed that he had a duty to maintain constitutional government, and that this required preventing a government governing without Supply. So Kerr dismissed Whitlam and appointed the Opposition Leader, Fraser, as caretaker Prime Minister on condition that he immediately call an election. Fierce passions were aroused on both sides, Whitlam urging his supporters to "maintain your rage". But in the election of 1975, Fraser received the largest majority in Australian history.

Whitlam and his supporters, seeking a scapegoat, attacked Kerr on increasingly personal grounds, and boycotted him, but he stayed on as Governor-General until December 1977. Early in 1978, Kerr was appointed as Australia's Ambassador to UNESCO, but savage attacks on this appointment led him to resign it before taking it up. By the end of the year, he had published a best-selling defence of his action, *Matters for Judgment*. Sir John and Lady Kerr lived quietly in England from 1978, before returning to Sydney in 1984.

Kerr was a gentle, even soft-hearted man, though he acted with courage in a grave crisis not of his making. His natural good humour and generosity of spirit made him a gregarious and engaging companion. Open-minded and capable of seeing issues from all sides, he believed that hatred harmed the hater more than the hated. Determined not to be embittered by the campaign against him in 1975, he was remarkably magnanimous about his critics. Recent years have seen reconciliation with some, and the "rage" has largely ended.

Obituary published as "Sir John Kerr"
(further to the obituary by Richard Hall, 26 March 1991)
The Independent, *30 March 1991*

During Australia's constitutional crisis of 1975, the Prime Minister, Gough Whitlam, told Sir John Kerr, the Governor-General, that the only way an election could occur was if Kerr were "to do a Philip Game". This was a reference to the dismissal in 1932 – when Whitlam and Kerr were young men – of the Premier of New South Wales, Jack Lang, by the Governor, Sir Philip Game. Whitlam's remark – one of a number along these lines – recognised the real possibility that Kerr might exercise the reserve powers of the Crown to resolve the deadlock between an elected Senate refusing to vote Supply to the government until an election was called and a Prime Minister refusing to call a general election.

In the aftermath of the Game-Lang dismissal, Dr H.V. Evatt, a future Labor leader, a mentor of Kerr's, and then a judge of the High Court of Australia, wrote a book, *The King and His Dominion Governors* (1936), about the reserve powers. For Evatt, Kerr, or Whitlam, or anyone familiar with Commonwealth constitutional history, the reserve powers of the Crown were not "obsolete", but powers to be used in those (fortunately) rare and extraordinary circumstances which demanded them. Kerr believed in 1975 that the maintenance of constitutional government in Australia demanded that he resolve the titanic constitutional struggle, and defeat Whitlam's attempt to subvert the Constitution by governing without Supply authorised by parliament. The ultimate safeguard of responsible government would be destroyed if a government could continue in office even though the parliament refused it Supply. Under Australia's written Constitution, the elected Senate has the right to refuse Supply. Whitlam had himself, in 1970 and 1974, accepted that a Senate denial of Supply must lead to an election. It was his refusal to act on this principle that forced the Governor-General to dismiss him, and bring on an election (in which Whitlam was overwhelmingly defeated).

Kerr gave a compelling defence of his actions in *Matters for Judgment* (1978). In articles in Sydney's *Bulletin* magazine in September 1985, he specifically refuted the charge that he had "deceived" Whitlam or his ministers. On the day he was dismissed, Whitlam was asked if he was "suggesting the Governor-General may have misled you". Whitlam answered: "No, I'm not saying that." It was only later, when Whitlam needed a scapegoat for his massive defeat, that allegations of deception gained currency.

Kerr's life was one of great industry and achievement. As a federal judge from 1966 to 1972 he achieved much, not least in conducting three important inquiries. One resulted in a major improvement in pay and conditions of the armed forces. Another led to the creation of an impartial tribunal on remuneration of parliamentarians. From 1968 to 1971, Kerr chaired a distinguished committee which proposed a new structure for the review of administrative decisions in the Australian federal bureaucracy. Whitlam lauded this "pioneering" report, and said it would "make a very great contribution to citizen rights in this country". And so in time, it did.

Facing death calmly, Kerr looked back on his life with satisfaction. He never doubted that he had done the right thing in 1975. But he greatly regretted the necessity for it, not least because he had many friends in the government he dismissed. Subjected to a long campaign of vilification, he generally turned the other cheek. He was determined not to be embittered by hatred, and he was remarkably generous about his critics. Recent years have seen reconciliation with some. This is one mark of his stature as a great Australian.

~

"A Reflection" at State Memorial Service for Sir John Kerr
St James's Church, Sydney
6 April 1991[20]

It was my very great privilege to develop a close friendship with Sir John Kerr in the last decade of his distinguished life. It is to the man as I knew him that I pay tribute today.

The man I knew was a man who enjoyed life – a serious-minded man, certainly, with a strong sense of duty, and a man of industry and achievement; but one whose seriousness was balanced by a buoyant sense of humour and of fun; a man who rejoiced in the joy of life. He was no exile, no embittered recluse.

My friendship with Sir John began when he and Lady Kerr were living in

[20] Published as "Sir John Kerr: a Reflection", *The Australian Journal of Forensic Sciences*, vol. 23, June-December 1991.

England. In 1982, I was one of a group of Australian students[21] – the Gang of Four, we were dubbed – who invited Sir John to speak at an Australian dinner in Oxford. We knew, of course, that Sir John's brilliant academic and legal career had culminated in his appointment as Chief Justice of New South Wales, and as Governor-General of Australia; and we knew, of course, of 1975: and we were pretty nervous about entertaining so great a figure. But it all went very well. There was immediate warmth between us, all reserve vanished, and an enduring friendship began. I saw a great deal more of Sir John and Lady Kerr before their return to Sydney in 1984, and after that, on their trips to Europe, and mine home to Australia.

Sir John's capacity for spontaneous and lasting friendship with a group of Australians 40 years or more his junior was a remarkable thing, and was for all of us something very special indeed. We learnt much from him, and we had many good times together. How well do I remember a picnic in Magdalen meadow in Oxford on a glorious summer's day; our discovery of an enchanting restaurant on the Thames just a few miles away, to which we loved to return; Sir John's ready willingness, in our early days of friendship, to join us in the Trinity College chant across the college wall to Balliol. How well do I remember many meals shared together when Sir John, warmly and happily, would evoke the spirits of judicial and political figures he had known over the years, with tantalising insights into their idiosyncrasies. And how he would relish our impersonations of one or two more recent figures.

Sir John was gregarious, down-to-earth, and sincere. I remember his ready and hearty laughter. His was a natural good humour and generosity of spirit. His close friend James McAuley once wrote: "He is in fact a soft-hearted person who greatly dislikes taking part in the infliction of hurt on anyone". The man I knew *was* a soft-hearted man, kind and compassionate. He took genuine interest in others. Open and liberal-minded, Sir John was strikingly receptive to opposing views. He was a good listener. He was thoughtful – thoughtful and conscientious about his own responsibilities; thoughtful and considerate about other people. When, a few years ago, one of his young friends from Oxford days[22] came from interstate to be admitted to the New South Wales Bar, Sir John – in a most gracious act of

[21] [George Brandis, Tom Harley, Timothy Potts, and myself. See Anne Kerr, *Lanterns Over Pinchgut*, Macmillan, Melbourne, 1988, p. 325.]
[22] [George Brandis.]

friendship – went to sit on the Court for what I believe was the only time since he had been Chief Justice.

When I came to know him, Sir John was enjoying an active retirement. He had already written one book, *Matters for Judgment*, and he was to go on to write a second, called *The Triumph of the Constitution*, which he completed just weeks before entering hospital.[23]

In June 1984, not long before returning to live in Sydney, Sir John wrote to me that he was considering writing an account of his life since leaving office. Every word he wrote rings true. He said:

> I want to show that one can have a life of fulfilment living, not in exile, but in a most pleasurable way as a Europhile who "still calls Australia home".

He referred to those who depicted him, in his words, as "sitting on the verandah watching the passing parade", and he continued:

> I don't see it that way. Am I wrong? In fact I have been a much more active person that most could imagine, exploring life and, with Anne, creating a new one, conducting what to me has been a stimulating correspondence, thinking continuously about politics in Europe – the UK, France, and Germany – and of course America, enjoying getting to know my grandchildren and indeed our two families combining now as one, ... enjoying exhibitions, discovering constantly new wonders in Europe, ... keeping in constant contact with my Australian friends both when they visit Europe and on visits by us to Australia, reliving 1975 and getting it into perspective, ... avoiding hatred and bitterness, being always amused by pomposity whilst trying to avoid it, refusing to change my own lifestyle, reconciling myself to retirement, which is necessary at 70, enjoying the newly found gang of four, loving life and laughter and conviviality and generally having a good time.

This was the man I knew.

Elsewhere, Sir John wrote of Lady Kerr – and I quote – that her "dignity and courage, loyalty and never wavering understanding and love sustained me always." More than once, he told me that he had promised her when they married that, when they left Yarralumla,[24] they would spend some years in Europe. Like so many people, they stayed because they loved it.

But Sir John was always proudly, and distinctively, Australian. I remember

---

[23] [The foreword to *The Triumph of the Constitution* is in the next chapter of this book.]

[24] [Government House, the Governor-General's principal official residence, is in the Canberra suburb of Yarralumla.]

once, when he and Lady Kerr were staying with me in Oxford, we went on a day trip to Cambridge. My car had broken down once already, and we were driving back through teeming rain, and thought – wrongly, as it turned out – that we were lost. We kept our spirits up by reciting *The Man From Snowy River* from beginning to end.

In Europe, as here at home, Sir John followed Australian affairs closely. A forward-looking man, he thought deeply about Australia's future. His abiding commitment to its well-being was unmistakeable to anyone who knew him.

Among other things which Sir John and I discussed, we naturally talked about his Governor-Generalship, and, of course, about 1975. In a crisis not of his making, he had done his duty as he saw it, conscientiously and courageously, even though he knew that he would suffer for it. Through all that followed, he never doubted, and never had cause to doubt, that he was right. Since then, the "touch of healing" and the balm of time have largely worked, and the rage of yesteryear has subsided. Recent years have seen a calmer understanding of the 1975 crisis developing. Even among those who disagree with Sir John's action, there is growing acceptance that he acted properly and courageously.

What struck me again and again in my talks with Sir John was his sense of duty, typified in his frequent references to his oaths of office, and how free of bitterness he was about the attacks on him. Though naturally angered by some things that were said or done, he generally turned the other cheek. He largely maintained a dignified policy of silence. He was determined not to be embittered by the campaign against him. In this he succeeded. It is one measure of his stature as a man that he was so remarkably magnanimous and generous about his critics. He spoke with *regret* of friendships cut off, and even occasionally with admiration of some of the activities of some critics. As Sir John said at one of our first encounters, "we all have to live on the same planet, you know".

It meant much to him that reconciliation was achieved in his lifetime with some. Early in our friendship, he showed me a letter from one of the ministers in the Whitlam government, apologising for his role in the attacks on Sir John. He told me from time to time of talks and meetings with others. It was characteristic of the man that he welcomed this with an instinctive generosity of spirit. With his death, the chance for personal reconciliation has passed, but the process of moderation and understanding continues.

From time to time over recent years, as his physical ailments worsened, Sir

John talked about the death he believed would not be long away. He looked back with satisfaction on a good life; sure in the love of his family, and of his friends; and at peace, certain in the knowledge that he had discharged the many mighty responsibilities entrusted to him over a long and varied life – as a barrister, administrator, judge, Chief Justice, and Governor-General – with steadfast devotion to duty.

He looked forward without fear.

I salute a dear friend, a fine and good man, and a great Australian.

Sir Zelman Cowen, Governor-General 1977-1982[25]

Speech of introduction to Sir Zelman Cowen
The 49ers Dinner, Melbourne
15 April 1997

Thank you for the opportunity to introduce to you Sir Zelman Cowen, a truly outstanding Australian whom I am honoured to claim as mentor and friend. Sir Zelman was born on 7 October 1919 in St Kilda. There are no prizes for guessing the football team of which he is proudly patron.

His parents both came from families which had fled Czarist Russia in the late 19th and early 20th centuries in the face of fierce anti-Jewish pogroms. He grew up in an inter-war Australia which still largely considered itself British, and he too felt the strong pull of Britain. After a brilliant undergraduate career at the University of Melbourne, he was in 1940 awarded the Rhodes Scholarship for Victoria which would take him to Oxford. Before taking it up, he served for four years in the Royal Australian Navy, including in Darwin during the 1942 bombing.

Going to Oxford in 1945 with his bride, Anna Wittner, he topped his year in his postgraduate law course, and became a permanent Fellow of Oriel College – an Oxford don. In 1951, the Cowens came home to Melbourne, and at 31 Zelman Cowen became Professor of Public Law at the University of Melbourne, also immediately becoming Dean of the Law School – then the

---

[25] On Sir Zelman Cowen (7 October 1919-8 December 2011), see also Donald Markwell, *"A large and liberal education": higher education for the 21st century*, 2007, pp. 259-67, and *"Instincts to lead": on leadership, peace, and education*, 2013, pp. 84-101, 290-313. The author and Geoffrey Browne undertook an extensive oral history project with Sir Zelman Cowen, sponsored by Victoria University, Melbourne, in 1996-1997. Details are at https://researchdata.ands.org.au/oral-history-recordings-don-markwell/123011. It contributed to the writing of *A Public Life: The Memoirs of Zelman Cowen*, Miegunyah Press, Melbourne, 2006.

only university law school in Victoria. Through the 1950s and early 1960s – as academic leader, teacher, and scholar – he in effect created the modern law school. He was helped in doing this by the generosity, which is not forgotten, of several Melbourne business leaders.

Somehow he combined this demanding work with a remarkably active public life – not least, many appearances on such radio and later television shows as *Any Questions*, *Brains Trust*, *Meet the Press*, and *Notes on the News*. Indeed, he helped to pioneer public affairs television in Australia.

In 1966, Professor Cowen stunned his colleagues by leaving Melbourne to take up the Vice-Chancellorship of the University of New England, then Australia's only rural university. From there he was headhunted, as we would now say, to be Vice-Chancellor of Queensland University – just as it would be engulfed, like several Australian universities, by waves of sometimes vicious student protests. Both my wife and I were undergraduates at the University of Queensland in the 1970s, and my first encounter with the bold, distinctive signature "Zelman Cowen" was on dire warnings about copyright infringement placed next to the photocopiers in the University library.

In 1977, in the bitter aftermath of the 1975 constitutional crisis, it was announced that Sir John Kerr was to retire as Governor-General, and on the day his successor was to be announced, an American visiting professor said to the Vice-Chancellor of Queensland University, "what damned fool would take that job?" A few days later the visitor wrote to apologise, lamenting that he had had the luck to say this to the one person in Australia least likely to be comforted by the thought. As Governor-General from 1977 to 1982, Sir Zelman worked tirelessly, as did Lady Cowen. They visited all parts of Australia, and Sir Zelman delivered almost innumerable speeches, which he researched and prepared himself. The Cowens brought what is rightly remembered as "a touch of healing" to the Governor-Generalship and to this country.

In 1982, Sir Zelman returned to his old Oxford college, Oriel, as Provost – head of the College – serving there and in other public offices in England, most importantly as chairman of the British Press Council, until 1990. On the Cowens' return to Australia, Sir Zelman became chairman of John Fairfax Holdings, again bringing a touch of healing, this time after a commercial rather than a constitutional crisis. He has been and is active in Australian life in many other ways – for example as foundation chairman of the Australian National Academy of Music, music being one of his first loves – and I am very pleased that he has now been persuaded, even prevailed upon, to write the story of his life and times in an autobiography.

There is no person better qualified to discuss the issues in the republic debate than Sir Zelman Cowen. He was a professor of public, or constitutional, law for 15 years; biographer of the first Australian-born Governor-General, Sir Isaac Isaacs; himself Governor-General for four and a half years; and someone who has spoken and written extensively on the Governor-Generalship since then. As so often in his career, he has served with great distinction in the offices he has held, but this "radical administrator", as he has been described, has always recognised the possibility that things could be done better than they now are; that change, if carefully considered, may bring improvement.

And so, ladies and gentlemen, it is a great pleasure to introduce to you a truly great Australian – Sir Zelman Cowen – to discuss the issues of an Australian republic.

~

Address at State Funeral for Sir Zelman Cowen
Temple Beth Israel, St Kilda, Melbourne
13 December 2011[26]

In August 1940, George Paton, Professor of Jurisprudence at the University of Melbourne and a Rhodes Scholar for Victoria 14 years before, wrote a reference for a 20-year-old candidate for the Rhodes Scholarship who had dreamed since boyhood of going to Oxford:

> I have known Mr. Z. Cowen well for some years. His academic record ... is one that has rarely been equalled. It is frequently the case that those who do brilliantly in Arts do not show quite the same aptitude for law, but Mr. Cowen shows the same skill in both fields. His mind is very keen and remarkably mature for one of his age. Very few could even attempt the task he is doing this year – finishing the law course and carrying a burden of University teaching as well. I have found his contributions in discussion classes very penetrating and interesting, and, although one is a poor student who can teach his mentors nothing, from Mr. Cowen I have learned a great deal.
>
> He has a rounded personality, broad interests and cultivated tastes. ... He has great energy and that intellectual integrity which refuses to accept anything which has not been investigated. ...
>
> ... He has the assured courtesy of a much older man, and, while he has no reticence in urging his own opinions, I have found him both respectful and willing to abandon his point of view, if its weakness

---

[26] Previously published as "Sir Zelman Cowen: Educational Leader and Healing Governor-General", *The Round Table: The Commonwealth Journal of International Affairs*, February 2012, and in Markwell, *"Instincts to lead"*, op. cit., pp. 84-91.

could be shown.

In short, I feel he has that quality which would benefit most from a period at Oxford. I have written many of these testimonials for the Selection Committee, but this is the first time that I can write for a candidate who has exactly that intellectual flair of which great things can be predicted.

Zelman Cowen won the Rhodes Scholarship for Victoria that year, but was not able to take it up until 1945, after war-time service in the Navy. In Oxford, where he went with his young wife and life partner, Anna, he was appointed a permanent Fellow and Tutor in Law at Oriel College even before he topped the postgraduate Bachelor of Civil Law degree in 1947. From this base, he also did legal work in the post-war occupation of Germany, and had his first exciting exposure to law teaching in the United States.

In 1950, George Paton, as Dean of the University of Melbourne Law School, wrote to Zelman to see if he was interested in applying for the Professorship of Public Law there. He was; and the Warden of Rhodes House, Oxford, C.K. Allen, an under-stated but highly distinguished Australian lawyer, wrote from Oxford expressing "both pleasure and confidence in supporting [Mr. Zelman Cowen's] application". Noting his "academic record, both in Australia and at Oxford", and that he had "more than amply justified his election [as a Rhodes Scholar] on all grounds, both personal and scholastic", Warden Allen reported that "since he was elected a Fellow of Oriel College I have ample evidence ... that he is a successful teacher who takes great trouble with his pupils, has a shrewd judgement of them, and is much appreciated by them. He is, in my opinion, a man not only of quick and extensive legal attainment, but of genuine scholarly interests." He commended Zelman as a constitutional lawyer who would be a "co-operative colleague ... efficient in ... administrative duties". Oriel College, the Warden privately noted, would be "very sorry to lose" this "excellent tutor".

Zelman Cowen was, of course, appointed to the Chair of Public Law, and as George Paton was almost simultaneously appointed Vice-Chancellor of the University of Melbourne, the 31-year-old Rhodes Scholar came home not only as Professor but also unexpectedly as Dean of the Melbourne Law School. Over the next 16 years, he truly transformed it into the modern law school, grounded in first-rate scholarship and teaching, and rich with international linkages, especially with the U.S. universities he visited. His own inspiring teaching and encouraging mentoring are, I know, still remembered with gratitude by many law students of that time, now very senior in their profession. It was in these Melbourne years that Simon, Nick, Kate, and Ben were born. At the same time, Professor Zelman Cowen also emerged as a public figure, including through radio and later television commentaries on public and international issues, opposing the Communist Party dissolution referendum in 1951 and the Victorian hangings of the 1960s, and contributing internationally to the development of legal education and building up administrative talent in various Commonwealth countries and territories.

The early references I quoted from Sir George Paton and Sir Carleton Allen give insight into the qualities of intellect and character that led Zelman Cowen to so distinguished a career as legal scholar, author of many articles and several books, of which clearly one of his favourites was his biography of Sir Isaac Isaacs; pioneer in legal education; academic leader as Dean, and then Vice-Chancellor of the University of New England and then of the University of Queensland; tireless healing Governor-General of Australia; and then back at Oriel College, Oxford, as Provost, where he was proud to be the first Rhodes Scholar to be head of Cecil Rhodes's own college.

In his application for the Rhodes Scholarship in 1940, the 20-year-old Zelman Cowen wrote:

> The [teaching] work as a member of the University staff has entailed fair experience in public speaking. While at Scotch College, I was a member of the School debating team, and since that time have been keenly interested in public speaking. I have found that the work [teaching] in the [University] Extension Board particularly, together with invitations I have from time to time received to address bodies, such as Public Schools and clubs has afforded invaluable experience in this very interesting work.

It was indeed "invaluable experience". As a Vice-Chancellor and Governor-General, and in other public roles, Zelman Cowen was to find speeches a powerful instrument of leadership and healing. When, as a young Rhodes Scholar from Queensland with a shared interest in constitutional conventions, I came to know Sir Zelman in Oxford in the early 1980s, beginning one of the greatest friendships of my life, I was struck by how vividly etched, even scorched, in his mind was his speech to a large crowd in the Great Court at the University of Queensland, my much-loved alma mater, during the Springbok protests and University disruption of July 1971. For such a speech-maker to describe this as "the speech of my life" reflects the tensions of those times. It also reflects that he was by nature a communicator. The late 1960s and early to mid-1970s were times of tumult and protest around the world, including at the University of Queensland, where the Vice-Chancellor had to steer the University between what was often abusive protest on the one hand and an overly assertive Premier on the other. During these troubles, Zelman and Anna Cowen showed "grace under pressure" – which is a definition of courage.

Through "the troubles" and beyond, Professor Cowen defended the rights and interests of students, and worked to build the University, engaging community support, including philanthropic support. Then, as before and later, he was an effective fundraiser. One important benefactor of the University of Queensland was a flamboyant grazier, Barney Joyce. When asked how he would like to be portrayed in the University's official portrait of him, Sir Zelman replied, somewhat cheekily: "with my hand in Barney Joyce's pocket". Her Excellency the Governor-General[27] has spoken of how, when she invited Vice-Chancellor Cowen at short notice to lecture to one of her law classes at UQ at that time, his was the best lecture she has ever heard, earning a standing ovation from the students.

Fulfilling his vision of the Vice-Chancellor as an "independent public figure" as well as leader within the University community, in various public addresses in Australia and overseas Vice-Chancellor Cowen spoke of how the tearing of the social fabric in countries around the world was threatening the fragile consensus – the acceptance of shared values and rules – on which what he called a "civil liberal society" depended.

The 1975 constitutional crisis and responses to it greatly strained the fragile consensus about crucial aspects of governance in this country. When in 1977 Sir John Kerr indicated his intention to resign as Governor-General, the Prime Minister, Malcolm Fraser, turned for his successor to a wholly non-partisan constitutional scholar and attractive public figure who, in thought and action, had grappled more profoundly than perhaps anyone else in this country with the issues of division, consensus, communication, and healing. In using Nehru's phrase "a touch of healing" to describe what he hoped to bring to the office, Sir Zelman set the theme of his four and a half years as Governor-General. Above all, the healing was done through reaching out to community groups in all corners of the country, endless visits and countless speeches, reflecting careful research and what seemed like boundless energy. I first saw Sir Zelman Cowen, of whom of course I had known for years, when in 1978 he came back to the University of Queensland, where I was

[27] [Ms (later Dame) Quentin Bryce AC.]

then an undergraduate, to give a major speech in the Mayne Hall, which he had been so determined and proud to build. His speeches aimed not least, in Sir Zelman's phrase, to "interpret the nation to itself". As we all know, this healing balm was a profound gift to the nation, for which we are right to remain grateful, and Sir Zelman's approach has been a model for a number of subsequent Governors-General.

On going back to Oriel College in 1982 as its Provost, Sir Zelman again brought healing – healing a college hurt by the sudden departure of its previous Provost, and presiding over the harmonious resolution of what had been the divisive issue of admitting women to Oriel, the last all-male college in Oxford. His speeches to rowdy undergraduates at dinners after rowing victories were legendary, showing his own depth of engagement in the full life of the College and enabling him humorously to encourage academic as well as sporting success. Sir Zelman combined the Provostship with other roles, including as chair of the British Press Council and of the Van Leer Jerusalem Institute, as well as speaking commitments around the world.

His extensive speech-making about the role of Governor-General and other Commonwealth issues reflected the fact that, although he had written on issues of monarchy and republic since the mid-1960s, he – along with most Australians – then believed that Australia had sufficiently achieved the substance of independence and had no need to change to a republic. But within five years of coming back to Australia in 1990, he believed that Australia's national journey and sense of itself now required that its head of state be, in words he liked, "one of us" – unequivocally symbolising Australia itself. And so in the republican debate of the mid- to late 1990s, the constitutional lawyer who had brought healing to the nation in the position of Governor-General was advocating, including in speeches over which he laboured, an Australian president chosen by special majority in the parliament.

By that time, with strong support from Victoria University, where he was a Distinguished Visiting Professor, Sir Zelman and his team were hard at work on his memoirs, *A Public Life*. They were launched by Justice Michael Kirby on Sir Zelman and Lady Cowen's 61st wedding anniversary, in June 2006. It is in these memoirs that one can read of many diverse interests that can barely be touched on today – music (especially Mozart), architecture, the press, his work on radio and television, adult education – and other aspects of his life, from the Jewish migrant experience of his forebears, his St Kilda boyhood and interest in ships and early aviation, and the joys of student days, through to his retirement work for Griffith Law School and the National Academy of Music, and for editorial independence at Fairfax newspapers, and much else besides. In recent days so many institutions and organisations have expressed their deep gratitude to him, and rightly so.

Both in his memoirs and in countless speeches and deeds over many decades are reflected the liberal values for which Sir Zelman Cowen was a beacon – individual liberty under law, including the rights to privacy and to free speech in a civil and tolerant society; the rule of reason, with a preference for moderation, collegial leadership and consensus-building, and even-tempered public and private discourse, with disagreement without rancour; uncompromising and scrupulous integrity; and education – in a college, a law school, or the wider university – that both broadens and sharpens the mind. In one such speech, he spoke of "the study and reflective and speculative thinking which lies at the heart of good teaching" – something he exemplified, expected, and encouraged. Spending 34 of his 92 years leading educational institutions, while ceaselessly interested in broad public issues, he never lost his commitment to the interests of students, and was always delighted when any former student remembered his teaching or help that he had given.

George Paton in 1940 wrote of Zelman Cowen having "exactly that intellectual flair of which great things can be predicted" – great things fulfilled beyond prediction, perhaps even beyond the prediction of his mother, who expected him to be a King's Counsel – and of his having "that intellectual integrity which refuses to accept anything that has not been investigated". For me, conversation with him was often a Socratic dialogue, an investigation – the pursuit of a topic beyond what I thought possible – marked by this experienced raconteur's sudden bursts of humour and an anecdote or three. He brought clarity of mind, charity of spirit, and civility of expression to all he did; erudition and elegance; wisdom in judgment; energy, single-minded determination, efficiency, and dignity in action; and a remarkable capacity for friendship – intensely loyal, warm and kind friendship, expressed in the most generous hospitality by him and Lady Cowen, in conversation that encouraged as well as stretched, and in correspondence that spanned the world.

Zelman Cowen was for me and for others, not only a truly exceptional academic and public figure at home and abroad, but a uniquely special friend and mentor, and a profound and wise influence on our lives. We remember him with love and gratitude, and we will miss him more than we can say.

6

THE 1975 CONSTITUTIONAL CRISIS AND THE CONVENTIONS OF RESPONSIBLE GOVERNMENT

Review of Sir John Did His Duty
by Sir Garfield Barwick (1983)
Published as *"By reference to the voters"*
The Times Literary Supplement
20 April 1984

The actions last year of the Governor-General of Grenada, Sir Paul Scoon,[1] have renewed debate on the discretionary "reserve powers" of the Queen and her representatives. In very different circumstances in Australia, such debate was generated by the constitutional crisis of 1975. Australia's then Governor-General, Sir John Kerr, exercised his reserve powers to resolve a deadlock between two elected houses of parliament. He dismissed the Prime Minister, Gough Whitlam (whose government could not get money from parliament), and appointed the Opposition Leader, Malcolm Fraser, as caretaker Prime Minister specifically and solely to get Supply and to call immediate elections for both houses.

Kerr (himself a former Chief Justice of New South Wales) acted with the advice of the then Chief Justice of Australia, Sir Garfield Barwick. Barwick, now in retirement, has written a concise but compelling justification of Kerr's action: "what he did was both the only course he could have taken and the course he was in duty bound to take".

By late 1975, because if its record on unemployment and inflation, the departure from office of two senior ministers over a loan-raising venture of doubtful legality, and its general air of incompetence, the Whitlam Labor government had become massively unpopular. The Senate, in which the non-Labor Opposition had a majority, refused to grant Supply to the government

---

[1] [In 1983, Sir Paul Scoon, in the midst of a revolutionary coup, requested U.S. military intervention to restore order in Grenada.]

until an election was held. The Prime Minister refused to call an election. The House of Representatives (in which he had a majority) and the Senate (with ten senators from each state, elected on proportional representation) were deadlocked. Whitlam proposed to govern without Supply – to try to continue spending without the parliamentary authorisation the Constitution requires. His proposals were of dubious legality, and offered no guarantee that government employees would be paid or government contracts met. Australia faced the chaotic prospect of public services grinding to a halt.

The stark constitutional and practical reality was – as Australia's first Prime Minister, and a distinguished lawyer, Sir Edmund Barton, once put it – "without money you cannot govern". So, on 11 November 1975, with Supply running out and the need to act if an election were to be held before the following February, Kerr, with Barwick's backing, dismissed Whitlam and called elections in which the caretaker Fraser government received the largest majority in Australian history. The Labor Party was routed – returning to power only in 1983, three elections and two leadership changes later.

Barwick, an uncompromising advocate, argues from first principles about the fundamentals of Australia's (written) Constitution. His greatest weapon is an incisive common sense. For Barwick, the constitutional crisis of 1975 consisted of three "events": the Senate's deferral of Supply, the Prime Minister's refusal to call an election, and the Governor-General's dismissal of him to enable a general election to be held.

Barwick argues that the Senate did indeed have the power to deny Supply; that its exercise of that power was reasonable given its judgment (vindicated by the election landslide) that the government had lost the confidence of the people; that a Prime Minister who cannot get Supply must either resign or call an election; and that, with Whitlam's refusal to do either, the Governor-General acted correctly in dismissing him and, through a caretaker Prime Minister, referring the political dispute to the Australian people.

It is Barwick's view that the Australian Constitution embodies the democratic theory which sees a reference to the voters as the means to resolution of major disputes: there is a procedure (though inadequate to deal with a Supply crisis) for dealing with deadlock between the two houses over legislation, which is to call elections for both houses; the Australian Constitution, born of referendums, can only be amended by referendum. Barwick places great stress on the argument that the Senate's deferral of Supply represented the government's loss of "the approval of the parliament" which it needs if it is to govern. This is less compelling than the simpler, starker argument that he later uses: it is the Governor-General's constitutional duty to "ensure the carrying on of the ordinary services of government", and he must obtain ministers who can get the money needed for this from parliament.

The Senate's deferral of Supply, itself a legitimate action, became part of a prolonged crisis because of Whitlam's refusal to call an election. Barwick now places the guilt for the crisis back where it belongs – with Whitlam. He describes Whitlam's intention to govern without Supply, rather than face the people, as "the very antithesis of democracy and a denial of the requirements of the Constitution".

There has been little attempt since 1975 to justify the actions of the Senate in deferring the Budget. Barwick's defence of that action has an important cutting edge: it reflects how intertwined the political and constitutional issues remain. But Barwick does not make the fundamental point that if the Senate has the power to block Supply and so to force an election, its judgment that the Whitlam government was a disaster was of itself sufficient justification for its exercising that power, which it judged would produce a new government.

Barwick explains how Sir John Kerr, perfectly properly, sought his advice. That advice confirmed Kerr's own judgment of the right constitutional course to take. Barwick convincingly shows that Kerr had no duty to warn Whitlam of his intention beyond what he did. It might be added that, had Kerr done more, Whitlam would almost certainly have sought the Governor-General's dismissal by Buckingham Palace, thus dragging the Queen into an Australian political quagmire.

One might reasonably quibble with some of Barwick's points. For example, his dogmatic defence of the Senate as an expression of "our federalism" will annoy many readers. Nonetheless, his justification of Sir John Kerr's action has a ringing clarity and an inescapable logic.

This book review sparked extensive debate in The Times Literary Supplement *and then* Quadrant *on the 1975 constitutional crisis. References are given in footnote 15 to the next piece in this chapter.*

Foreword to The Triumph of the Constitution
Unpublished second book by Sir John Kerr
Foreword completed June 1992

Early in the morning of Palm Sunday, 24 March 1991, Sir John Kerr died in the Kirribilli Private Hospital, Sydney, at the age of 76. He had entered hospital two months before after a massive attack, and was diagnosed as having a terminal brain tumour. He approached death with calmness and courage.

To spare his family from media intrusion in their grief, he was buried the day after his death in a private funeral service, after which his death was publicly announced. A State Memorial Service was held in St James's Church, King Street, Sydney, a fortnight later (6 April). It was attended by the Governors-General of Australia and of Papua New Guinea, three former Governors-General of Australia, the state Governors, the then Prime Minister, and many hundreds of others, including what David McNicoll called "the biggest covey of legal eagles ever assembled".[2]

The Eulogy at this service, given by the Chief Justice of Australia, Sir Anthony Mason, a close friend of Sir John's, is reprinted as an appendix to *The Triumph of the Constitution*, as are two shorter "reflections" on Sir John (by his son, Philip Kerr, and by me) also delivered at the Memorial Service.[3] They give an account of the life, career, and character of this remarkable Australian.[4] Amongst other things, they make clear that his period as Governor-General (1974-1977) was but the culmination of a distinguished career that had already taken him from working class Balmain, where he grew up, to the Chief Justiceship of New South Wales; and that, although his dismissal of the Whitlam government during the 1975 constitutional crisis was outstandingly important in his own life, as in the life of the nation, there was very much more to his life, after 1975 as well as before it, than that dismissal.

For some considerable time before the attack in January 1991 that foreshadowed his death, Sir John had been working on *The Triumph of the Constitution*. We do not, of course, know how he would have revised it had he had the opportunity.[5] He had written an earlier book, *Matters for Judgment*

---

[2] David McNicoll, "Fitting finale for Sir John", *The Bulletin*, 23 April 1991.

[3] [My "reflection" is reprinted in the previous chapter of this book.]

[4] See also, e.g., obituary in *Australian Law Journal*, vol. 65, no. 6, June 1991, p. 367.

[5] In preparing the text for publication, some editing has necessarily been done. Lady Kerr, with some advice from me, undertook this work. This has been comparable to the process by which, for example, Hedley Bull and Carsten Holbraad prepared Martin Wight's *Power Politics* (Penguin, 1979) for posthumous publication.

(1978), which combined autobiography with a detailed exposition and defence of his role in the 1975 crisis. This was republished in 1988 with a new preface by Sir John.[6]

He had also, in 1985, to mark the tenth anniversary of the crisis, published two articles in *The Bulletin*, and given an interview to Bruce Stannard of *The Bulletin*.[7] Although Bruce Stannard's interview contains much excellent material, I think myself that his portrayal of Sir John as conservative misses the strong reformist streak in him that was seen, for example, in the pioneering work of the Kerr Committee which in 1971 laid the basis for radical reform of Australian administrative law, and in his term as Chief Justice of N.S.W.[8]

Sir John's *Bulletin* articles are also reprinted as appendices to *The Triumph of the Constitution*. They give a direct explanation of why he acted as he did in 1975, and a response to various criticisms of his action.

Although Sir John's was deliberately a private retirement, he also made occasional speeches, wrote a small number of letters to journals or magazines, and gave some interviews; some of these are touched on at points in *The Triumph of the Constitution*. Sir John also engaged in an active correspondence with many friends in various parts of the world, including notably with one of the great authorities on constitutional law and practice, the Canadian senator and socialist, Dr Eugene Forsey.[9]

The Triumph of the Constitution was conceived as following on from Sir John's earlier writings, not repeating (except where necessary) their points, but surveying much of the public debate on the Australian Constitution from 1975 to 1990 (especially in the 1980s); drawing out the implications of that debate for a view of 1975; producing further thoughts on aspects of 1975; and responding more fully to some of the stranger stories about it than he had previously done. Although there is much in it that will be of interest to an academic and legal audience, *The Triumph of the Constitution* was not intended primarily for that essentially specialist readership, but is aimed at the general

[6] Sir John Kerr, *Matters for Judgment: An autobiography*, Macmillan, Australia, 1978, U.K., 1979; Sun/Macmillan, Australia, 1988.
[7] *The Bulletin*, 3 & 10 September 1985 (articles); 17 September 1985 (interview).
[8] See, e.g., *The Sydney Morning Herald*, 11 November 1972, p. 8.
[9] On Dr Forsey, see *A Life on the Fringe: The Memoirs of Eugene Forsey*, Oxford University Press, Toronto, 1990, esp. pp. 198-9. D.J. Markwell, "Canada's Best", *The Round Table: The Commonwealth Journal of International Affairs*, October 1991, pp. 502-5 [reprinted in appendix 3 of this book]. Obituary, *Australian Law Journal*, vol. 65, no. 7, July 1991, p. 430. Dr Forsey's obituary of Sir John Kerr was published after both had died: *The Daily Telegraph* (London), 26 March 1991. Very useful is *Evatt and Forsey on the Reserve Powers*, Legal Books, Sydney, 1990.

reader – ordinary Australians with an interest in the Constitution under which their country has been, and in future will be, governed. I believe that *The Triumph of the Constitution* will be of particular interest and value in at least five ways, on which I shall touch in turn.

First, *The Triumph of the Constitution* provides a good overview of debate on constitutional reform, specifically as affecting the Senate and the Governor-Generalship, in the 1980s. Sir John helps us to retrace the steps that led to the Constitutional Commission, the development of its thinking through its "New Scheme on Parliament" and subsequent rethinking, and the unsuccessful referendums of 1988 and their aftermath. He makes pithy but fair-minded remarks on the debates and proposals.

The aspects of constitutional reform on which Sir John focuses are, of course, those which were most in play during the 1975 crisis. Here is an exploration of the debates on, and attempts to reform, those aspects of the Constitution from the perspective of the man in the hot seat of Australia's greatest constitutional crisis. For that reason alone, *The Triumph of the Constitution* is a unique historical document. Reminding ourselves of work on constitutional reform in the 1980s should help us think about it intelligently in the 1990s and beyond. And we should not forget that Australian experience is watched with interest by, for example, those in Canada and the United Kingdom actively interested in creating elected upper houses there.

Secondly, as well as giving a useful guide to the recent debate, this book represents an important contribution to that debate on the future of the Australian Constitution, and especially concerning the monarchy. When Sir John died, the Australian Labor Party had not yet adopted the policy of seeking a referendum on Australia's becoming a republic by the year 2001. Nor had Mr Keating (not then Prime Minister) embarked on his campaign of speeches and comments giving his view of the Australian national identity – stressing Australian independence, advocating a republic, attacking Britain's past behaviour towards Australia in World War II and over the European Common Market, attacking the attitude of past Australians towards Britain (which many in earlier generations regarded affectionately as their mother country), proposing a new Australian flag, and seeking to shift attention from Gallipoli to Kokoda. All of this makes this book even more topical now than when Sir John was working on it; and he has much to say on some of these matters.

Sir John stresses early in this book that Australia is "entirely independent of the United Kingdom", and he later quotes Mr Hayden as saying that becoming a republic would not make "one difference to the way this country runs its affairs, or in which decisions are taken, or the independence it has". This important point is sometimes lost sight of. Australia has, and has had for many decades, total independence in all areas of national policy — foreign affairs, defence, and trade, as well as in all aspects of domestic policy. The British government plays absolutely no role whatsoever in any aspect of the Australian Constitution or policy-making (except, of course, that, like all foreign countries, it can make representations to Australia on its policies, as Australia can to them). The Queen is Queen of Australia, and she acts on Australian matters on the advice solely of Australian ministers. Indeed, with only the most trivial exceptions, the Queen herself actually plays no role in Australian constitutional life other than appointing the Governor-General and state Governors on the advice of the Prime Minister of Australia and state Premiers, respectively: other powers under the federal Constitution are exercisable by the Governor-General (or Governor-General in Council). Sir John touches on the process of "Australianisation" of the Crown in this century.[10] The fact that the Queen is simultaneously Queen of the U.K., Canada, New Zealand, Papua New Guinea, and several other entirely independent countries does not in the least detract from Australia's total independence.

This book makes clear that, for this and other reasons, Sir John did not believe it was necessary for Australia to become a republic. Believing that Australia's constitutional monarchy works well, and that seeking a republic would be deeply divisive, he did not support moves towards becoming a republic. Sir John, who was very proudly Australian, did not believe that Australian national identity was compromised by recognising and valuing highly the historical influence of British traditions on Australia (not least in our legal and parliamentary systems). This is especially significant coming from a man who took so keen an interest, and played various important roles,

---

[10] Sir John refers to my account of this in *The Crown and Australia (The Trevor Reese Memorial Lecture, 1987)*, University of London, 1987 [reprinted as ch. 3 of this book]. Some further specific aspects are discussed in, e.g., "Another residual constitutional link with the United Kingdom terminated; diplomatic letters of credence now signed by Governor-General", *Australian Law Journal*, vol. 63, no. 3, March 1989, pp. 149-53. Alex C. Castles, "The Tasmanian constitutional crisis and State Governors' powers after the Australia Acts", *Australian Law Journal*, vol. 63, no. 11, November 1989, pp. 781-5. On the Australianisation of the Constitution generally, see R.D. Lumb, "The Bicentenary of Australian Constitutionalism: The Evolution of Rules of Constitutional Change", *University of Queensland Law Journal*, vol. 15, no. 1, 1988, pp. 3-32. See also: W.J. Hudson & M.P. Sharp, *Australian Independence: Colony to Reluctant Kingdom*, Melbourne University Press, 1988.

in Australia's relations with its neighbours in the Asia-Pacific region.

It is also striking that Sir John believed that Australia would remain a constitutional monarchy for a very long time, and that moves towards a republic would not gather sufficient support to carry a referendum for the foreseeable future. This view was supported by the remarkably stable level of support for retaining the monarchy shown in opinion polls over some decades. However, in the wake of the prominence given to the Australian Republican Movement in 1991, and to comments by Mr Keating in early 1992, opinion polls suggested a major shift of support in favour of a republic. But, at the time of writing this foreword [June 1992], the latest poll suggests that public support for a republic has declined again, and that more people are against than in favour of becoming a republic.[11] Future polls may well show further oscillations. Interestingly, opinion polls before the 1988 referendums showed strong support for the proposals put then;[12] but all were soundly defeated. Indeed, the reluctance of most Australians to support at referendum much less important changes to the Constitution than the switch to a republic has been demonstrated in the defeat of 34 of the 42 constitutional questions put to the people since 1901. Given this, it still seems highly likely that Sir John was right to think that a referendum on becoming a republic is unlikely to succeed for a long time to come. Time will tell.

Sir John believed — as do many of those advocating a republic — that the year 2001, the centenary of federation under the existing Constitution, is a suitable time for considering what change is needed to it. Although he believed that the present Constitution has served Australia very well, he recognised that some changes may be desirable. For example, in chapter 4, he appears to support the idea of a four-year maximum (not fixed) term for the House of Representatives (without setting this out in sufficient detail to explain what term senators should have — which, as he knew, is the main stumbling block for moves to a four-year term at the federal level). In his *Bulletin* articles, Sir John supported the proposal to amend the Constitution to provide that if the Senate denies Supply for, say, 30 days, there must automatically be an election for both houses of parliament. Sir John also there supported

---

[11] *The Australian*, 5 May 1992.

[12] *The Sydney Morning Herald*, 8 August 1988. See Enid Campbell, "Southey Memorial Lecture 1988: Changing the Constitution – Past and Future", *Melbourne University Law Review*, vol. 17, no. 1, June 1989, pp. 9-10. "The failure of the Bicentennial Referendum to amend the Constitution, 3 September 1988", *Australian Law Journal*, vol. 62, no. 12, December 1988, pp. 976-8.

provisions for greater security of tenure for the Governor-General, saying more about this in Chapter 7 of *The Triumph of the Constitution*.

Although he favoured some reforms, Sir John opposed setting 2001, or any other date, as a target date for wholesale change to the Constitution. In the debate between those who believe that the Constitution needs a major overhaul and those who advocate more modest, incremental change, Sir John is clearly on the side of modest, incremental change. Indeed, where some critics believe that the lead-up to the centenary of the Constitution should be used to focus our attention on what they see as its gross inadequacies, Sir John believes we should combine careful thought about reform with celebration of just how well the Constitution serves us.[13]

Sir John is keen to encourage his fellow Australians to think calmly and carefully about constitutional reform, not entering into it lightly, and not being swayed by emotion. Over the course of his life, Sir John had seen much emotion (including much bitterness and hatred) in public life – in his Balmain youth, in his legal work in the struggle against communism in many trade unions in the 1950s, and, of course, in the aftermath of the dismissal of the Whitlam government. Sir John touches on some of this here. He writes from his own experience. He speaks from the heart when he urges Australians not to allow their views of the great constitutional issues facing the country to be swayed by violent emotions. And surely he is right.

Instead, Sir John shares the hope of those who believe that constitutional reform will come about through consensus. Experience suggests that a proposal opposed by one of the major parties (and even perhaps, as in 1967, a minor party) will not be carried at referendum.[14] There is no sign that the Liberal and National Parties will support moves for a republic (and it is unfortunate that it has become a partisan issue). At the time of writing [June 1992], there are growing signs of organised action amongst those wishing to retain the monarchy, with leadership from such respected figures as the former Chief Justice of Australia, Sir Harry Gibbs; Dame Leonie Kramer, Chancellor of Sydney University; and Michael Kirby, President of the N.S.W. Court of Appeal. Certainly there is no sign of a consensus behind a republic.

The third way in which I believe this book will be of interest is that it

---

[13] Cf. Sir Daryl Dawson: "The Constitution – Major Overhaul or Simple Tune-up?" (The Southey Memorial Lecture, 1983), *Melbourne University Law Review*, vol. 14, 1984, esp. p. 354.
[14] See, e.g., Campbell, op. cit.

provides readers with access to much of what has been written about the 1975 constitutional crisis in diverse newspapers, magazines, journals, and elsewhere. (It is not, however, intended as an academic survey of academic writings, although Sir John did keep himself abreast of such writings.)

An enormous amount of material has been written on the 1975 crisis, and a vigorous debate has been conducted.[15] Sir John followed the debate closely, considering seriously (without agreeing with) what his critics said, and thinking carefully about their arguments. For the most part, he believed it was better that he not enter the debate personally, but maintain his policy of silence.

As the years have passed, this debate about 1975 has been less influenced by the emotions of the time. Similarly, as debate and research have continued, some propositions could not be sustained, and have faded away, and other propositions have become more clearly established. I believe (as Sir John clearly did) that these processes have largely worked to the advantage of a sympathetic view of his role in the 1975 crisis, and that the serious debate on 1975 has shifted more and more in his favour. I believe that any fair-minded person who reads a substantial part of the serious writing on 1975 will be struck by how strong the case for Sir John's action is. The key constitutional points now seem very hard to dispute.

As his position on these key constitutional issues has been more and more clearly recognised, some critics of Sir John's action have tended to move their fire to the way in which he dismissed Mr Whitlam. Sir John's *Bulletin* articles provide a powerful, and in my view convincing, defence of his actions against attacks on these grounds, and others have also vigorously defended him.[16]

Of course, many people remain firmly attached to the strong contrary

[15] One strand of this debate began in The *Times Literary Supplement*: Don Markwell, "By reference to the voters", 20 April 1984 (review of Sir Garfield Barwick, *Sir John Did His Duty*, Serendip Publications, Sydney, 1983) [reprinted earlier in this chapter]; letters: 25 May (L.L. Robson), 22 June (Gareth Evans), 29 June (Don Markwell), 20 July (J.B. Paul), 27 July (L.L. Robson), 17 August 1984 (Sir Garfield Barwick); and resumed in *Quadrant*: Gareth Evans, "Repatriating the Debate", *Quadrant*, November 1984; letter from Sir Garfield Barwick, January-February 1985; Don Markwell, "On Advice from the Chief Justice", *Quadrant*, July 1985, and letters October 1985 & April 1986, and from Richard Lucy, September 1986.

[16] E.g., Edward St John, "The Dismissal of the Whitlam Government", *Quadrant*, September 1976. Edward St John, "1975", *Quadrant*, November 1979. J.B. Paul, "The Constitutional Crisis 1975", in Richard Lucy (ed.), *The Pieces of Politics*, 2nd ed., 1979. J.B. Paul, "Judgment of the Matter", *Quadrant*, January-February 1980. Peter Coleman, "Behind the Rage", *Quadrant*, January-February 1979. Sir Garfield Barwick, *Sir John Did His Duty*, ch. 6. Don Markwell, "The Dismissal", *Quadrant*, March 1984.

views they have long held, many commentators remain critical, and many people have not had the chance to follow the serious debate on 1975. But as Sir John shows in this book, the work of the Constitutional Commission implicitly accepted the key constitutional principles on which his view of 1975 is based. As time has gone by, research has demolished the case of Sir John's critics on key points: for example, where it was said that before 1975 a Governor-General had consulted a Chief Justice on only one occasion,[17] it has now been shown that there were very many such precedents.[18] As time has gone by, more and more distinguished authorities have expressed the view that Sir John was right to act as he did: the posthumous article, which appeared in 1985, by Sir David Derham, a pre-eminent Australian legal scholar and Vice-Chancellor, is a most impressive example.[19] The chapter in *The Triumph of the Constitution* on "Men of light and learning" will, I think, strike fair-minded readers as demonstrating a very considerable body of authoritative support for Sir John Kerr — and there are other important endorsements Sir John could well have added.[20] (It will be realised that some

[17] See, e.g., Geoffrey Sawer, *Federation Under Strain*, Melbourne University Press, 1977, p. 157. E.G. Whitlam, *The Truth of the Matter*, Penguin, 1979, p. 91.

[18] See chapter 6 [of *The Triumph of the Constitution*], where sources are given. Many of the precedents are set out in fuller detail in Don Markwell, "The Governor-General Consults: Griffith, Barton and the Early Governors-General", working paper presented at seminar, Dept. of Politics, Univ. of Western Australia, 5 October 1984 [see ch. 4 of this book]. On the 1967 Casey-Barwick consultation, see also W.J. Hudson, *Casey*, Oxford University Press, Melbourne, 1986, p. 309. Contrary to at least one media report, the former Governor of N.S.W., Sir Roden Cutler, told the Constitutional Commission's Advisory Committee on Executive Government that in his view it was correct for the Governor-General to consult the Chief Justice if he so wished: letter from Sir Roden Cutler to the author, 3 September 1986.

[19] See chapter 10 [of *The Triumph of the Constitution*]. Sir David Derham, "The Dismissal of the Prime Minister on 11 November 1975", *Law Institute Journal*, vol. 59, no. 11, November 1985, pp. 1174-86. See also Columb Brennan, "Sir David Derham's legacy to law and learning", ibid., pp. 1166-7.

[20] E.g., Sir Kenneth Wheare, "Australia's Constitutional Crisis", *The Parliamentarian*, vol. 59, 1978. H.V. Hodson, "The Constitutional Consequences of Mr Whitlam", *The Round Table*, April 1976. Don Aitkin, "Sir John Kerr acted properly — but nothing can excuse the politicians", *The National Times*, 13 November 1976. Malcolm Mackerras, "Kerr earns a good place in history", *The Age*, 20 November 1975. Very important is the opinion prepared in October 1975 by Keith Aickin QC, long the leader of the Melbourne Bar and later a High Court judge; Murray Gleeson QC, now Chief Justice of N.S.W. [and later Chief Justice of Australia]; and Professor P.H. Lane. It argued that, on denial of Supply, the Governor-General could dismiss the incumbent ministers and appoint ministers who would advise an election, and that "the Governor-General is entitled to seek advice on his powers from sources outside the Ministry ..., for example, ... from the Chief Justice of Australia". K.A. Aickin, A.M. Gleeson, P.H. Lane, *Ex parte J.M. Rothery* (23 October 1975); see Michael Sexton, *Illusions of Power*, George Allen & Unwin, 1979, p. 220. Another joint opinion worthy of study is by J.S. Lockhart QC, now a Federal Court judge, and R.P. Meagher QC, now a judge of the N.S.W. Court of Appeal, 1976, in *The Facts and the Law*, Institute of Public Affairs (N.S.W.), Sydney, c. 1976, pp. 14-8.

of the authors Sir John cites were not specifically addressing themselves to whether he was right to act as he did in the circumstances of 1975, but to the general principles underlying his action.) The publication of *The Triumph of the Constitution* should make it even harder for commentators to write about 1975 without having themselves read some, at least, of the extensive literature in support of Sir John Kerr.

Media discussion after Sir John's death contained, as was to be expected, many inaccuracies and some adverse comments on his action in 1975. Yet it was striking just how much comment there was which was sympathetic to, if not fully in support of, his action. To give but a few examples. The day after Sir John's death was announced, the ABC radio programme, *PM*, devoted a lengthy session to an interview with the former Chief Justice, Sir Garfield Barwick, in which Sir Garfield explained with great clarity his support for Sir John.[21] Sir Garfield said that today "nobody who really knows, is really skilled and knowledgeable" in the law could say that the dismissal was wrong. This interview made a deep impression on many people. So too did a moving tribute to Sir John by the retired judge Kenneth Gee in *The Weekend Australian*.[22] An editorial in *The Australian* strongly backed Sir John.[23] Sir David Smith, who had recently retired as Official Secretary to the Governor-General, in which post he served five Governors-General, gave media interviews explaining why he supported Sir John. (He is preparing further research for publication.[24]) An opinion poll in April 1991 suggested that, while a smaller proportion of people had a view on the rightness or otherwise of the dismissal in 1991 than had a view in 1975, a considerably higher proportion of those with a view believed that Sir John Kerr was right.[25] In both 1975 and 1991, more people believed Sir John was right than believed

[21] 26 March 1991.

[22] *The Weekend Australian*, 30-31 March 1991. See also Kenneth Gee, "Sir John Robert Kerr – Patriot", *Quadrant*, May 1991, p. 10.

[23] "Kerr and the myths of dismissal", *The Australian*, 1 April 1991.

[24] See *ANU Reporter*, Canberra, 24 April 1991. Sir David Smith, "Myths and Legends – The Stuff of History, (or 1975 Revisited)" (The Nan Phillips Memorial Lecture, 17 October 1991), *Canberra Historical Journal*, no. 29, March 1992. Sir David quotes Michelle Grattan giving reasons why "the historians will probably be kinder to Sir John than the contemporary commentators": ibid., p.9. [See also Sir David Smith, *Head of State: The Governor-General, the Monarchy, the Republic and the Dismissal*, Macleay Press, Sydney, 2005.]

[25] Peter Hartcher, "Gough's Last Word", *The Sydney Morning Herald*, 13 April 1991, p. 39.

that he was wrong.[26]

Indeed, Mr Whitlam (who had maintained silence when Sir John's death was first announced) was moved to give an interview to *The Sydney Morning Herald* to respond to what were to him the disconcerting signs of support for Sir John.[27] The gracious way in which the then Prime Minister, Mr Hawke, spoke of Sir John, in a press release on the announcement of his death and in the subsequent House of Representatives condolence motion debate, contrasted with a bitter attack on Sir John by Mr Paul Keating (prompted, Mr Keating said, by the vigorous defence of Sir John by the Leader of the Opposition, Dr Hewson).[28] The allegation, which Mr Keating repeated, that Sir John deceived Mr Whitlam is dealt with in Sir John's second *Bulletin* article. Suffice it to say here that Sir John reminds us of what Mr Whitlam himself said on the afternoon of his dismissal when asked in a press conference if he was "suggesting the Governor-General may have misled you": "No, I'm not saying that." Mr Keating's claim that "the Labor Party makes the political heroes in this country" is hardly a balanced view of Australian history; and it is the more balanced view that is likely ultimately to prevail.

It is very difficult for anyone reading this book and what many other writers have said (or even just reading section 53 of the Constitution) to doubt that the Senate was constitutionally entitled to deny Supply, as it did in October-November 1975.[29] There is, however, a surprising and persistent misconception in some circles that the Senate did not in fact deny Supply in 1975, and that therefore there was no constitutional crisis for the Governor-

---

[26] Hartcher (ibid.) gives the 1975 figures as: Kerr right 49%, Kerr wrong 48%, no opinion 3%. He does not give the exact dates of this poll. (Figures for a Gallup poll in March 1976 were: Kerr right 52%, Kerr wrong 42%, Don't know 6%: *The Melbourne Sun*, 25 March 1976.) Hartcher gives the Saulwick poll figures for April 1991 as: Kerr right 43%, Kerr wrong 34%, no opinion 23% (*SMH*, 13 April 1991).

[27] Ibid.

[28] *Commonwealth Parliamentary Debates: House of Representatives*, 9 April 1991, pp. 2127-39. See also *CPD: Senate*, 9 April 1991, pp. 2039-52.

[29] On the legal power, see *P.M.A. Case* (1975) 134 CLR 81 at 121-2, per Barwick CJ; 143, per Gibbs J; 168-9, per Stephen J; 185, per Mason J. On the absence of a convention that this power not be used, see, esp., J.E. Richardson, "The Legislative Power of the Senate in Respect of Money Bills", *Australian Law Journal*, vol. 50, June 1976; and Paul in Lucy, op. cit. As Sir John points out, such a convention, if it existed, could not over-ride the actual text of the Constitution. Far from its existing, there have been frequent assertions of the Senate's right to deny Supply since the framing of the Constitution.

General to resolve.[30] The implication appears to be that the Governor-General might have been entitled to act if the Senate had actually rejected the appropriation bills, but that he was not entitled to act when it was only refusing to pass them. This is, of course, in the circumstances, a distinction without a difference.

In 1975, taking the same view on three separate occasions (16 October, 22 October, and 6 November), the Senate adopted in respect of both appropriation bills amendments along these lines:[31]

> That this Bill be not further proceeded with until the Government agrees to submit itself to the judgment of the people, the Senate being of the opinion that the Prime Minister and his Government no longer have the trust and confidence of the Australian people because of [the Loans Affair, Mr Whitlam's leadership, and economic "mismanagement"].

Four things may be said in response to the suggestion that passage of these amendments did not amount to denial of Supply. First, precedents show beyond doubt that this is quite sufficient to constitute denial of Supply, and that it does not require the out-and-out rejection of the appropriation bills. On 30 November 1909, the House of Lords refused the second reading of the Finance Bill by accepting Lord Lansdowne's amendment: "That this House is not justified in giving its consent to this Bill until it has been submitted to the judgement of the country".[32] All agreed that passage of this amendment amounted to denial of Supply: so must the Senate's strikingly similar amendment in 1975. And in Britain in 1909, it was not doubted by Prime Minister Asquith and his cabinet that this denial of Supply required an immediate election.[33]

[30] Variations on this view can be found in: Gordon Bryant, "Don't Blame Whitlam, Blame the System", *Quadrant*, January-February 1985, p. 103. L.J.M. Cooray, *Conventions, the Australian Constitution and the Future*, Legal Books, Sydney, 1979, p. 118. *Commonwealth Parliamentary Debates: House of Representatives*, 9 April 1991, pp. 2133, 2138. *CPD: Senate*, 9 April 1991, p. 2048. Hartcher, op. cit. G.S. Reid & Martyn Forrest, *Australia's Commonwealth Parliament 1901-1988: Ten Perspectives*, Melbourne University Press, 1989, pp. 330-1.

[31] *Commonwealth Parliamentary Debates: Senate*, 16 October 1975, p. 1221.

[32] Neal Blewett, *The Peers, the Parties and the People*, Macmillan, 1972, p. 99.

[33] See: *Parliamentary Debates: Commons*, 2 December 1909, cols. 549-50. Roy Jenkins, *Asquith*, Collins, London, 1964, p. 202. Roy Jenkins, *Mr Balfour's Poodle*, Heinemann, 1954, p. 70. Stephen Koss, *Asquith*, Allen Lane, 1976, p. 116. A. Lawrence Lowell, *The Government of England*, vol. 1, Macmillan, New York, 1914, p. 427. Ivor Jennings, *Parliament*, Cambridge University Press, 1948, p. 406. Reference to the Asquith papers, Bodleian Library, Oxford, further illustrates this: 5, folios 150, 158, 167-68, 169-70, 172-73; 12, folios 43-50, 64-5; 22, folios 218-223, 229, 231, 236-37. On Churchill's recognition, notwithstanding his bitter hostility to the Lords' action, that it forced a dissolution, see, e.g., Randolph S. Churchill, *Winston S. Churchill*, vol. 2, Houghton Mifflin, Boston, 1967, p. 312. Robert Rhodes James (ed.), *Winston S. Churchill: His Complete Speeches 1897-1963*, vol. 2, Chelsea House, 1974, pp. 1446, 1458, 1470, and elsewhere.

For example, Churchill, a member of cabinet, wrote to Asquith in July 1909: "... the necessary outcome of a constitutional deadlock consequent upon the Lords insisting on their amendments to the Budget must be Dissolution and an appeal to the constituencies. That is a truism so obvious that it requires no argument."[34] In 1974, the Whitlam government had regarded the defeat of the government in the Senate on a procedural motion ("that the question be put") as "a denial of supply" − then Senator Murphy's words − and had "thereupon" and "therefore" − Mr Whitlam's words − advised a dissolution.[35] If defeat on a procedural motion can constitute denial of Supply, how much more so did the 1975 Senate votes.

Secondly, the passage of the Senate's amendment had exactly the effect of denying Supply: it meant that no Supply was forthcoming, that no money would be available to pay public service salaries and wages, and so on. The actual rejection of the appropriation bills could do no more. As Sir John points out, the money was fast running out in November 1975. The government needed money; the Senate was asked to approve the appropriation of such money; the Senate refused to do so until an election was called. That it was denying Supply to the government was as clear as day.

Thirdly, the Senate amendment expressed its attitude precisely: it was prepared to provide Supply when the government agreed to an election. There was nothing more appropriate it could say or do. Finally, the Constitution (section 57) clearly envisages that the Senate's "fail[ing] to pass" a bill can have the same effect as its rejecting it. In 1975, the Senate was clearly "fail[ing] to pass" the appropriation bills. The hypothetical question of whether the Senate would ever actually have rejected the bills outright does not alter the clear constitutional and practical reality that the Senate had denied Supply.

It is a measure of how much it is accepted that Senate denial of Supply requires resignation or an election that some of the critics who assert that the Senate did not in fact deny Supply in 1975 have fallen back on this silly idea. (In the case of some writers, this error appears in more carefully considered, but still in my view quite wrong, critiques of Sir John's handling of the crisis.)

It is hard for anyone reading this book, or what many other writers have said, to doubt that a Prime Minister unable to get Supply through the Senate (or, of course, the House of Representatives) must either resign or call an

[34] Churchill to Asquith, 20 July 1909, in Asquith papers, 12, fol. 46.
[35] *Simultaneous Dissolution of the Senate and the House of Representatives 11 April 1974*, Commonwealth Parliamentary Paper No. 257, 1975, pp. ii, 6.

election for the House of Representatives (or for both houses of parliament – a double dissolution). Sir John cites various authorities for this, and there are others.[36] In 1975, of course, the Senate exercised its power to deny Supply, and the Prime Minister refused to take the constitutionally necessary step of either resigning or calling an election.

Similarly, it is very hard for anyone reading this book, or what many other writers have said, to doubt that the Governor-General does have "reserve powers" which include the power to dismiss a Prime Minister, and that these powers exist to be exercised where necessary for the maintenance of constitutional government. Section 61 of the Constitution gives the Governor-General the power, which carries with it the duty, to ensure "the execution and maintenance of this Constitution". Of course, in all but the most extraordinary circumstances the Governor-General acts on and only on the advice of the Prime Minister. But the reserve powers exist for those extraordinary circumstances, and are the exception to the general constitutional principle that the Crown acts only on ministerial advice. Sir John believed, as do many other distinguished authorities, that it was necessary in the circumstances of 1975 to exercise the reserve power of dismissal. The chapter in *The Triumph of the Constitution* on "Men of light and learning" draws together comments from many such writers.

The 1990s are seeing various attempts, not only to debate the case for constitutional reform, but also to commemorate and study the work of the Federation Conventions of the 1890s which, through long and complex debates, drafted the Constitution.[37] Sir John quotes in his *Bulletin* articles from some speeches in those conventions, and in *The Triumph of the Constitution* he expresses the hope that the work of our founding fathers will be properly

[36] E.g., Sir John Marriott, *Second Chambers*, Clarendon Press, Oxford, 1927, pp. 119-22. F.L.W. Wood, *The Constitutional Development of Australia*, 1933, pp. 216, 221. L.F. Crisp recognised this as a reality, though he did not like it: *Australian National Government*, Longmans, 1965, p. 294. J.D.B. Miller, *Australian Government and Politics*, 2nd ed., 1959, pp. 97, 99. D.J. Killen, "A fine flourish of 17th-century vigor?", *The Australian*, 19 October 1973, p. 10; "The possible danger in rejecting Supply Bills", *The Sydney Morning Herald*, 11 April 1974, p. 9. (Killen supported the denial of Supply in 1975.) On discussion of denial of Supply if Labor won the 1953 Senate elections, see "Test for Mr Menzies", *The Times*, 8 May 1953; "The Australian Senate", *The Times*, 5 May 1953. DO35/5185, Public Record Office, London; also DO35/5270.

[37] See, e.g., "Centenary of entry into force of the Federal Council of Australasia Act 1885", *Australian Law Journal*, vol. 59, no. 11, November 1985, pp. 647-8. Sir Zelman Cowen, "Is It Not Time", Commemorative Lecture on the National Australasian Convention of 1891, Parliament House, Canberra, 7 March 1991. Other events of note include the Constitutional Centenary Conference, Sydney, 2-5 April 1991, and the launch of the Constitutional Centenary Foundation in April 1992: *The Australian*, 15 April 1992.

celebrated. The Federation Convention debates have been subjected to various interpretations. But, having studied the relevant debates, I believe that the more they are intelligently studied, the more clearly the key constitutional principles relevant to 1975 will be recognised. The Convention debates must, of course, be read bearing in mind the specific proposals before the delegates, and the fact that they came with widely varying political views and from colonies with differing interests.

It is clear from the official reports of the Conventions that the Senate — both as the states' house[38] and as a popularly elected house — was intended to be more powerful than the House of Lords or colonial upper houses.[39] As Sir John points out, it was deliberately given the power to reject money bills, including appropriation bills.[40] J.A. La Nauze recorded of the 1891 Convention, which reached the compromise on Senate powers over money bills which became section 53 of the Constitution: "There was no opposition to the proposition that while money bills must originate in the popular house, the Senate might in an extreme case reject such bills in toto."[41] This power was part of the deal that made federation possible. The Senate was expected to exercise that power, though to do so judiciously. It was accepted that if the Senate denied Supply, and compromise on any specific issue could not be reached with the House of Representatives, then the government must either resign or the dispute must be referred to the people — either as a double dissolution, or a dissolution of the House of Representatives alone.[42] The need to obtain Supply from both houses, and the liability to resignation or dissolution if it were denied, were regarded as

---

[38] Deakin (p. 584), Sir John Forrest (p. 854), Charles Kingston (p. 870), Sir George Turner (p. 879), and W.A. Trenwith (p. 947) were amongst those who foresaw that the Senate would divide party against party rather than state against state. *Official Record of the Debates of the Australasian Federal Convention*, Sydney, 1897 (hereafter *Convention Debates*). La Nauze says this was an unrepresentative view: J.A. La Nauze, *The Making of the Australian Constitution*, Melbourne University Press, 1972, pp. 44, 119, 148.

[39] See, e.g., *Convention Debates*, Adelaide, 1897, pp. 512-3 (Deakin).

[40] See, e.g., Richardson, op. cit. Sawer, op. cit., pp. 115-6.

[41] La Nauze, op. cit., p. 43.

[42] See, e.g., *Convention Debates*, Adelaide, 1897, pp. 22-3, 557 (Barton); pp. 295, 507ff. (Deakin). These passages from Barton and Deakin show clearly that, contrary to C.J.G. Sampford, the Senate's legislative power over money bills was regarded as giving it power, in La Nauze's words, "affecting the life of a government": La Nauze, op. cit., p. 145. The U.S.-style separation between legislative and executive powers is not to be found in the Australian Constitution, or in the intentions of its drafters, in the way Sampford suggests. C.J.G. Sampford, "Reconciling Responsible Government and Federalism", in M.P. Ellinghaus, J. Bradbrook, & A.J. Duggan (eds), *The Emergence of Australian Law*, Butterworths, Sydney, 1989, pp. 355-75.

compatible with the primary responsibility of the government to the House of Representatives, which was provided for in giving it the sole power of initiation of all, and of amendment of almost all, money bills.

Despite opposition, these were the views that prevailed in the Federation Conventions.[43] There are at least two reasons why some analyses of the Convention debates go astray.[44] First, some writers assume that the expression "responsible government" denotes a system of government in which nothing the Senate could do could affect the life of the government – when clearly the Senate's capacity to deny Supply and so compel resignation or dissolution was accepted by delegates, who believed themselves to be adopting a system of "responsible government".[45] I shall say more on this below. Secondly, some commentators regard the objective of House of Representatives "control" of Supply as meaning that the Senate should have no right of veto, when the real issue of contention in the Federation Conventions was whether or not the Senate could amend money bills, its right to reject them being readily agreed.[46]

---

[43] Some delegates did not want the Senate to have such power, and wanted the government to be solely, not just primarily, responsible to the House of Representatives. But they did not succeed. It was partly because the Constitution, section 53, gave the Senate the means of "rejecting the measures absolutely which are necessary to keep the Government going" (p. 16) and with it the power to "make and unmake ministries" (p. 118F) that H.B. Higgins campaigned against acceptance of the Constitution. See H.B. Higgins, *Essays and Addresses on the Australian Commonwealth Bill*, Atlas Press, Melbourne, 1900, esp. pp. 16, 18, 47-8, 79-81, 91-2, 110-1, 118F-G, 129-31. His fears were exaggerated. Once the Constitution was adopted, he accepted that it was necessary to work within it, even though he did not like it: see below.

[44] Cf. ibid. Brian Galligan, "The Founders' Design and Intentions Regarding Responsible Government", in Patrick Weller & Dean Jaensch (eds), *Responsible Government in Australia*, Drummond, 1980. H.O. Browning, *1975 Crisis: An Historical View*, Hale & Iremonger, Sydney, 1985.

[45] See Richardson, op. cit., pp. 288-9.

[46] The "compromise of 1891" survived to become section 53 of the Constitution. G.B. Barton's exposition of the 1891 draft said that "it follows the English practice by saying that the Senate may reject a money bill, but may not amend it" (pp. 39-40). He clearly regarded this as compatible with "responsible government", which he said the draft embodied (pp. 48-50). "Responsible government" meant to him that the executive government, comprising a Federal Executive Council including ministers who were members of parliament, would be responsible to parliament. G.B. Barton (ed.), *The Draft Bill to Constitute the Commonwealth of Australia as Adopted by the Convention of 1891*, Government Printer, Sydney, 1891. See also Cowen, op. cit., pp. 17-9. La Nauze, op. cit., pp. 39, 40, 43-4, 53, 70-2, 126, 139-49. On Sir Samuel Griffith's views, see letter, *Quadrant*, June 1985. Especially interesting are *Convention Debates*, 1891, pp. 31-40 (Griffith), 44-53, 74-85 (Deakin), 427-31 (Griffith), 471 (Duncan Gillies), 526 (where Griffith set out the compromise of 1891), 527 (where he said the draft embodied government responsible "to the parliament of the Commonwealth"), 538 (Wrixon).

At the 1897 and 1898 Conventions,[47] which are the relevant ones for section 57 of the Constitution, there was overwhelming agreement that deadlocks between the houses should be resolved by reference to the people. Several delegates presented a dissolution in response to deadlock as being fundamental to "the British Constitution".[48] It was not generally believed that a dissolution of the House of Representatives or of both houses arising from such deadlock damaged "responsible government".[49] The view that a government can or should refuse to go to the people on a denial of Supply is totally at odds with all that transpired in the Convention debates on deadlocks. The action of Sir John Kerr in bringing on such a referral to the voters in 1975 was entirely in keeping with both the letter and the spirit of the Constitution as its framers, diverse as they were, intended it. The more the 1890s debates are carefully studied, the more, I believe, this will be recognised.

The Constitution drafted at those Conventions, though not loud with ringing proclamations of the principle of direct popular sovereignty, actually embodied it in many provisions − including, as Sir John points out, in the provision for double dissolutions, and for amendment of the Constitution solely by referendum. The Constitution's emphasis on the role of the people is a point Sir John Kerr frequently stressed. He saw the reserve power of dismissal as referring an otherwise irresolvable crisis back to the people to resolve. This is what he did in 1975.

In his first *Bulletin* article, Sir John says that "in 1901, the two houses engaged in a serious dispute over the form of the first supply bills". This was the new Constitution being put into practice in a parliament dominated by men who had led the process of framing it in the 1890s. These vigorous parliamentary debates in 1901 show several points central to 1975.[50]

[47] The debates are at: *Convention Debates*, Adelaide 1897, pp. 1150-73. Sydney 1897, pp. 541-773, 807-981. Melbourne 1898, pp. 2104-2249. Good summaries are at: J.E. Richardson, "Federal Deadlocks: Origin and Operation of Section 57", *Tasmanian University Law Review*, vol. 1, November 1962, pp. 716-32; John Quick & R.R. Garran, *The Annotated Constitution of the Australian Commonwealth*, Angus & Robertson, Sydney, 1901, pp. 138-9, 180-2, 189-93, 202-4, 218.

[48] E.g., *Convention Debates*, Sydney 1897, pp. 822, 832, 912, 961. Melbourne 1898, pp. 2112, 2208.

[49] See, e.g., Sydney 1897, pp. 624, 735, 907. Melbourne 1898, pp. 2108-9.

[50] There are subsequent debates also worth reading which reflect the views that the Senate is entitled to reject money bills, and that denial of Supply requires resignation or an election. See, e.g., the debates on the 1902 and 1933 *Customs Tariff Bills* (September 1902 and November 1933), and the *Income Tax Bill* 1943 (March 1943). E.g., Sir Josiah Symon at *Commonwealth Parliamentary Debates*, 9 September 1902, pp. 15813ff., and Deakin, 10 September 1902, p. 15923.

1. Several senators[51] and some Members of the House of Representatives[52] – including, as Sir John pointed out, the Prime Minister (Edmund Barton) and H.B. Higgins – explicitly declared the Senate's power to reject Supply.

2. Some stated and others implied that by so doing the Senate could force the government to resign or call an election.[53] As best I can see, no one contradicted this.

3. The rights that the House of Representatives was concerned to claim as its exclusive rights were the right to originate money bills and the right to amend them.[54]

4. It was universally acknowledged that no legal appropriation could be made without the assent of the Senate.[55]

5. It was not argued that there was any constitutional reason why the Senate should not reject Supply or that it would be improper for them to do so.

6. It was argued by many members of both houses, including Barton, that there was no analogy between the Senate and the House of Lords or the upper houses of the states as would restrict the Senate's rights.[56]

7. It was not countenanced by any member of either house that a government should be able to govern without Supply.

8. It was said by a number of members – including H.B. Higgins, who had campaigned against acceptance of the Constitution – to be their obligation to operate within the Constitution as it was, even if they would rather see it modified.[57]

9. A number of members of both houses, again including Barton, said that any "precedents" created by their actions would not destroy the rights each house had under the Constitution; the written word of the Constitution safeguarded them.[58]

---

[51] E.g., *Commonwealth Parliamentary Debates*, June 1901, pp. 1025, 1027, 1036, 1037, 1042, 1043, 1321, 1345.

[52] E.g., ibid., pp. 1176, 1473-4, 1501-2, 1504.

[53] Ibid., pp. 1183, 1326 (Senator Charleston, whom Sir John quotes), 1328 (Senator Sir John Downer), 1334, 1347ff.

[54] Ibid., pp. 1175, 1187, 1473-4, 1477, 1481, 1484; see also pp. 1342-3.

[55] E.g., ibid., pp. 1187, 1189, 1345, 1347, 1349-51, 1472-3, 1478, 1481-2, 1484.

[56] Ibid., pp. 1023, 1025, 1026, 1028, 1029, 1030, 1043, 1311, 1314, 1330, 1336, 1341, 1342, 1345-9, 1358, 1480-1.

[57] E.g., ibid., pp. 965, 1504.

[58] Ibid., pp. 1314, 1325, 1474, 1475, 1486.

It is sometimes said, following John Winthrop Hackett,[59] that there is an incompatibility between federalism, as embodied in a powerful Senate, and "responsible government".[60] Parallel to this is the claim that the principle of "responsible government" means that Senate denial of Supply cannot require a government with a majority in the House of Representatives to resign or go to an election. These claims show a misunderstanding of the term "responsible government". As Holroyd J of the Victorian Supreme Court said in the 19th century, "we must not be misled by abstract terms... There is no cut-and-dried institution called responsible government, identical in all countries where it exists."[61] The most fundamental meaning of "responsible government" as it relates to the relations of government to parliament is, not the notion that the government is responsible to the lower house alone, but that it is responsible to the legislature, as against, as in the American system, the separation of executive and legislature. This point is clear in, for example, the famous joint judgment of Knox CJ and Isaacs, Rich and Starke JJ in *The Engineers Case*:[62]

> In the words of a distinguished lawyer and statesman, Lord Haldane, when a member of the House of Commons, delivered on the motion for leave to introduce the bill for the [Commonwealth of Australia Constitution] Act ..: "The difference between the Constitution which this bill proposes to set up and the Constitution of the United States is enormous and fundamental. This bill is permeated through and through with the spirit of the greatest institution which exists in the Empire... − I mean the institution of responsible government, a government under which the Executive is directly responsible to − nay, is almost the creature of − the Legislature. This is not so in America ..." With these expressions we entirely agree.

---

[59] *Convention Debates*, 1891, p. 280. Hackett said that "responsible government" was impossible to define (pp. 280-1), and that "the Senate is the hinge of federation" (p. 277). On Hackett's often misquoted prophecy, see Sawer, op. cit., p. 122. Sir Robert Garran, *Prosper the Commonwealth*, Angus & Robertson, Sydney, 1958, pp. 116-7.

[60] See, e.g., David Wood, "The Senate, Federalism and Democracy", *Melbourne University Law Review*, vol. 17, no. 2, 1989, pp. 292-306. Of course, if there is a problem, and there need not be, it is in reconciling a strong upper house with "responsible government". A federal system does not necessarily have a strong upper house (e.g., Canada); and strong upper houses can exist in non-federal systems (e.g., Britain before 1911; the French Third Republic: see below). See, e.g., Sampford, op. cit., esp. pp. 355-6. D.J. Markwell, *The Federal State: Lessons from North American and European Experience*, Ditchley Conference Report, 1991, p. 4.

[61] Quoted from K. Bailey in *Cambridge History of the British Empire*, vol. 7, Cambridge University Press, 1933, p. 395. See also G.B. Barton's 1891 discussion of the term: Barton, op. cit., pp. 48-50.

[62] *Engineers Case* (1920) 28 CLR 129 at 147. See also, e.g., *Boilermakers Case* (1956) 94 CLR 254 at 275.

Leaving aside its meaning for the relationship between the Crown and ministers, to say that Australia has responsible government is to say that the executive is responsible to the parliament;[63] it does not specify the exact nature of that responsibility. The form of responsible government adopted in Australia certainly means that the government's "main responsibility"[64] (as Sir Robert Garran put it) or "primary responsibility"[65] (as Sir Harrison Moore put it) is to the House of Representatives. So, for example, so long as the government is able to get Supply from parliament, the question of who forms the government will be determined solely by reference to who can best command the confidence of the House of Representatives. But it was also accepted that the Senate could deny Supply and by so doing force either the resignation of the government or a dissolution. This was – and is – the form of responsible government adopted in Australia.[66]

We should not imagine, as some people do,[67] that this arrangement was unique or unprecedented. In 1909, Lord Curzon, in defending the right of the House of Lords to reject the Budget, declared it "inherent in the rights of any Second Chamber ... that in the last resort a Second Chamber can compel a reference to the polls."[68] Churchill was one of the most vigorous Liberal assailants of the Lords' rejection of the Budget in 1909; but Churchill assailed the action of the Lords, not as an attack on responsible government, but as an attack on representative government, because the Lords was unelected and unaccountable.[69] It was because the Lords was unelected that in 1911 it was deprived of the power to reject money bills.[70] This objection did not apply to the Australian Senate, and it was not then or later deprived of the power to reject such bills.

In the French Third Republic, "the two houses had equal rights in

---

[63] See, e.g., Colin Howard, *Australian Federal Constitutional Law*, Law Book Coy, 1972, pp. 135-6. Geoffrey Marshall & G.C. Moodie, *Some Problems of the Constitution*, Hutchinson, London, 1959, p. 47. A.C. Castles, "Constitutional Conventions and the Senate", *Australian Current Law*, 1975 DT 285.

[64] Garran, op. cit., p. 117.

[65] Harrison Moore, "The Political System of Australia", in Meredith Atkinson (ed.), *Australia: Economic and Political Studies*, Macmillan, 1920, p. 109.

[66] See J.B. Paul, "An Epistle from Paul", *Quadrant*, April 1984, for an exposition of the views of Sir Harrison Moore on this.

[67] "No other country would have a situation where an upper House could reject a Budget": E.G. Whitlam, *The Truth of the Matter*, p. 77.

[68] Curzon in House of Lords, 30 November 1909. Quoted from C.S. Emden (ed.), *Selected Speeches on the Constitution*, vol. 1, Oxford University Press., 1939, p. 160.

[69] Rhodes James, op. cit., pp. 1416-8, 1441, 1449-50, 1451-2, and passim.

[70] The *Parliament Act* of 1911 is at, e.g., Jennings, op. cit., p. 52lff.

legislation and finance (except that the Senate had no power of financial initiative) ... [T]he Senate forced three ministries out of office between 1875 and 1929, four between 1930 and 1940."[71] The Third Republic, like Australia, combined an upper house capable of forcing a government from power with "the Parliamentary System which she borrowed from Britain."[72] Its "Constitution-makers", like Australia's, "were determined that the Senate should have more power than the British House of Lords."[73]

It is very hard for anyone now to imagine that Sir John Kerr acted as he did for any reason other than purely constitutional ones. Sir John deals very convincingly with the incredible proposition that the CIA or some other foreign intelligence agency somehow procured his dismissal of the Whitlam government. It would hardly be worth devoting any space to this conspiracy theory were it not that it has continued to be repeated in the face of all the evidence.

John Pilger is the main propagator of it. One of the most prominent places in which he has recycled this story is his book lambasting Australia, *A Secret Country*.[74] In a single paragraph of this book,[75] I have found the following inaccuracies. Pilger claims that "Kerr's intelligence career and his association with the CIA are matters of record." Sir John did not have an intelligence career, nor any association of which he was aware with the CIA.[76] Pilger claims that "on Sunday, November 9", "Kerr travelled to the ultra-secret headquarters near Melbourne of Australia's most important spy organisation, the Defence Signals Directorate, DSD, where he was briefed on the 'security crisis'." On Sunday 9 November, Sir John travelled from Melbourne to Sydney. On Saturday 8 November, he had reviewed a parade to mark the 50th Anniversary of the foundation of the Royal Australian Corps of Signals at Watsonia Barracks, near Melbourne, and opened the Corps Museum. This mission was so "secret" that the Vice-Regal News sections of several Australian newspapers, to which the Governor-General's office routinely sent the information, broadcast it to the world. In a footnote, Pilger gives a source for this alleged information: but that source,

[71] Philip M. Williams, *Crisis and Compromise: Politics in the Fourth Republic*, Longman, London, 1972, p. 186.

[72] Paul Vaucher, *Post-War France*, Thornton Butterworth, London, 1934, p. 31.

[73] J. Hampden Jackson, *Clemenceau and the Third Republic*, Hodder & Stoughton, London, 1948, p. 50.

[74] John Pilger, *A Secret Country*, Jonathan Cape, London, 1989.

[75] Ibid., p. 167.

[76] See *Matters for Judgment*, pp. 99-100, 176-7, 183-6.

a newspaper article,[77] does not actually contain the claim which Pilger makes that the Governor-General "was briefed on the 'security crisis'". Pilger has added it himself.

Pilger then goes on to allege that the Governor-General actually made a telephone call during his visit, and that the Governor-General wished to be sure his conversation was not overheard or listened in on. What possible significance can there be in that? Pilger finally asserts that Sir John never "allowed himself to be subject to public scrutiny on these or any other matters". Sir John has given interviews "on these and other matters" to such diverse public figures as Geoffrey Robertson QC, Bruce Stannard of *The Bulletin*, and Gerard Henderson.[78] Pilger in effect concedes that his spies-and-traitors story is, at best, speculation, and neither he nor anyone else has produced any proof for it. His only "evidence" consists of regurgitation of unsubstantiated allegations made by other polemicists, without proof, and already denied by those involved. To discuss the dismissal with no reference to the Australian Constitution, or to the voluminous writings on the dismissal's constitutionality, as Pilger does, is to miss the point of it altogether.

The fourth feature of *The Triumph of the Constitution* which I think will interest many people is that, as well as drawing the attention of readers to much of what has been written on 1975, Sir John draws attention to aspects of the crisis that have been largely neglected, or not known, before. For example, he mentions in chapter 7 that he had "good reason to believe" that the Prime Minister's Department "was in fact ready to act on the instant if required" if Mr Whitlam had decided to advise the Queen to dismiss Sir John as Governor-General. To the best of my knowledge, this has not been public knowledge before. Indeed, Sir John's very acute discussion of

---

[77] *Times on Sunday*, 21 February 1988. William Pinwill's article "The Dismissal: still seeking the whole truth" refers to the Governor-General being at the "ultra-secret headquarters [of the Defence Signals Division, as DSD was then called] in Watsonia, near Melbourne, a few days before he sacked Whitlam". He does not say, what Pilger has produced from thin air, that the Governor-General "was briefed on the 'security crisis'". Sir John, of course, has denied ever being briefed on any "security crisis", and those alleged to have briefed him have denied having done so.

[78] Geoffrey Robertson, lengthy television interview, 1987. The Henderson interviews of which I am aware are: "The Kerr Testimony", *The Weekend Australian*, 30-31 January 1988. "Sir John Kerr: The dismissal: What I told Malcolm Fraser", *The Weekend Australian*, 7-8 November 1987. "Kerr note found – record of what he told Fraser", *The Weekend Australian*, 14-15 November 1987. On the topic of Sir John's telephone conversation with Mr Fraser on the morning of 11 November 1975, it is also worth reading the letter from R.J. Ellicott QC, "The rewriting of Nov 11, 1975", *The Weekend Australian*, 5-6 December 1987.

dismissal of a Governor-General highlights a point very few people have considered: from his point of view, as Governor-General, the issue was not (as some commentators would have it) how soon advice from the Prime Minister to the Queen to dismiss the Governor-General would be accepted by her, but that Sir John would not have believed himself free to dismiss the Prime Minister once such advice (which the Queen would be bound sooner or later to accept) was given by the Prime Minister. (Sir John touched on this in *Matters for Judgment*,[79] but deals with it more fully here.) Events in Papua New Guinea in September-October 1991, when the Governor-General's resignation pre-empted the Prime Minister's declared intention to advise the Queen to dismiss him, reminds us yet again that the possibility of a Governor-General being dismissed is not an academic one (though in the P.N.G. case, unlike in Australia, there was a strong case for seeking the Governor-General's dismissal).[80]

Similarly, Sir John's discussion of what he refers to as Mr Whitlam's "Goulburn doctrine" brings into even sharper focus the fact that the novel constitutional doctrine in 1975 was not that the Senate could deny Supply, nor that the Governor-General had reserve powers, but that no constitutional consequences flow from a Senate denial of Supply. This was, of course, a revolutionary doctrine in a parliamentary system such as Australia's: for a government governing without Supply granted by parliament (which in Australia requires the consent of both houses of parliament) destroys the one means the parliament has for holding the government to account – denying it the money to carry on. If a government can continue to govern even though Supply has not been passed by the Senate, it can continue to govern even though Supply has not been passed by the House of Representatives. Sir John's first *Bulletin* article is especially striking in listing nine instances prior to September 1975 where Mr Whitlam had implicitly or explicitly accepted that denial of Supply must lead to resignation or an election – the constitutional axiom his "Goulburn doctrine" sought to subvert.

Chapter 12 of *The Triumph of the Constitution* contains new information on the failure of Mr Whitlam to advise the Governor-General of the possible need for an Executive Council meeting on 13 December 1974 to authorise loan raisings. This gives further insight into Mr Whitlam's approach to the Governor-General and the established procedures of constitutional

[79] *Matters for Judgment*, p. 331.
[80] *Keesing's Contemporary Archives*, 1991, pp. 38534-5.

government.

There are, of course, issues concerning 1975 that have not been fully covered even in all the millions of words written about it to date, and further material is yet to come into the public domain. It is clear that Sir John wished to see his correspondence with Buckingham Palace made public at an appropriate time (which would presumably have to be agreed between the monarch and the Australian Prime Minister). The clear implication of what he writes is that this will show that the version of events which he recorded in *Matters for Judgment* was what he recorded at the time of the events in his reports to the Queen.[81] Similarly, Sir John urges the private banks to make public the legal opinions which they received on the scheme devised by the Whitlam government to try to enable it to govern without Supply. This scheme relied on the cooperation of the banks. Sir John believed, and with good reason, that this scheme was unconstitutional, illegal for other reasons also, and (at least in the time available) unworkable, and that "the private banks would not feel able to participate and would not".[82] Although there has been useful writing on this scheme,[83] more remains to be said.

The fifth way in which I believe *The Triumph of the Constitution* will be of interest is the insight it gives us into the mind and character of its author, a figure of towering importance in Australian history. Though he deliberately quotes extensively from others, Sir John's own voice comes through clearly. He wishes to bring to the attention of readers what others have written, including acknowledging where they disagree with him. This reflects one of his most striking features – his fair-mindedness. This is also evident in the generous remarks he makes about some of those who have attacked him most bitterly (though, naturally, he has clear views on their behaviour in and since 1975).

Although *The Triumph of the Constitution* is not intended as autobiography, it gives many insights into Sir John's life – for instance, comments about his boyhood and youth (especially in chapter 8); his anti-Stalinism; his advocacy in the 1940s of using the external affairs power to expand Commonwealth

[81] See also J.B. Paul, "Judgment of the Matter", *Quadrant*, January-February 1980, pp. 52-3.

[82] *Matters for Judgment*, pp. 300, 326. See also "Statements of the Australian Bankers' Association Research Directorate issued 5th and 11th November 1975", in *The Facts and the Law*, Institute of Public Affairs (N.S.W.), Sydney, c. 1976, pp. 19-20.

[83] H.W. Arndt, "The Economics of the 1975 Constitutional Crisis", *Quadrant*, July 1984. Reply by Sir Garfield Barwick, *Quadrant*, March 1985. Letters from H.W. Arndt, April 1985; Sir Garfield Barwick, June 1985; Don Markwell, June 1985.

power; his thinking in 1975 about what impact his action might have on the monarchy in Australia; the attention with which he followed the constitutional debate of the 1980s; and the joy of life together with Lady Kerr in Europe and Australia after 1975. Once or twice there are intimations of approaching death.

This book was written by Sir John Kerr in the final years of his life. He put it aside late in 1990, just weeks before entering hospital. It is a fitting memorial to a man with a unique place in Australian history — a man of outstanding intellect, integrity, and courage.

~

"Nothing improper in advice to Kerr"
Letter to The Sydney Morning Herald
7 January 1994

Sir John Kerr's consultation of Sir Garfield Barwick and Sir Anthony Mason, both then High Court judges, in 1975 before dismissing the Whitlam government was proper in principle and well supported by precedent.

In the rare cases where a Governor-General (or state Governor) has an independent discretionary power to exercise (as over dismissal of a government), he [or she] is entitled to seek advice about exercising his [or her] discretion from whomever he [or she] believes appropriate in the circumstances. It must be for the people whose advice he [or she] seeks to decline if they believe it improper for them to give advice.

The eminence and distinction of Sir Garfield and Sir Anthony as constitutional lawyers are sufficient explanation for the Governor-General's seeking their individual advice before taking such an important constitutional decision in 1975. As such an exercise of the reserve powers of the Crown was not open to review by the courts, there was no reason of principle why such judges should not advise the Governor-General. (It is worth noting that Mr Whitlam made no attempt to challenge his dismissal before the High Court.) There was no compromising of the independence of the judiciary.

The matter Bruce Donald (*Herald*, January 4) suggests might have come before the High Court – the dissolution of both houses of parliament – was not, strictly speaking, an issue on which the Governor-General sought advice from Sir Garfield, or as I understand it, Sir Anthony. Had any case come before the Court about which these judges believed themselves to be "compromised", they could have disqualified themselves from sitting. But no such case arose, nor was one ever likely.

Many Governors-General and Chief Justices since federation have held, and acted on, the view that a Governor-General is entitled to seek advice from High Court judges, and that they are entitled to give it, at least on non-justiciable issues. This was the view of at least eight Governors-General (Northcote, Dudley, Denman, Munro Ferguson, De L'Isle, Casey, Hasluck, and Kerr) and at least four Chief Justices (Griffith, Dixon, Barwick, and Mason).[84]

The actions of Kerr, Barwick, and Mason in 1975 are in line with a very extensive history of earlier consultations of High Court judges by Governors-General. For example, several of the early Governors-General frequently consulted the first Chief Justice, Sir Samuel Griffith, and also another distinguished High Court judge, Sir Edmund Barton, including over whether or not to agree to requests by Prime Ministers to dissolve the House of Representative or both houses of parliament. In most cases, as with Sir Anthony Mason in 1975, such advice was given confidentially, and without reference to the Prime Minister of the day.

In 1975, the Governor-General dismissed a Prime Minister who was unable to get money from parliament but who, contrary to constitutional principle and practice, refused to call an election. Rather than criticise Sir Garfield Barwick and Sir Anthony Mason for giving advice to the Governor-General as he was considering how to fulfil his constitutional responsibilities, we would do well to reflect on the fact that both the then Chief Justice and the present one believed that the Governor-General did what was both proper and necessary in the extraordinary circumstances of the 1975 crisis.

---

[84] [Sir Harry Gibbs, a High Court judge in 1975 who succeeded Barwick as Chief Justice, supported this view: Joan Priest, *Sir Harry Gibbs: Without fear or favour*, Scribblers Publishing, 1995, p. 75. Another future Chief Justice, Murray Gleeson QC, and another future High Court judge, Keith Aickin QC, also supported this view in 1975: K.A. Aickin, A.M. Gleeson, P.H. Lane, *Ex parte J.M. Rothery* (23 October 1975). See Sexton, op. cit, p. 220.]

"The Case for Kerr"
The Weekend Australian
11-12 November 1995

Why did the Governor-General dismiss the Prime Minister in November 1975, and bring on an election? The key to understanding what happened is to be found, not in what Rupert Murdoch did or did not say to John Menadue,[85] but in Sir John Kerr's understanding of the Constitution, which it was his duty to uphold. The constitutional argument, all too often lost sight of in more sensational discussions, merits careful thought by all Australians interested in the way their country is governed.

Under the Constitution, the Governor-General has a duty to maintain constitutional government. This requires having a government that is able to get Supply – money for government services – passed by the parliament.

Gough Whitlam was unable to get Supply from parliament, and refused to take the one step – advising the Governor-General to call an election – that would get it. It was therefore necessary for Kerr to obtain other ministers who could get Supply.

In replacing a Prime Minister who could not get Supply with one who could, Kerr averted the chaos of government funds completely running out, and ensured that an immediate election was held for both houses of parliament, giving the people of Australia the final say.

This was the democratic outcome to the crisis. An election enabled the people to choose a new parliament. Had they wished, they could have reinstated Whitlam as Prime Minister. Moreover, the need for governments to get Supply from parliament, and not to govern without Supply, is, as we shall see, a fundamental safeguard of our parliamentary democracy.

November 11 was the climax, and the resolution, of a great crisis that had deadlocked the parliament for weeks, and was already seeing money for government services begin to run out. The crisis comprised three elements. First, the Senate's continuing refusal since mid-October to pass Supply until the government agreed to call an election. Second, Whitlam's continuing refusal to call an election. Third, after four weeks of this stand-off, Kerr's dismissal of Whitlam to enable an election to be held.

The crisis was caused, not by Kerr's action, but by Whitlam's refusal,

---

[85] [John Menadue, Whitlam's former private secretary and Permanent Secretary of the Prime Minister's Department in 1975, later claimed that Rupert Murdoch had indicated to him extensive foreknowledge of the dismissal and subsequent events.]

given the Senate's denial of Supply, to do what he knew was constitutionally the only proper course – to advise an election (or to resign) when he was unable to get Supply from the parliament.

Looking back over 20 years, it is striking how debate on those events has progressed.

- It is now generally accepted that the Senate has the power which it exercised in 1975 to deny Supply, and that there was no convention that it should not do so.

- It is now also generally accepted that the Governor-General has the reserve power of dismissal which he exercised in 1975. Under Paul Keating's proposals for a republic, it is proposed that "the Head of State will retain those very few powers now held by the Governor-General which, in the most exceptional circumstances, may be exercised without, or possibly contrary to, ministerial advice". That is a very good description of the reserve powers. They exist to uphold parliament's control of the government and the people's control of parliament.

- It is now established as historical fact there were many precedents before 1975 for Sir John Kerr's consulting the Chief Justice, Sir Garfield Barwick, and another judge of the High Court and later Chief Justice, Sir Anthony Mason. A number of Governors-General had consulted Chief Justice Sir Samuel Griffith and puisne judge Sir Edmund Barton on several occasions. These cases included whether to agree to requests from Prime Ministers to dissolve the House of Representatives, and over the resignations of two Prime Ministers. Chief Justice Sir Owen Dixon had been consulted by the Governor of Victoria in 1952. Lord Casey had consulted Barwick in 1967 after the death of Harold Holt, and Chief Justice Sir John Latham had been consulted by senior ministers in 1939 after the death of Joseph Lyons.

- Some of the more absurd conspiracy theories have largely disappeared (though new ones seem in danger of growing up to replace the old).

- It is now widely acknowledged that Whitlam's handling of the crisis was unwise and seriously at fault. His manifest and misplaced contempt for the office of Governor-General and his unwillingness to consider views other that his own made frank discussion between him and Kerr impossible. It also led him to ignore the warnings he received of what Kerr might feel duty bound to do.

What is the Governor-General's duty? Under section 61 of the Constitution it includes "the execution and maintenance of this Constitution, and of the laws of the Commonwealth".

First of all, this requires that the wheels of government are kept turning. Second, it requires that the Governor-General do what he can, subject to constitutional practice, to prevent the subversion of the Constitution and the law.

Keeping the wheels of government turning requires money – to pay public servants, suppliers and contractors and others. Section 83 of the Constitution provides that "no money shall be drawn from the Treasury of the Commonwealth except under appropriation made by law". Under sections 1 and 53, money can only be lawfully appropriated by vote of both houses of parliament.

Without the Senate's agreeing to an appropriation, not a dollar of public money may be spent. The Senate may refuse to grant such appropriation, as it did in 1975. In the absence of such an appropriation, it is impossible for the processes of government to continue. This is why Kerr, in 1975, needed to have ministers who, unlike Whitlam, could get parliament to appropriate money for government services.

The constitutional requirement that no money be spent without authorisation by parliament is a crucial safeguard of our parliamentary system. The fundamental principle that government (the executive) is responsible to parliament and through them to the people depends upon parliament having the ultimate weapon of driving a government from office by making it impossible for it to govern. As Sir Isaac Isaacs, later Chief Justice and subsequently Governor-General, said in 1922, "The parliamentary guardianship of taxation and expenditure is the pivot of the Constitution and the keystone of the arch of personal liberty."

For a government to be able to govern without Supply would destroy parliament's control of government. That was what Whitlam was seeking to do in 1975. That was what Kerr prevented.

For most purposes the government is responsible only to the lower house of parliament. But the Australian Constitution was deliberately written to require that Supply must come from both houses. As part of the compact under which federation took place, the Senate was deliberately given power, through denying Supply, to force a government to resign or go to an election.

In 1902, soon after the writing of the Constitution, the leading constitutional lawyer Sir Harrison Moore wrote, "One of the checks upon the Ministry and the Lower House lies in the fact that the Upper House might in an extreme case refuse to pass the Appropriation Bill, and thereby force a dissolution or a change of ministry. These are the conditions recognised by the Constitution."

The Australian people could remove the Senate's power over money bills if they wished, but they have not done so.

The principle that Senate denial of Supply requires an election (or the government's resignation) was recognised many times by politicians and constitutional authorities over the decades from 1901 to 1975. Whitlam had himself acknowledged it in 1970 when, as Opposition Leader, he tried to get the Senate to block the Budget and so force the Gorton government to an election. He did so again in 1974 when, as Prime Minister, he immediately advised as election after a Senate vote the government had said it would treat as a denial of Supply. He said in April 1974 that he did not object "to the Senate or an Upper House refusing Supply if it also faces the people at the same time" as the House of Representatives. In March 1975, Whitlam said that "if there is again a refusal of a Supply Bill, there will certainly be an election".

It was only later in 1975 that Whitlam sought to deny this fundamental constitutional principle.

During the 1975 crisis, Whitlam knew that he was risking dismissal. There was media discussion of this possibility. A former Solicitor-General, then an Opposition MP, Robert Ellicott QC, had publicly said that Kerr should dismiss Whitlam immediately if Supply was denied. Kerr had asked Whitlam for the views of the law officers on the Ellicott statement. As Kerr showed in his book *Matters for Judgment*, Whitlam referred more than once during the crisis, in conversation with him, to the possibility of being dismissed. Whitlam has acknowledged that some of his parliamentary statements were made in response to growing "speculation about possible intervention by Sir John Kerr".

Some say, perhaps rightly, that Whitlam did not take the possibility seriously, and rejected warnings (for example, from Bill Hayden) that it was a serious possibility.

Whitlam may have been surprised by being dismissed, but that is a comment on his misjudgment, not any failing on the part of Kerr.

In the lead-up to the denial of Supply, Kerr at least twice suggested to Whitlam that he should respond to such a denial by going to an election. Whitlam rejected the idea. He did so also when others, including Labor ministers such as Senators Ken Wriedt and John Wheeldon, tried to persuade him to call an election.

Whitlam seems not to have understood fully that there were few ways in which the crisis could end. Either he would back down, or the Opposition's united front in the Senate would crack, or a compromise would be reached between government and Opposition, or Kerr would resolve the crisis. Kerr tried unsuccessfully to help bring about a compromise between government and Opposition. As the days of stand-off turned into weeks, and other solutions to the crisis did not happen, the chances became greater and greater that the crisis would have to be resolved through the Governor-General.

By November 11, government money had already begun to run out. On October 21, the Minister for Housing and Construction had told parliament that "within three weeks" – that is, by November 11 – "the Government will not be able to meet its commitments in respect of certain works and construction". Other ministers said that funds would run out by mid-November for salaries for Northern Territory school teachers, tertiary students, Aboriginal children, and reconstruction from the Darwin cyclone. Newspapers reported on November 11 that "the Federal Government has run out of money to pay subsidies for aged people's homes and for facilities for the handicapped".

In their conversations at Yarralumla that day, Whitlam had the opportunity to go to an election as Prime Minister. Kerr warned him that, since he proposed to govern without parliamentary Supply, it would be necessary to dismiss him. If Whitlam had been willing to advise an election, this was the moment to say so: but he did not. He threw away the chance.

Later that afternoon, after he was dismissed, Whitlam was asked in a press conference if he was "suggesting the Governor-General may have misled you". He replied, "No, I'm not saying that." The idea that Kerr "misled" Whitlam, for which there is no foundation, only arose subsequently, when it was necessary for Whitlam to find a scapegoat for his electoral defeat.

Much has been written, to no clear conclusion, on whether some Opposition senators would have "cracked" and voted to grant Supply had Kerr not resolved the crisis when he did. It is impossible to know now, and it was impossible to know when Kerr had to decide what to do in 1975, whether (and if so, when) this would happen. In deciding how to act, Kerr could not gamble on rumours that this might happen. For an Opposition senator to have voted to grant Supply would almost certainly have brought about the end of his or her political career. In fulfilling his duty to maintain constitutional government, Kerr could hardly rely on the highly uncertain chance that this backbench senator or that would commit political harakiri on the floor of the Senate.

Although some journalists seem willing only to report criticisms of Kerr, it is striking how many of the leading constitutional authorities in Australia, Canada, and Britain have endorsed Kerr's approach to the 1975 crisis. To give just two of many possible examples: Sir Victor Windeyer, a former High Court judge, said in 1977 that "the validity in law and constitutional propriety of the Governor-General's action in the circumstances is not seriously questionable". Sir David Derham, the former Vice-Chancellor of Melbourne University, wrote a detailed and powerful article explaining why he believed Kerr's action was constitutionally right and necessary.

The onus is on those who think Kerr was wrong to act as he did to suggest how else the crisis could have been resolved. They must take into account, not least, the implacable quality in Whitlam's personality that made calm discussion with him impossible.

The dismissal of Whitlam resulted in an election. The Australian Constitution embodies the democratic theory which sees a reference to the voters as the means to resolution of major disputes. The Constitution, born of referendums, can only be amended by referendum. The "double dissolution" procedure for dealing with deadlock between the two houses over ordinary legislation is to call elections for both houses.

The writers of the Constitution a century ago took it as axiomatic that a denial of Supply would result in an election or a change in government. Ultimately, that is what happened in 1975: the Constitution was upheld. It was, however, a tragedy, not least for Whitlam himself, that his intransigence meant that this result only came with much pain and causing many wounds. Even now, some of those wounds are yet to heal.

7

DEBATING THE HEADSHIP OF STATE – MONARCHY TO REPUBLIC?

While Australia has been a monarchy since British settlement in 1788, there have been recurrent bursts of republican sentiment. This was most conspicuous in the 1990s, when Paul Keating (Prime Minister, 1991-1996) vigorously advocated a republic, including making detailed proposals in 1995. The promised referendum on moving to a republic was overseen in 1999 by monarchist John Howard (Prime Minister, 1996-2007). That referendum was defeated, and – although frequently arising in public discussion – the push for a republic has not yet regained its pre-referendum momentum.

The first piece below was a speech in 1997 seeking to set out, as impartially as possible, the key issues in the republic debate. The second piece, jointly written with Dr Jon Ritchie in 2006, discusses republicanism in both Australia and other Commonwealth countries.

"An Australian Republic?"
Background address to the Constitutional Centenary Foundation's
National Schools Constitutional Convention, Parliament House, Canberra
1 March 1997

Should Australia become a republic? As my purpose is to set out issues and not to push one view or another, I hope that you will not be able to tell what my view is on whether Australia should become a republic, or indeed on most other key issues.

In discussing these issues, we should bear in mind that for Australia to become a republic requires approval of changes to the Constitution by a referendum. This requires support of the proposed change from a majority of voters throughout Australia, including a majority in at least four states. In talking about proposals for a republican system, I am only going to discuss ideas which have been part of the "mainstream" debate and seem to me to have some chance of support at a referendum. Because it is the term most commonly used abroad and in Australian debate, I will use the word "president" to indicate the head of state in a republican system, though Australia could certainly become a republic with a head of state called something else – even, as some have suggested, keeping the title "Governor-General".

The key issues are:

1. Should Australia change from being a constitutional monarchy to being a republic?
2. If so, what form should that republic take? For example: what would be the powers of the president? How would the president be chosen, and how removed?
3. Does our view on whether to become a republic depend on the proposed form of the republic?

All of these are questions to which I will return. But before considering change, we should understand the system we have at present.

What is the present system?

Australia is a constitutional monarchy. That is, we have a monarchy which operates according to constitutional rules and limitations which are either set out in the text of the Constitution or are embodied in unwritten but binding rules called "conventions" based on past practice and constitutional principles. These rules ensure that, except in rare cases, the powers of the Crown are exercised only on the advice of ministers.

In Australia's monarchy, our head of state is the Queen, who is formally designated Queen of Australia, and whom we share as head of state with the U.K., Canada, New Zealand, Papua New Guinea, and eleven other countries. But almost all her roles with respect to Australia – ceremonial and constitutional – are performed by her representatives in Australia – the Governor-General at the federal level, and Governors in each of the states.

Let us focus on the federal level. Section 61 of the Constitution says that "The executive power of the Commonwealth [of Australia] is vested in the Queen and is exercisable by the Governor-General as the Queen's representative ..." The Governor-General is appointed by the Queen on the nomination of the Prime Minister of Australia. The nomination is that of the Prime Minister alone, though by convention there is prior discussion with the

Queen as to who will be nominated. The Governor-General usually serves for around five years, and can be dismissed as Governor-General by the Queen again acting on the advice of the Prime Minister – though advice for dismissal of a Governor-General of Australia has never been given.

Until the 1960s, most Governors-General were British, but since the 1960s, every one has been Australian. It is now impossible to imagine a non-Australian appointed as Governor-General. Some, such as Lord Casey, Sir Paul Hasluck, and Bill Hayden, have been drawn from Australian political life, and some, such as Sir John Kerr, Sir Zelman Cowen, Sir Ninian Stephen, and Sir William Deane, have been Australians eminent in the law. Although there is no requirement that a Governor-General has a background in either field, it has been thought that political or legal knowledge greatly assists the Governor-General in the performance of the office. Sir Zelman Cowen also had a distinguished career in university education.

The Governor-General exercises his constitutional functions without consulting the Queen, though he will report to the Queen on key events. The Governor-General exercises almost all his powers on the advice of ministers in a government which is formed because it commands the confidence of, or has a majority in, the House of Representatives. In normal circumstances, the Governor-General appoints as Prime Minister the person who leads the majority party or coalition in the House. The Governor-General appoints and removes individual ministers on the advice of that Prime Minister, and performs a host of other executive functions on ministerial advice. The Governor-General is free to question that advice, though he must do so with care, and this questioning and other discussions between ministers and the Governor-General can be of great value. But on almost all matters the Governor-General must, sooner or later, act on the advice ministers give him. It is they after all who face the parliament and the people to take responsibility for what happens.

There are certain very limited matters on which the Governor-General has an independent discretion – on which he has to make up his or her own mind – and can act without or against ministerial advice. These are so-called "reserve powers" – powers held in reserve for extraordinary circumstances. For example:

- Where a Prime Minister no longer has the confidence of the House of Representatives, and there is an alternative leader who now does have majority support, the Governor-General could refuse a request from the incumbent Prime Minister for an election and instead appoint as Prime Minister the person who does have the confidence of the House.

- In a parliament where no party has a majority, or immediately after the death of a Prime Minister, the Governor-General must decide whom to appoint as Prime Minister.

- In very rare cases, the Governor-General may dismiss the Prime Minister if he believes this is constitutionally necessary, and appoint someone else as Prime Minister, probably – as in 1975 – on a caretaker basis until there is a federal election.

Reference to 1975 reminds us that there is much debate about the reserve powers, including about the conventions governing their use, and their use may arouse fierce controversy.

What do we mean by talking of changing to a republic?

A republic, as discussed in Australia, would replace the Queen and Governor-General with a single person performing all the ceremonial, symbolic, and constitutional functions of the head of state, and probably called a "president". Whereas the Queen is Queen as a result of heredity – because her father was King, and his brother and father before him – there would be no hereditary element in a republic. The process of appointment of the president would also be a purely Australian one. Beyond saying this, a republic could take one of many forms, and I will return to those options after a brief discussion of whether Australia should become a republic. It may be useful to set out briefly two opposed views.

Supporters of retaining the constitutional monarchy say that it is a system that works well, and since it works well, we should leave it as it is. "If it isn't broken, don't fix it." The monarchy, they argue, provides us with a headship of state which is above party politics. It is a system which arises from our history and heritage; a system which has adapted over time – been Australianised – to suit Australia's changing aspirations, making the Queen truly Queen of Australia, or alternatively making the Governor-General in reality our head of state. Constitutional monarchists argue that we can rely more confidently on this system to serve us well into the future than we could rely on a republican system, as the move to a republic would risk undoing the carefully worked out balance in our present system, and might create either an over-powerful presidency, or on the other hand, a rubber stamp not serving the safeguard role the Governor-General does at present. It is argued that there are strong ties of attachment within Australia to the monarchy, and that the proposed move to a republic needlessly divides the community, including threatening to divide pro-monarchy states from republican states. Some monarchists argue that Australia is already a de facto republic – a fully democratic political system – adorned with the valuable and historic symbols of monarchy which it would serve no useful purpose to remove. Constitutional monarchists argue that Australia is fully independent, and has been for half a century or more, and the move to a republic would not enhance our independence one bit, while it would nonetheless needlessly damage our historic and important ties with Britain.

Supporters of a change to a republic argue, by contrast, that Australia should have a head of state who truly symbolises and stands for Australia; that the Queen, as an English person, cannot now do this, especially for an Australia which is ethnically and culturally diverse and which is keen to be seen internationally as distinctively Australian and fully part of the Asia-Pacific region; that the Governor-General's capacity to stand for Australia within Australia or abroad is seriously impaired because he is the stand-in for an absentee; in other words, that Australia should have a head of state who is "one of us". Australia should have a head of state who is not first and foremost the head of state of another country, Britain, as the Queen is. Republicans say that it is an insult to our intelligence to believe that this generation of Australians, the successors of those who devised a new Constitution a century ago, is unable to design the modest changes needed for a republican Constitution that can be relied on to work as well as the present one. Perhaps, they say, it would work even better. They also argue that, given the degree of opposition in modern Australia to the monarchy, the only way the headship of state in Australia can again be a truly unifying force is if Australians come, over time, to be united under a home-grown headship of state.

In short, the argument is between those who say that we should not needlessly change a system that works, and those who think we should and safely can adopt a headship of state which more truly reflects Australia's national identity.

If we are to become a republic, what sort of a republic might we have?
We could have a republic in which the president, unlike our Governor-General, has real, substantial, day-to-day executive power – combining in a sense the roles of the present Governor-General and Prime Minister, a system in which the president is both the formal head of state and the powerful head of government. A number of countries – such as the U.S., Russia, and South Africa – have executive presidents of this sort. Alternatively, we could have a parliamentary republic – like Germany, Italy, Ireland, India, Israel, indeed like most republics – in which the separation is kept between the president as formal head of state and a Prime Minister or equivalent, with a majority in parliament, who is the head of government.

Almost all prominent advocates of a republic in Australia oppose our developing a U.S.-style executive presidency, and favour our retaining our parliamentary system, with the president playing the sort of role the Governor-General does now, and the Prime Minister retaining the role he now has. I will assume from here on that we are talking about a parliamentary republic of that kind.

How, then, should the powers of the president be set out in the Constitution? Should they be spelt out more clearly than now, saying more fully than at present which powers are to be exercised only on ministerial advice, but setting out the areas in which the president has "reserve powers"? Should the conventions of the Constitution on the role of the Governor-General be "codified" into clear written rules for the president?

There has for decades been debate amongst constitutional experts as to whether such codification of the reserve powers is desirable. The battle lines are drawn between those who say that codification would bring greater clarity and certainty to the options open to a president in different situations, and those who believe it impossible to write down these powers in a way that covers every contingency, does not create new controversies, and leaves room for the gradual evolution of the conventions. It is also feared that codifying conventions would be an invitation to the High Court to interpret them its own way, and interfere in what should remain the discretion of the president.

In any event, it seems to me likely that it would be very difficult to agree on a codification that would gain strong support across the political spectrum. Most obviously, there is keen disagreement on what circumstances, if any, justify the dismissal of a Prime Minister.

In 1995, Mr Keating suggested in his detailed proposal for a republic that it be stated explicitly that all the constitutional duties of the Governor-General which have by convention been exercised on ministerial advice *must* be exercised only on such advice; but that the "reserve powers" be left as they are, with the conventions governing their exercise not spelt out.

A similar, alternative idea would be to write into the Constitution a provision along the lines that "the powers of the president will be exercised subject to the same conventions as governed the exercise of the powers of the Governor-General prior to Australia's becoming a republic".

How powerful a president is may, in practice, be significantly affected by how the president is appointed. The "Issues Paper" you have sets out three options:

1. Appointment of the president by the Prime Minister – which I think is very unlikely to be accepted by the people of Australia in making the shift to a republic, even though as our present system has evolved the Governor-General is in reality the personal choice of the Prime Minister.
2. Election of the president by a special majority in the parliament.
3. Direct election of the president by the people of Australia

The advocates of election by a special majority in parliament often suggest that for a person to be elected president they must get the votes of, say, two-thirds of both houses of parliament. This could be two-thirds of the houses sitting together, as a joint sitting, or two-thirds of both of them sitting separately. It is argued that to get two-thirds of both houses of parliament will always require that a nominee be acceptable to both major political groupings – both Labor and the Coalition – and that this is the best safeguard there can be that a nominee will be a distinguished Australian who is non-partisan and impartial and who can symbolise Australia "for all of us". It is argued that such figures as Sir Zelman Cowen, or Sir Ninian Stephen, or Sir William Deane would be willing to allow their names to be put to parliament with the support of both or all major parties, but not to engage in a hotly-fought and controversial nation-wide election campaign.

Opinion polls suggest that there is, however, strong public support for direct election of the president by the people. If the president is to stand for the people of the Australia, it is argued, then she or he should be chosen by the people of Australia, and not merely by elite and partisan political leaders.

Against this, it is argued that direct election would mean that the president would be the only person with the democratic legitimacy of direct election by the people. He or she would have a clearer, more direct vote of personal support even than the Prime Minister. Armed with this personal vote, this democratic legitimacy, it is feared, the president would be likely in a crisis, or gradually over time, to assert his or her powers ever more forcefully. In a parliamentary democracy, the people elect a parliament, and a government – led by a Prime Minister – is formed out of the elected parliament. For the people *also* to elect a president would risk a fundamental change in our constitutional system from a parliamentary democracy to one with a powerful, interventionist head of state. It is also argued that direct popular election, unlike selection by parliament, would make it inevitable that a politician is chosen as president, because only nominees of political parties will have the immense resources needed to campaign for votes across the country.

Most republics around the world do not have direct election of the president. The U.S. and Russia do, but they are not *parliamentary* democracies. France does, but it has a system where it is not known from one election to the next whether the more powerful person will be the President or the Prime Minister. Amongst major states, only Ireland combines direct election of the president with retaining a parliamentary system, and it does so by strictly defining and limiting the President's powers to prevent a powerful presidency from emerging. That sort of codification of powers is something which many of us here in Australia put in the "too hard" basket, or oppose on other grounds.

The effective power of the president will also be determined by how he or she can be removed – how much security of tenure the Governor-General has. Mr Keating's 1995 proposal was that the Governor-General be appointed on the single nomination of the Prime Minister by two-thirds of both houses of parliament and be removable only by vote of two-thirds of both houses. This would mean that he or she could only be removed if some factor, such as inappropriate conduct, seemed to both major parties to warrant removal. Some people think this security of tenure would improve on the present situation where the Governor-General is removable by the Queen on the advice of the Prime Minister alone. Such people think that, for example, Sir John Kerr would have been better placed in handling the 1975 crisis if he had been sure that he could not himself be dismissed at Mr Whitlam's say-so. On the other hand, Mr Hayden has worried that if a president can only be removed by two-thirds of both houses of parliament, he or she is in effect irremovable, since one party or the other would want to prevent a change; and so the president would become over time, or in a crisis, an excessively powerful figure.

The "Issues Paper" asks the question: "Should the Commonwealth and the States move to a republic at the same time?" Arguments for and against are given.

We need to remember that, just as the Commonwealth of Australia is a constitutional monarchy, so each of the states is also a monarchy in its own right. So, at least, most constitutional lawyers believe. The Queen is said to be Queen of each state just as much as she is the Queen of the Commonwealth of Australia. It has been argued that it would be deeply divisive, even a threat to federation, to try to force states whose people do not wish to give up the monarchy to do so because there is a republican majority in the rest of Australia. Mr Keating's model was to propose a republic for the Commonwealth of Australia, and to let each state decide for itself whether or not it wished to retain the Queen within the state.

My own guess, for what it is worth, is that if the Commonwealth of Australia became a republic, the Queen would herself regard it as inappropriate to remain Queen of only one or two states within that. I think it is likely that she would abdicate as Queen of those states, just as – for example – she in effect abdicated as Queen of Fiji after the *coup d'état* there a decade ago. It would be reasonable and sensible for people advocating a republic to urge that all states move simultaneously with the Commonwealth of Australia towards a republic – just as, of course, it would be reasonable for monarchists to urge that neither the Commonwealth nor any state make this change.

The great word "Commonwealth" refers both to the Commonwealth of Australia, the proper name of this country, and to a long-standing and valuable association of 53 independent nation states known as the Commonwealth, once the "Commonwealth of Nations", and before that the "British Commonwealth of Nations". Few Australians wish Australia to leave that international Commonwealth. I believe it is right that we should wish to remain in – active in – it, and it would be good if this were reiterated on Monday, which is Commonwealth Day. But becoming a republic is no obstacle to Australia's continuing active – even enhanced – involvement in the Commonwealth. There have been republics in the Commonwealth for nearly fifty years, and although the Queen has the title "Head of the Commonwealth", over two-thirds of Commonwealth countries – such as India, South Africa, and Malaysia – do not have the Queen as their own head of state.

Whether we support Australia's becoming a republic or not will, for some people, depend crucially on what type of republic is proposed. For example, it would be very reasonable to support Australia's becoming a republic if the president were chosen by two-thirds of both houses of parliament, but to oppose becoming a republic if the president were to be directly elected in the manner of the U.S. or French or Russian presidents. That is certainly the private view of some prominent Australian republicans. Some people, I'm sure, take exactly the opposite view.

There are many other options for a republican system which I have not had time to discuss. For example, there might be restrictions on who could be nominated to the headship of state. Mr Keating proposed that no one who had served in a parliament in the previous five years be eligible. This was aimed to ensure a non-partisan, unifying, and impartial president.

While I cannot cover this and other issues now, I hope that this presentation has helped to clarify for you some of the most important questions: Should Australia stay a constitutional monarchy, or become a republic? If a republic, then what form of republic? And finally: does your view on whether we should become a republic depend in any major way on the form the republic would take?

~

"Australian and Commonwealth Republicanism"
by Jonathan Ritchie and Don Markwell
The Round Table: The Commonwealth Journal of International Affairs
October 2006

When republics, beginning with India in 1949, were first admitted to the Commonwealth of Nations, Australia remained strongly attached to the Crown and the King's (later the Queen's) role as Head of the Commonwealth. Indeed, many Australians had seen a shared Crown as axiomatic, and a symbol of Commonwealth unity. Despite bursts of republicanism in Australia during the 19th and 20th centuries it was not until the 1990s that a republic appeared likely. One historic driver of anti-British Australian republicanism has been the Irish heritage of many Australians. As republicanism grew, it was important that Australia could remain in the Commonwealth as a republic. The past decade has seen a stronger sentiment in Australia than in the other "old Dominions" – New Zealand and

Canada – that national independence and identity require the symbol of a home-grown head of state, rather than one seen as British. The growth of republicanism in such countries, and in Britain itself, would be likely to encourage republicanism in Australia. Australia's republican majority has been frustrated by its inability to agree on a model for parliamentary selection or direct election of the president. No Commonwealth country provides a model which Australians find compelling.

The "New Commonwealth" – including republics

Among the many momentous events of 1949 was a vexed decision made by the leaders of the Commonwealth to allow India to remain within the Commonwealth as a republic. This ran counter to the doctrine, prominent in Australia, that the Crown should be indivisible, and that shared allegiance to the Crown was essential to Commonwealth unity. This controversial 1949 decision, enshrined in history as the London Declaration, served as a precedent for constitutional arrangements in the wave of decolonisation that was gathering momentum in the British Empire. It permitted many former British colonies to adopt republican status and choose their own head of state, while becoming or continuing as "free and equal members of the Commonwealth of Nations, freely cooperating in the pursuit of peace, liberty and progress".[1] The London Declaration helped ease the transition to independence of many of the former colonies and helped lay the foundations of the contemporary Commonwealth, in the words of the Singapore Declaration of 1971, as a "voluntary association of independent sovereign states, each responsible for its own policies, consulting and cooperating in the common interests of their peoples and in the promotion of international understanding and world peace".[2]

Nearly six decades after the London Declaration the majority of Commonwealth members are republics, with their heads of state being chosen from among their own citizens. Of the rest, some are monarchies in their own right, and 16 have remained as constitutional monarchies with Queen Elizabeth II as head of state. These are predominantly small developing nations, located in the Caribbean or the South Pacific, but also include the three former Dominions of Australia, Canada and New Zealand, as well as the U.K. itself. The question of whether each of these four larger nations should

---

[1] L.F. Crisp, *Ben Chifley: A Biography,* Longman, Melbourne, 1963, pp. 285-6.
[2] Declaration of Commonwealth Principles, issued at Heads of Government Meeting in Singapore, Commonwealth Secretariat, 1971.

similarly become republics has arisen from time to time during their recent histories, and today a debate continues in each country.

Australia has had a prominent republican movement over the past 15 years, culminating in a 1999 referendum on whether to amend the Constitution and make Australia a republic. While the failure of the constitutional amendment proposal at this referendum has helped to relegate the issue to the sidelines for the time being, the question of whether Australia should become a republic has not entirely disappeared. A recent Senate inquiry has made a number of recommendations that, if followed, will see further consultation and the promise of another referendum. Many people in other member states of the Commonwealth, not least those which, like Australia, have remained as constitutional monarchies but with an active republican movement, are observing developments in Australia with interest.

While the London Declaration enabled republics to be members of the Commonwealth, states which transform from constitutional monarchies into republics need to reapply formally for such membership. In practice this has not represented a significant hurdle, providing that the process of becoming a republic has been seen as expressing the popular will. Nevertheless, and particularly in the 1990s, some Australians have been concerned that transformation to a republic might jeopardise Australia's membership of, and relations within, the Commonwealth. This reflects a continuing warmth in Australia, at least in the 1990s, among a significant body of people for the Commonwealth as an association and as a web of familiar, almost familial, international relationships. Allaying concerns that Australia's membership of the Commonwealth might be threatened, the Commonwealth Secretary-General at the time of the republic referendum, Chief Emeka Anyaoku, explained succinctly that "whatever the outcome of the referendum, there is no question of Australia's membership of the Commonwealth being in doubt".[3] The Queen, too, following the referendum, reminded Australians in a speech at the Sydney Opera House on 20 March 2000 that "the future of the monarchy in Australia is an issue for ... the Australian people ... alone to decide by democratic and constitutional means", and reassured Australians that, "whatever the future may bring", her "lasting respect and deep affection for Australia and Australians everywhere will remain as strong as ever". For

[3] Emeka Anyaoku, "Australian Commonwealth membership not in doubt, says Commonwealth Secretary-General", Commonwealth News Release 99/64, 2 November 1999.

some states, among which Australia is prominent, the question of whether to become a republic is closely connected with perceptions of national identity. The basis for the Commonwealth as established by, and since, the London Declaration means it can be assumed that, if a referendum is held making Australia a republic, Australia's membership of the Commonwealth would continue. Australia has been described by Secretary-General Don McKinnon as "a mainstay of our Commonwealth"[4] (a phrase to be used sparingly, so as not to identify and alienate the "non-mainstays"). Should this "mainstay" become a republic, this is likely to have some ramifications for the development of republicanism elsewhere in the Commonwealth, not least in the three other large and economically developed constitutional monarchies, Canada, New Zealand, and the U.K.

Australian republicanism

Australian republicanism has a long pedigree, and has historically been essentially about asserting Australian independence from Britain and a separate Australian identity unencumbered by what is widely seen as a British monarchy. There has been only very limited popular sense of the Crown as one that is shared with many other countries, or that has become a specifically Australian monarchy, despite the Queen for decades being titled "Queen of Australia". The waxing and waning of republicanism has been intertwined with the course of Australia's relationship with Britain, and one historic driver of anti-British Australian republicanism has been the Irish Catholic heritage of a significant minority of Australians.

Prominent in the last part of the 19th century, when it was bound up in concepts of Australian identity, nationalism and xenophobia, Australian republicanism was left to wither for most of the 20th century. With Australian federation in 1901, the ambitions of many Australians concerning their national identity were fulfilled, and the obvious benefits of retaining the imperial defensive shield, as well as economic relationships (especially with Great Britain), favoured the continuation of the imperial link. Successive agreements, such as those made at Imperial Conferences in 1926 and 1930, the 1931 Statute of Westminster, and the 1932 Ottawa trade agreements, led

---

[4] Don McKinnon, *Future directions of the Commonwealth*, Commonwealth Lecture for the Commonwealth Round Table in Australia, Trinity College, University of Melbourne, 22 March 2006.

to a more refined understanding of Australia's separate identity, while it still remained an integral part of the British Commonwealth (as it then was) – like Canada, New Zealand, South Africa, the Irish Free State and Newfoundland – as a Dominion. The 1949 conference of Commonwealth Prime Ministers, which resulted in the London Declaration, saw the Australian Prime Minister, Ben Chifley, playing an important role in what was to determine the constitutional structure of the Commonwealth; this debate did not seriously question the continuing reliance of Commonwealth members on the Crown in some form.[5] From 1949 the conservative leadership of Prime Minister Robert Menzies (1949-1966) saw a continuing strong relationship between Australia and the monarchy, despite great social change, including significant non-British immigration to Australia.

Towards the end of Menzies's Prime Ministership there were signs that the status quo was changing, however, shown not least in Australian willingness to participate with the U.S.A. in conflict in Indochina. During the 1960s the relationship between Australia and the monarchy was again questioned: Donald Horne's *The Lucky Country*[6] and Geoffrey Dutton's symposium on *Australia and the Monarchy*[7] were two influential books that gave prominence to the issue. By the early 1970s, and especially with the election of Gough Whitlam's Labor government in 1972, many Australians were reconsidering their national identity, evident both in politics and in a resurgence of focus on Australianness in film, music, writing, and in other ways.

Although not in itself sufficient to create a powerful republican movement, the dismissal in November 1975 of Whitlam by the Governor-General, Sir John Kerr, to resolve the parliamentary deadlock on Supply, prompted more Australians to question the continuing links with the Crown. The factors that had been emerging in the previous decades – such as increased non-British immigration and greater affluence – were joined by multiculturalism at home and a more multilateral foreign policy, and in the 1980s republican sentiment was increasingly evident. Legislative changes were made, such as the *Australia Acts* of 1986, which removed the role of the British government in the appointment of state Governors and ended the last vestiges of appeals

---

[5] F. Bongiorno, "'British to the bootstraps?': H.V. Evatt, J.B. Chifley and Australian policy on Indian membership of the Commonwealth, 1947-49", *Australian Historical Studies*, 36(125), 2005, pp. 18-39.

[6] Donald Horne, *The Lucky Country: Australia in the Sixties*, Penguin, Melbourne, 1964.

[7] Geoffrey Dutton (ed.), *Australia and the Monarchy: A Symposium*, Sun Books, Melbourne, 1966.

from Australian courts to the Privy Council. A Constitutional Commission was established in 1985, and asked to undertake a comprehensive review of the Constitution, to report by the bicentenary year of 1988. Its Committee on Executive Government was chaired by the Governor-General who succeeded Kerr from 1977 to 1982, Sir Zelman Cowen. Although this committee explored the question of a transition to a republic in some depth, it recommended against proceeding in this direction at that stage, judging that the time for this was not yet right.[8]

By the mid-1980s it was clear that the process of the Australianisation of the Crown had moved a considerable distance.[9] The Queen was by then formally Queen of Australia. Her federal representative in Australia was invariably an Australian who was appointed on the advice of the Australian Prime Minister, and her representatives in the states were appointed on the advice of the relevant state Premier. It was possible in the 1980s to argue that this process of Australianisation of the Crown meant that it was not necessary to a strong sense of independent Australian identity to take the further step of becoming a republic. Indeed, this interpretation has persisted: one (factually inaccurate) argument of some monarchists is that the Governor-General has somehow become Australia's head of state, and that Australia thus already has a home-grown head of state.[10] On the other hand, some argued that the process of Australianisation pointed towards the next, supposedly "inevitable" step of Australia's becoming a republic; the core argument is that the full expression of Australia's national identity requires a head of state who is Australian.

Despite the cautious approach advocated by the Constitutional Commission in 1988, republican sentiment continued to grow in the early 1990s. In 1991 the Australian Republican Movement (A.R.M.) was established, with the aim that "Australia's Head of State would be an Australian citizen chosen by Australians, and that this could be achieved in time for the centenary of Australia's federation on 1 January 2001".[11] Support for a republic – which had averaged around 28% in opinion polls across the years from 1975 to 1988

[8] *Final Report of the Constitutional Commission*, Canberra, 1988. Sir Zelman Cowen, *A Public Life: The Memoirs of Zelman Cowen*, Miegunyah Press, Melbourne, 2006, p. 376.

[9] D.J. Markwell, *The Crown and Australia (The Trevor Reese Memorial Lecture, 1987)*, University of London, 1987 [reprinted as ch. 3 of this book].

[10] Sir David Smith, *Head of State: The Governor-General, the Monarchy, the Republic and the Dismissal*, Macleay Press, Sydney, 2005, p. 230.

[11] Australian Republican Movement, "The history of republicanism in Australia", A.R.M. website, 2001.

– jumped to 36% in mid-1991.[12] Later that year Paul Keating became Prime Minister, the sixth since federation of Irish Catholic background (all bar one of them Labor). Keating was a firm republican, who was seen by some as drawing on the history of anti-British sentiment among Australians of Irish descent in his support for republicanism (although he has said that his support for a republic was not linked to his Irish heritage[13]). It has been said that, although not one of his cabinet ministers was a monarchist, he was the only avowed republican.[14] Keating's approach, the high profile of the A.R.M., and the salacious revelations appearing at the time in the media about members of the Royal Family, stimulated further support for a republic among Australians: by April 1993 this had reached 52%.[15] A Republic Advisory Committee was appointed, and asked to produce options for making the transition to a republic with the least constitutional change. It concluded that "the only constitutional change ... required to make Australia a completely republican system of government is to remove the monarch", and put forward proposals to achieve this.[16]

In parliament on 7 June 1995 Keating connected the push for a republic in the 1990s with that of a century earlier, reiterating his belief that "our Head of State should be one of us", and proposing parliamentary selection of a president.[17] The following day, John Howard, the leader of the Liberal and National Party Coalition, then in opposition, pledged that, should the Coalition win the next election, a constitutional convention to consider the question of whether Australia should become a republic, and what form this should take, would be convened. In 1996 the Coalition took office, and the promised convention assembled in February 1998.

Following 10 days of sometimes bitter debate the convention adopted the motion "that this Convention supports, in principle, Australia becoming a republic". It also adopted a further resolution on the method of choosing the president that involved the nomination by the Prime Minister and Opposition Leader of a candidate and required a two-thirds majority of the

[12] Roy Morgan Research, "Support for a republic stable – however Australians divided on three constitutional convention options", 17 February 1998 (Finding No. 3054).
[13] Address by the Prime Minister of Australia Paul J. Keating to the Parliament of Ireland, 20 September 1993, Houses of the Oireachtas/Parliament of Ireland.
[14] M. Kirby, "The Australian referendum on a republic – ten lessons", *Australian Journal of Politics and History*, 46(4), 2000.
[15] Roy Morgan Research, 1998, op. cit.
[16] Republic Advisory Committee, *An Australian Republic: The options*, AGPS, Canberra, 1993, vol. 1, p. 1.
[17] *House of Representatives Debates*, 7 June 1995, p. 1434.

Australian parliament, sitting in joint session.[18] This model was put to the people in a referendum in November 1999 amid vigorous debate. Both during the convention and the referendum campaign an important factor was the disappointment of many Australians that the president was not to be directly elected by the people. There was concern expressed that the model agreed by the convention was a hasty compromise by a group of "elites".[19] Despite a clear majority of Australians being supporters of a republic, many republicans joined with those advocating the "No" case, rather than opting for a republic that they considered less than satisfactory. Such disagreement among republican supporters led to the defeat in the referendum both of the republic proposal (with 45% of the vote), and of the proposal to insert into the Constitution a preamble about Australian identity (with 39% of the vote).[20]

The defeat of the republic proposal was a major blow to the republican movement in Australia. Although support for a republic has continued to be strong, with 51% of Australians in a 2005 opinion poll still in favour,[21] it has been difficult for the pro-republican forces to retain the momentum gained before the referendum. The "minimalist" model that was offered in the referendum failed to galvanise the Australian electorate, and attempts within the republican movement to overcome this have not resulted in a clearly articulated statement of a single preferred model for a republic likely to attract broad support across varying strands of republican sentiment. Shortly after the referendum Prime Minister Howard played down any possibility of the issue arising again "in a hurry";[22] subsequent events have proved his prediction to be correct, although following a convention in the country town of Corowa in December 2001 and a Senate inquiry in 2004 there has been some further attention to the issue.[23]

A notable public convert to republicanism in the mid-1990s had been Sir Zelman Cowen, the Governor-General who had brought a "touch of healing" after the 1975 dismissal. In June 2006, media attention was given

---

[18] Constitutional Convention, Transcript of Proceedings, 13 February 1998, pp. 946, 982.
[19] Kirby, 2000, op. cit. H. Irving, "Commentary", *Australian Journal of Political Science*, 35(1), 2000. M. Lavarch, "The way forward", speech from Australian Republican Movement website, February 2000.
[20] Australian Electoral Commission, *Referendum 1999 Report and Statistics*, 1999.
[21] Roy Morgan Research, "51% now want Australia to be a republic, but 61% would want a republic if Prince Charles were king", 22 February 2005 (Finding No. 3835).
[22] "Howard plays down fallout from republic referendum", transcript of interview on ABC TV *7.30 Report*, 8 November 1999.
[23] Australian Republican Movement, 2001, op. cit. Senate, *The Road to a Republic*, AGPS, Canberra, 2004, pp. 1, 4.

to the statement in his memoirs that, whereas he had previously supported a republic only if the selection of the president was by special majority of parliament, he was now willing to support a directly elected presidency if this was the only means to secure a republic.[24] Soon afterwards Peter Costello, the conservative but republican Treasurer and potential Prime Minister, again publicly asserted the ultimate inevitability of a republic.[25] Having learned the lessons from the failure in 1999, he and other republicans acknowledge that success, should it arrive, will not be in keeping with an artificial deadline such as the 2001 centenary of federation.

Republicanism in the Commonwealth

Of the 31 republics currently in the Commonwealth, only 12 were so constituted on gaining their independence or joining the Commonwealth.[26] This means that 19 current Commonwealth member states have followed the precedent established by India in 1949, and become republics following a period with the monarch as head of state. With few exceptions, this has been accomplished without disturbing relations of the country within the Commonwealth; the process by which a country in this situation was required to reapply for membership has been regarded generally as a formality only. Only when other, and particularly egregious, factors have been in existence has the Commonwealth taken action against the continued membership of states becoming republics. This was the case, for example, of South Africa in 1961, when Prime Minister Verwoerd withdrew the application to rejoin the Commonwealth rather than risk rejection as a result of the racist policy of apartheid and heavy-handed response to internal dissent.[27] Other members have left the Commonwealth from time to time, including Fiji in 1987 when its membership was allowed to lapse after its conversion to a republic following two *coups d'etat*.[28] Generally, however, a decision by a member state to adopt a republican form of government is not considered to constitute, of itself, reason for the country to leave the Commonwealth.

[24] Michael Kirby, "Launch of *A Public Life: The Memoirs of Zelman Cowen*", book launch, Melbourne, 7 June 2006.

[25] "Australia a republic by 2016: Costello", *The Age*, 27 June 2006.

[26] "Members", Commonwealth Secretariat website, 2006.

[27] J. Hamill, "South Africa and the Commonwealth. Part one: the years of acrimony", *Contemporary Review*, 267(1554), 1995, p. 13.

[28] "Country profiles – Fiji Islands", Commonwealth Secretariat website, 2006.

In the Commonwealth member states that are not republics the extent of republicanism varies. In the Caribbean both Barbados and Jamaica have shown indications of moving to a republic, and there is some interest in this in Antigua and Barbuda, and Grenada.[29] In the Pacific a referendum on a republic has been promised in Tuvalu but so far has not taken place.[30] In other small nations in both locations, however, support for the continuation of the constitutional monarchy remains strong.

Following Australia, the strongest interest in republicanism is evident in New Zealand, where there is an active republican movement. As in Australia, this movement has a lengthy history but has gained momentum in recent decades, linked not least to observation of events in Australia. New Zealand Prime Ministers from both the major political parties have expressed support for a republic: Jim Bolger of the National Party in 1994, and the current Prime Minister, Labour's Helen Clark, who in November 2004 established a parliamentary select committee to review aspects of New Zealand's constitution. The committee's inquiry was regarded by many at the time as a way of considering becoming a republic.[31] Its 2005 report made three recommendations on the discussion of constitutional change and the improvement in public understanding of these issues. Several submissions to the inquiry took up the matter of a republic, and arguments for and against have echoed, to a degree, developments in Australia. On the other hand, popular support for a republic, as measured in opinion polls (albeit of varying reliability) has remained relatively low. In one poll in July 2005 it was reported that only 27% of New Zealanders considered the country should become a republic,[32] while a more recent poll, in January 2006, showed public support for a republic at 35%, with 46% against changing from the current constitutional monarchy.[33]

In Canada support for a republic has also been significantly less than in Australia. To a large extent this has been thanks to the close proximity of the U.S.A., with its long history of republican government, and the need of

---

[29] E. MacAskill, "Republicanism grows in the old empire: sun setting on Queen's role as head of state", *The Guardian*, 7 December 2000. N. Thomas, "Barbados to vote on move to republic", *Caribbean Net News*, 7 February 2005.

[30] "Tuvalu begins process towards a referendum on whether to become republic", *Tuvalu News*, 9 August 2002. [A referendum in 2008 was defeated.]

[31] J. Rowan, "Goodbye Queen, we're keeping all the power", *New Zealand Herald*, 18 November 2004.

[32] S. Scanlon, "Support slim for republic", *The Press*, 18 July 2005.

[33] "Kiwis say it's King Charles the worst", *Sunday Star Times*, 1 January 2006.

Canadians to differentiate themselves from their North American neighbours. In Canada the issue of republicanism has been kept to the margins of political discourse for most of the recent past. Most Canadians pay little attention to the possibility of a republic.[34]

As with Australia and New Zealand, Canada's history has been as a "Dominion" within the Commonwealth and its relationship with the U.K. has evolved in a way that has meant greater and greater independence of its legislatures and courts. *The Canada Act*, passed by the British parliament in 1982, ended any legislative relationship between the U.K. and Canada, but it also established that changes to the Canadian Constitution require the approval of all 10 Canadian provinces, and this has made any transformation to a republic extremely difficult. Events in Australia during the 1990s as the republican movement developed were noted, and there was a diminution of support for the monarchy as the decade unfolded. An opinion poll taken in 1997, when support in Australia for a republic was growing, suggested that 41% of Canadians were in favour of abolishing the monarchy on the death of the current Queen, although nearly as many (39%) were indifferent to the matter. Only 18% of those surveyed still believed that the link with the monarchy should remain.[35] This level of anti-monarchical feeling has continued to grow, to the extent that 55% of Canadians in 2005 favoured a separation from the monarchy at the end of the Queen's reign.[36] In 2002 a group similar to the Australian Republican Movement, Citizens for a Canadian Republic, was formed, aiming to "promote discussion and help raise awareness of the clear advantages of amending The Constitution to allow for a democratically chosen Canadian to serve as head of state".[37] In April 2004 the Canadian House of Commons Standing Committee on Government Operations and Estimates recommended an inquiry that would take into account "the mandate, constitutional role, responsibilities, and future evolution of the Office of the Governor-General of Canada (the

---

[34] D.E. Smith, *The Republican Option in Canada, Past and Present*, University of Toronto Press, Toronto, 1999.

[35] J. Aubry, "Support for monarchy plummets: 80 per cent don't care about royals, Citizen-Global poll shows", *The Ottawa Citizen*, 17 December 1997.

[36] "In the end, most (55%) hope for a national divorce from British monarchy when Queen Elizabeth's reign ends – up 7 points from October 2002 (48%)", IPSOS News Center, 9 April 2005.

[37] "Our goals", Citizens for a Canadian Republic website, 2006.

Head of State)".[38] Hopes among Canadian republicans for such a review were dashed when the government chose to focus on the budgetary aspects of the Governor-General instead of looking more broadly at the evolution of the office.[39]

While the appeal of republicanism to Canadians reflects a degree of indifference to the monarchy, and indeed some concern about some members of the Royal Family, there is a substantial admiration in Canada (as elsewhere) for the Queen herself[40] and at the same time a widespread lack of recognition of the Governor-General. There has been no factor in Canada comparable to the 1975 dismissal in Australia, which brought the role of the Governor-General into greater public attention, and controversy, than ever before. A stronger factor in the way of any potential move towards a Canadian republic is that the relationship with the monarchy has helped, rather than hindered, Canadians to define their own identity in the face of the U.S.A.: "it is a symbol of Canadian sovereignty, and evidence of a tradition that marks Canadians off as North Americans with a difference".[41] Some in Canada have noted the confusion and disputation which have surrounded the hitherto unsuccessful moves towards a republic in Australia, and the absence of a republican model able to command general consensus there, and have wished to avoid that fate for Canada, with its own complex issues of national unity.

As in other parts of the Commonwealth, turmoil within the Royal Family itself has led some Britons to question the continuation of the monarchy in the U.K. – the latest in the very occasional waves of British republican sentiment. In opinion polls in high-circulation newspapers such as *The News of the World* and *The Daily Mirror*, significant numbers of those surveyed favoured either the election of a head of state once the Queen dies, or at least the passing of the Crown to her grandson, Prince William, bypassing the Prince of Wales.[42] Other newspapers, including *The Guardian* and *The Independent*, have actively questioned the continuing relevance of the monarchy to contemporary British

---

[38] House of Commons, Canada, Standing Committee on Government Operations and Estimates, *Second Report, the Governor-General of Canada: Role, Duties, and Funding for Activities*, Ottawa, 2004.

[39] Citizens for a Canadian Republic, 2006, op. cit.

[40] D. Watts, "Hail the nurturers of our dominion", *Edmonton Journal*, 20 May 2006.

[41] J.A. Evans, "The Canadian monarchy", *Contemporary Review*, 281(1641), 2002.

[42] ICM Research, "Royal Poll" (published in *The Daily Mirror*), August 1998. "Young People and the Monarchy" (published in *The News of the* World), October 2003.

life,[43] and there is an apparently growing body of opinion in favour of a move to a republic. A wide range of anti-monarchist groups has been established but, despite disenchantment with members of the Royal Family among the British public, it is unlikely that there will be republican support in the U.K. comparable to that in Australia, at least during the Queen's reign. The present authors doubt if the accession of Prince Charles to the throne will prove as problematic as many people have speculated.

An interesting development is the linkage, under the umbrella of "Common Cause", of the principal republican movements in the U.K., Canada, New Zealand, and Australia. This alliance brings a Commonwealth perspective to the question of republicanism, and is intended to provide a framework through which republicans in the four states can share ideas and resources, acknowledging their common heritage.[44]

Australian republicanism and the republicanisation of the Commonwealth?

As well as widespread indifference and some hostility, the Commonwealth continues to exert some attachment – from mild to strong – among many people in Australia: this, as well as keen sporting competitiveness, was reflected in the great interest in Australia in the 2006 Melbourne Commonwealth Games. It is widely considered important that membership of this association not be jeopardised, and a part of the ambivalence surrounding Australia's move to a republic in the past has been the concern that this might prejudice the continuing good relations enjoyed by Australia with other Commonwealth member states. Indeed, one argument was that sharing a Crown with several other countries was a modest but desirable form of internationalism – an element of international cooperation and harmony in a divided world. Given the strong support shown by both the Queen and other Commonwealth leaders for Australia to make its own mind up about its constitutional arrangements, rupture of Commonwealth relations is unlikely to take place should Australia become a republic. However, it is probable that this would provide some encouragement to republican movements in other parts of the

---

[43] R. Hattersley, "Why the Queen drags us all down: the monarch's personal conduct is a good advert for republicanism", *The Guardian*, 11 November 2002. "Time for a republic", *The Independent*, 18 February 1996.

[44] Australian Republican Movement, "Common Cause: an alliance of Commonwealth republican movements", A.R.M. website, 2006.

Commonwealth, not least in New Zealand, Canada, and even potentially in the U.K. Australian republicans, for whatever reason, have not identified a model for an Australian republic in any other Commonwealth country. Indeed, undemocratic presidential systems in Commonwealth, as in other, countries have been used by opponents of an Australian republic as examples of the risks of a republic. But a successfully established Australian republic may provide a kind of model for other "old Commonwealth" countries.

Would the development of an Australian republic, and indeed of republics in such other "mainstays" of the Commonwealth, endanger the relevance and vitality of the organisation as an association? For several decades in the 20th century it was argued by constitutional conservatives – for example, Sir Robert Menzies – that any dilution of the unity of the Crown, let alone development towards a republic, would fatally weaken the unity of the Commonwealth. Since 1949, however, the Commonwealth has evolved as an association of modest but real and continuing importance in world affairs, as an expression and in some ways upholder of shared values and common heritage, and as an agency of practical cooperation in a wide range of fields, including education. The movement of Australia and other "mainstays" of the Commonwealth towards republican status may test, as may the death of the present Queen, whether the Commonwealth has achieved viability as an association which does not rely on the Crown as the glue that holds it together. The present authors are optimistic that a Commonwealth of republics would remain a Commonwealth of relevance.

8

THE OFFICE OF GOVERNOR-GENERAL (2014)

Paper for conference in memory of Sir Zelman Cowen
Melbourne Law School
March 2014[1]

The office of Governor-General, previously analysed by Sir Paul Hasluck and Sir Zelman Cowen, has evolved as part of the "Australianisation of the Crown" since 1901. It has been consolidated as a de facto headship of state with important constitutional, ceremonial, and community functions, while the Queen remains Australia's de jure head of state. Among desirable attributes of a Governor-General is the ability to "interpret the nation to itself". Doing this, Cowen brought "a touch of healing" after 1975, and Dame Quentin Bryce balanced the traditional and contemporary. Their subsequent returns to universities have been appropriate for former Governors-General. Bryce's actions in 2010 and 2013 reflect the occasional need for the Governor-General to have independent advice, on which the Governor-General retains an important discretion.

March 2014 saw events to farewell and thank Dame Quentin Bryce on her retirement as Governor-General, and the swearing-in of her successor, General (now Sir) Peter Cosgrove. I have no doubt that, while wishing the new Governor-General well, Sir Zelman Cowen would celebrate the great success in office of Dame Quentin Bryce, and think that the office of Governor-General was handed on in good shape.

The title of this short paper, "The Office of Governor-General", was the title given by Sir Paul Hasluck to his Queale Memorial Lecture delivered in Adelaide in October 1972, republished with additional material in 1979 after increased interest in the office arising from the 1975 constitutional crisis and its aftermath.[2] Sir Zelman himself published under the title "The Office of

---

[1] Published as "The Office of Governor-General" (2015) 38(3) *Melbourne University Law Review*.

[2] Sir Paul Hasluck, *The Office of Governor-General*, Melbourne University Press, 1979.

Governor-General" in a symposium on Australia published in 1985 in *Daedalus*, the journal of the American Academy of Arts and Sciences.[3]

Sir Zelman's paper began with much discussion of the then relatively recent circumstances that gave the Governor-Generalship prominence in 1975; so I thought that I might similarly begin with some assessment of developments of recent years relating to the office of Governor-General. I then want briefly to discuss three aspects of the office: first, its existence, and the notion of the headship of state; secondly, occupants of the office; and thirdly, sources of advice to the Governor-General.

In a public lecture on "The Crown and Australia" in London in 1987, presided over by Sir Zelman Cowen, I argued that there had been "a very considerable 'Australianisation' of the Crown".[4] This was reflected in four major developments in the 20th century:[5]

> the abandonment of any imperial role for the Governor-General; the appointment of the Governor-General on the advice of the Australian Prime Minister; the appointment of Australians as Governor-General; and [what I called] the "Australianisation" of the Queen.

The latter point was illustrated by what Prime Minister Gough Whitlam said in moving a vote of thanks to Governor-General Sir Paul Hasluck for opening the Constitutional Convention of 1973. Mr Whitlam said of the Governor-General:[6]

> He holds a great office; he represents the Head of State of our nation. In this century how much that office has grown. The first Governor-General swore fealty to the Queen of the United Kingdom of Great Britain and Ireland. Henceforth the Governor-General will swear fealty to the Queen of Australia and her other Realms and Territories, Head of the Commonwealth. In this office and in those titles is shown the development of our nation.

Much has, of course, happened in the 27 years since that reference to the "Australianisation" of the Crown, including "the evolution of the office of Governor-General to one much more distinctly Australian",[7] with "the Crown ... developing an Australian identity in line with the growth of

---

[3] Sir Zelman Cowen, "The Office of Governor-General", *Daedalus*, (1985) 114(1).

[4] D.J. Markwell, *The Crown and Australia (The Trevor Reese Memorial Lecture, 1987)*, University of London, 1987, p. 10 [reprinted as ch. 3 of this book]. A more recent balanced and judicious account may be found in Peter Boyce, *The Queen's Other Realms: The Crown and Its Legacy in Australia, Canada and New Zealand*, Federation Press, 2008; see especially chs 6, 9.

[5] Markwell, *The Crown and Australia*, op. cit., p. 15.

[6] Ibid., p. 10.

[7] Ibid., p. 4.

Australia as a nation".[8] There has, of course, been the rise and the near triumph, especially in the 1990s, of republicanism, now in some form of abeyance. But I also think that we have seen the consolidation of the office of Governor-General as one that is widely respected and valued in Australian constitutional, ceremonial, and, perhaps especially, community life. One sign of this consolidation is that so much was made in early 2014 of the retirement of Dame Quentin Bryce and of valuing her contribution, and of the appointment of Sir Peter Cosgrove as her successor.

By "consolidation" I do not mean consolidation against republicanism. I mean that I think we have come as a nation more fully to respect and appreciate a distinguished Australian serving in our nation's highest office and playing, as I have said, a valued constitutional, ceremonial, and especially community role. The office has been consolidated as a de facto headship of state which could, I think quite readily, convert to a respected presidency.

This consolidation of the office of Governor-General in the decades since it became generally accepted that – Royalty perhaps excepted – only an Australian would serve as Governor-General, and since the tumult of 1975, has of course seen its own ups and downs: what seem from a distance to have been the "touch of healing" of Sir Zelman Cowen (1977-1982), the further calming and dignified energy of Sir Ninian Stephen (1982-1989), the initially controversial but then largely quiet years of Mr Bill Hayden (1989-1996), the energetic – some say too energetic – focus of Sir William Deane on Indigenous issues and reconciliation and the clever symbolism of the Deane years (1996-2001), the controversy that unfairly engulfed Dr Peter Hollingworth (2001-2003),[9] the stabilisation and energetic if unobtrusive conscientiousness of Major General Michael Jeffery (2003-2008), and the vibrant inclusiveness of Dame Quentin Bryce (2008-2014). Prime Minister Abbott recently said: "No one has added more to the office than the current Governor-General [Dame Quentin Bryce] who has lent enormous grace and style to our national life".[10]

Before discussing aspects of the Governor-Generalship of Dame Quentin Bryce, I ought to issue the disclaimer that it is always possible that my views are influenced by the fact that she was my tutor in administrative law at the University of Queensland in, I think, 1979. She has been remarkably kind

---

[8] Ibid., p. 25.
[9] See, e.g., Boyce, op. cit., pp. 197-201 [and appendix 2 of this book].
[10] Tony Abbott, "Press Conference", 25 March 2014.

in keeping in touch at many points over the subsequent decades. Like Sir Zelman Cowen, she has a great gift for friendship and for mentorship, and for nurturing her students — even decades on.[11]

Dame Quentin Bryce left office to very widespread acclaim for having, in the words of the Prime Minister [Tony Abbott], "discharged her duties as Governor-General with distinction and grace".[12] Others have commented on her ability to combine both empathy and dignity, and on her effective inclusiveness. The tributes to her from so many groups and individuals throughout Australia show how effectively she has acted as encourager and affirmer of countless activities around the country, including those in her particular interests of women and children, and human rights.

Dame Quentin Bryce has sought, in her own words in the Boyer Lectures in late 2013 (reiterated in her farewell speech at Parliament House in March 2014), "to strike a balance between observing traditions and protocol and being thoroughly contemporary".[13] Those Boyer Lectures also, of course, reflect progressive instincts and advocacy on her part which some more conservative Australians do not welcome. This was, of course, especially true of the closing words of the Lectures in which she imagined a future Australian nation "[w]here people are free to love and marry whom they choose. And where, perhaps, my friends, one day, one young boy or girl may grow up to be our nation's first head of state".[14]

While the apparent endorsement by the incumbent Governor-General of gay marriage and of a republic seemed to some as entering too far into controversy, and indeed of disowning the office in which she was serving, others warmly welcomed these and other statements. They may reflect in our time what Sir Paul Hasluck in his Queale Memorial Lecture had in mind when he said: "I have received encouraging indications ... that Australians both expect and appreciate statements by a Governor-General on matters of current concern at a level different from that of party political controversy".[15]

My understanding is that Governor-General Bryce sent the text of her Boyer Lectures to Prime Minister Tony Abbott well in advance of delivery,

---

[11] See Donald Markwell, *'Instincts to lead": on leadership, peace, and education*, Connor Court, 2013, pp. 102-6.

[12] Tony Abbott, "Appointment of the Governor-General", Media Release, 28 January 2014.

[13] Dame Quentin Bryce, *Boyer Lectures 2013: Back to Grassroots*, HarperCollins, 2013, p. 74.

[14] Ibid., p. 87.

[15] Hasluck, op. cit., p. 23.

and that he expressed no unhappiness with her proposed words. He spoke well of her when she was attacked for these particular remarks. I return later to the notion of the "headship of state", on which Dame Quentin's formulation ("our nation's first head of state") is somewhat surprising.

There is no doubt in my mind that Dame Quentin Bryce has been extremely successful in her speech-making, honouring and delighting audiences around the country and overseas with carefully prepared speeches which reflect both human empathy and considered thought. I cannot imagine that, in her focus on her speech-making, Dame Quentin was uninfluenced by the example, which she knew well, of Sir Zelman Cowen. He, of course, gave such care to his speeches that three volumes of his speeches from his years as Governor-General were published under the title *A Touch of Healing*.[16] As I mentioned at Sir Zelman's funeral, Dame Quentin Bryce knew of his genius as a speaker from at least when in the 1970s she invited him, at little notice, to give a lecture to one of her lecture groups in the law school at the University of Queensland, and he gave what she described as the best lecture she ever heard anyone give.[17] In her speech-making, I think that Dame Quentin Bryce has undertaken the role of the Governor-General described in words variously attributed to Sir Zelman and to Sir Ninian Stephen as "interpreting the nation to itself".[18] Her speech-making, travelling around Australia embracing community groups and diverse individuals, and welcoming so many to Yarralumla and Admiralty House, have helped her fulfil this role. I especially note her acceptance of the Patronage of the New Colombo Plan after it was clear that it had bipartisan support (a Patronage enthusiastically continued by her successor, Sir Peter Cosgrove).[19]

A number of other episodes from Dame Quentin's tenure as Governor-General merit mention. She was criticised for travelling to several African countries as Governor-General by critics concerned that she may have sought to encourage support for Australia's bid for a seat on the United

[16] See W.G. Walker (ed.), *A Touch of Healing: Speeches by Sir Zelman Cowen 1977-1982 – Society*, University of Queensland Press, 1986, vol. I. M.D. Kirby (ed.), *A Touch of Healing: Speeches by Sir Zelman Cowen 1977-1982 – Law and Society*, University of Queensland Press, 1986, vol. II. H.S. Houston (ed.), *A Touch of Healing: Speeches by Sir Zelman Cowen 1977-1982 – Education and Society*, University of Queensland Press, 1986, vol. III.

[17] Markwell, *"Instincts to lead"*, op. cit., p. 88 [and ch. 5 of this book].

[18] See, e.g., ibid., p. 93.

[19] For the speeches at New Colombo Plan events by both Governors-General, see Quentin Bryce, "Speech on the Occasion of the Launch of the New Colombo Plan", Parliament House, Canberra, 10 December 2013; Sir Peter Cosgrove, "Speech on the Occasion of the New Colombo Plan Scholarship Presentation Dinner", Canberra, 25 June 2014.

Nations Security Council.[20] Whatever criticisms may be made of that bid, it seems to me they should be directed at the government of the day, not at the Governor-General. Sir Paul Hasluck in his Queale Memorial Lecture spoke of what were then still early precedents of a Governor-General representing the country overseas — in Sir Paul's case, at the 2500th anniversary celebrations of Iran's imperial dynasties (less than eight years before the overthrow of the Shah, of course). Over subsequent decades, the ability of a Governor-General usefully to represent Australia overseas has, I think, become well-established.

In late 2013, the unusual circumstance arose that a son-in-law of the Governor-General became Leader of the Opposition. It is obviously not sustainable for long to have such a situation. My view is that the Governor-General acted wisely in offering to resign, and that Prime Minister Abbott acted wisely in declining that offer, given that the Governor-General had agreed to the extension of her term to see the country through an election, that she would serve only for a few further months, and that no matter calling for exercise of a vice-regal discretion was likely to arise in that time.

A brief note on the extension of Dame Quentin Bryce's term: there is strictly speaking no term of office for the Governor-General, who serves at Her Majesty's pleasure. But the practice has been to regard the appointment as being for approximately five years, and Dame Quentin Bryce's term was extended by a little over six months beyond that, so that her term — which commenced in September 2008 — did not end around the date of the September 2013 election. I believe that she agreed to serve longer than five years to see the nation through a period of political instability and intensity.

Earlier in her Governor-Generalship, of course, there was a real risk that the Governor-General might have to exercise her individual discretion or reserve powers. When the 2010 election failed to produce a majority government, had it not become clear through the statements of Independent and Green members of parliament which leader could command the confidence of the house, the Governor-General might have been faced with difficult choices: though my own view is that she would in that case have been right to allow the incumbent Prime Minister to test on the floor of the

---

[20] Troy Bramston, "Abbott Stands to Gain as Cosgrove Steps Up", *The Australian*, 25 March 2014, p. 10. [See also Paul Kelly, *Triumph and Demise*, Melbourne University Press, 2014, pp. 210-14.]

House whether she could command its confidence. I will return to the 2010 post-election episode.

As the leadership question resurfaced within the government from time to time during the years 2010-2013, it was also evident that the Governor-General might conceivably be faced with a need to exercise an independent discretion. This might have arisen had, for example, the incumbent Prime Minister, facing loss of the leadership of her own party, sought the dissolution of the House of Representatives to pre-empt a leadership challenge to herself. This did not happen; but, as will be discussed further later, when Mr Rudd replaced Ms Gillard as Leader of the Labor Party in June 2013, with the Labor government in a minority and dependent on Independent and Green members of parliament in the House of Representatives, the Governor-General did have the question of whether to commission Mr Rudd as Prime Minister and, if so, on what conditions if any. These circumstances show that on appointment and dismissal of Prime Ministers, and regarding dissolution of the House of Representatives and (I should add) regarding a double dissolution, the Governor-General retains an individual discretion or reserve power – infrequently arising, but crucial when it does. I would add that I think it is an element of wise statesmanship for political leaders to act so as to minimise, and if possible wholly to avoid, the need for the exercise of that discretion, because its exercise is almost always liable to be divisive.

At the time of Dame Quentin's retirement as Governor-General, a newspaper columnist pointed to two instances in which, in his view, the office of Governor-General may have been shown inadequate respect by Prime Minister Gillard: Ms Gillard announcing in January 2013 what she intended to be the election date in September 2013 without prior consultation with the person who would in fact need to dissolve the House of Representatives, the Governor-General; and the announcement of the sacking of a minister, Simon Crean, in March 2013 without reference to the Governor-General whose unhappy lot it was formally to undertake that dismissal.[21] I think that both criticisms are justified, but I do not think there is much likelihood that the prescription of the writer – the Prime Minister treating the Governor-General as a sort of mentor-confidant – is likely to be sustained for long, even if there is between Prime Minister Abbott and Governor-General Cosgrove that "tightness of confidence and ready communication" which

---

[21] Bramston, op. cit.

Sir Paul Hasluck said existed between him as Governor-General and his three Prime Ministers (Gorton, McMahon, and Whitlam).[22] Sir Zelman thought that Australian Prime Ministers just were not interested in, for example, the kind of regular conversations that British Prime Ministers have with the Queen.[23]

The re-creation in March 2014 of the titles of Dames and Knights in the Order of Australia, with Dame Quentin Bryce the first new Dame and her successor to be the first new Knight, attracted much comment, both favourable and critical. One aspect worth mentioning is that, for as long as this practice lasts, it is likely to resolve the question of title for a Governor -General. Indeed, in making the announcement, Prime Minister Abbott said that "[b]y virtue of appointment as Governor-General, henceforth the Governor-General will be a Knight or a Dame in the Order of Australia".[24] When Archbishop (as he then was) Peter Hollingworth was announced as Governor-General, Sir Zelman Cowen was not alone in puzzling over what title he would use; neither "Bishop" nor "Mr" seemed right. Sir Zelman regarded the award to Archbishop Hollingworth of a Lambeth doctorate so that he was then styled "Dr Hollingworth" as a fitting solution.[25] This may seem trivial to some, but in Sir Zelman's view, I believe, it affected the respect and warmth with which the new Governor-General was likely to be received, or not received, in diverse parts of the community. Some have expressed the view that it is better for the new Governor-General to be Sir Peter Cosgrove than "Governor-General General Peter Cosgrove".

On her retirement, Dame Quentin Bryce returned to her hometown, Brisbane, where she is basing her office at the Queensland University of Technology, with the intention of taking part in a range of activities there. Especially given her academic background, and her commitment to students, this seems particularly fitting. It raises the issue of what activities it is appropriate for a former Governor-General to undertake.

In 1979 notes additional to his Queale Memorial Lecture, written after controversy about Sir John Kerr's abortive appointment as Australia's Ambassador to the United Nations Educational, Scientific and Cultural

[22] Hasluck, op. cit., p. 32.

[23] Sir Zelman Cowen, *A Public Life: The Memoirs of Zelman Cowen*, Miegunyah Press, Melbourne, 2006, pp. 321-4.

[24] Abbott, 25 March 2014, op.cit. [Damehoods and Knighthoods were discontinued in late 2015 by Prime Minister Turnbull.]

[25] Boyce, op. cit., p. 199.

Organisation, Sir Paul Hasluck wrote:[26]

> As for further appointments after retirement I take a narrow view that
> for an Australian the Governor-Generalship is the apex. There is no
> office higher than it and one should not go below it. ... Furthermore, as
> in the case of a person like a Chief Justice, a Governor-General would
> imperil the reputation for detachment and independence necessary for
> his office if it were to appear that he was under an obligation to anyone
> or was inclined by his own hopes to seek special consideration in the
> future. While I take this strict view about appointment to new offices
> after retirement, it would not seem to me to be either inappropriate or
> improper for a retired Governor-General to accept public engagements
> [he mentioned public lectures as an example] which do not place him
> under an obligation or make him subject to the direction of another
> authority.

Sir Zelman rightly regarded his appointment as Provost of Oriel College,
Oxford, in 1982 as "solving" the post-retirement problem, and on his and
Lady Cowen's return to Australia in 1990, he was again active in Australian
public, academic, and commercial life. Sir Ninian Stephen in his retirement
represented Australia diplomatically and took part in international judicial and
other activities. It seems accepted that a former Governor-General may rightly
have an active retirement, continuing to contribute to Australian life but not
taking a role which they might have sought from the government when in
office.[27] Dame Quentin Bryce's retirement plans seem well-fitted to this −
though I suspect that she will sometimes stir controversy on issues close to her
heart through her advocacy and activism.

The existence of the office of Governor-General, and the "headship of state"

Had this conference been held 15 years ago, we would undoubtedly have been
considering the high possibility that the office of Governor-General would be
replaced by the office of president under the republican model presented to
the referendum of November 1999. This is not the place to detail the ups and
downs of Australian republicanism since 1788, or since 1975, or since Prime
Minister Keating's powerful advocacy of it − in which he convinced, amongst
others, Sir Zelman Cowen that Australia's head of state should be, in Keating's

---

[26] Hasluck, op. cit., pp. 46-7.
[27] Interesting discussions are in Boyce, op. cit., pp. 138-40, 195-6.

words, "one of us".[28] Nor is this the place to discuss why opinion polls suggest that support for a republic is at its lowest level in about 20 years, including how much such current sentiment may be attributable to the popularity of Prince William, the Duchess of Cambridge, and Prince George.

In this long debate, at present largely in abeyance, one proposition has been asserted that Sir Zelman Cowen strongly disputed. This is the proposition that, in the words of the distinguished former Official Secretary to successive Governors-General, Sir David Smith, "[t]he Governor-General is Australia's head of state".[29] I quoted Gough Whitlam earlier as saying that the Governor-General "represents the Head of State of our nation".[30] Sir Paul Hasluck in his Queale Memorial Lecture also treated it as clear that the Queen is our head of state. In describing the role of the Governor-General, he quoted s 61 of the Constitution:[31]

> The executive power of the Commonwealth is vested in the Queen and is exercisable by the Governor-General as the Queen's representative, and extends to the execution and maintenance of this Constitution, and of the laws of the Commonwealth.

Sir Paul spoke of "an Australian Governor-General, representing and acting on behalf of the Australian head of state, the Queen".[32]

In his 1985 *Daedalus* paper on "The Office of Governor-General", Sir Zelman Cowen wrote:[33]

> The Commonwealth constitution recognized the queen as head of state and the governor-general as her representative, charged with the performance of a variety of functions assigned by her. The constitution, however, vested important functions in the governor-general *without* reference to the queen, and these included power to appoint and dismiss ministers, to summon, prorogue, and dissolve Parliament, and to appoint judges.

Sir Zelman referred to the 1975 dismissal, and said: "On November 12, 1975, the Speaker of the House of Representatives, which had been dissolved the

---

[28] Cowen, *A Public Life*, op. cit., p. 378; see pp. 374-81. See also *Commonwealth Parliamentary Debates: House of Representatives*, 7 June 1995, p. 1435.

[29] Sir David Smith, *Head of State: The Governor-General, the Monarchy, the Republic and the Dismissal*, Macleay Press, Sydney, 2005, p. 85.

[30] Above n. 6, and accompanying text. [See also ch. 3 of this book.]

[31] Constitution s 61, quoted in Hasluck, op. cit., p. 11.

[32] Hasluck, op. cit., p. 24. [cf. W.G. Hayden, *Hayden*, 1996, part VII, e.g. p. 519.]

[33] Cowen, *The Office of Governor-General*, op. cit., p. 132 (emphasis in original).

previous day, made an approach to the queen as head of state of Australia".[34] Sir Zelman continued: "While the queen is unquestionably head of state and the governor-general her representative, the power to dismiss ministers is one which, by the constitution, is specifically vested in the governor-general".[35]

I quote Whitlam, Hasluck, and Cowen at length on the point to show that the classical view is that the Queen is Australia's head of state, and the Governor-General her representative. But in the republican debates of the 1990s, it came to be argued that Australia does not need to change to a republic to achieve an Australian head of state because we already have one: the Governor-General. Hence Sir David Smith's statement that "the Governor-General is [our] head of state".[36]

I would argue that, in any strict constitutional meaning of the term "head of state", the Queen is Australia's head of state – so to speak, de jure – but that the Governor-General has come to play such a role in our national life that the Governor-General has become day-to-day our de facto head of state.

The occupants of the office

In considering the desirable attributes of a person to be appointed as Governor-General, it is useful to start with observations of Sir Paul Hasluck in his Queale Memorial Lecture:[37]

> I have spoken on the assumption that Governors-General will be active and I fervently hope that Australia in the future will never have the misfortune to have an inactive one. It will also be plain that an active Governor-General would need to have some knowledge of both the theory and practice of government and the more he [or she] knows of Australian usage and of the Australian constitutional background and the Australian administrative structure the better he [or she] will be able to do his [or her] job. I fervently hope that Australia in the future will always have the good fortune to have Governors-General with some experience of the working of government. To be an eminent citizen is not a full enough qualification for this post. That does not mean that I

[34] Ibid.

[35] Ibid., p. 133.

[36] Smith, op. cit., p. 85. See also Boyce, op. cit., pp. 28-9, 216-7.

[37] Hasluck, op. cit., pp. 21-2. Hasluck's view of the Governor-Generalship has been criticised by some as requiring too active a role: see, e.g., Boyce, op. cit., pp. 127-8. For an interesting recent (if brief) account of the views of the great Canadian constitutionalist (and socialist), Eugene Forsey, see Helen Forsey, *Eugene Forsey: Canada's Maverick Sage*, Dundurn, 2012, pp. 77-81, 316-20.

suggest that every Governor-General has to be a specialist or an expert in public administration. His [or her] role requires qualities that would enable him [or her] to consider wisely advice given to him [or her], rather than to try to tell others what to do. ... He [or she] has to be free of partisanship. He [or she] cannot start promoting particular causes, for his [or her] dominant role is as one who uses his [or her] influence to ensure that there is care and deliberation, a close regard both for the requirements of the law and the conventions of the Constitution and for the continuing interests of the whole nation, and that the government which the Australian people choose should be a stable government acting consistently and responsibly.

In his notes additional to the Queale Memorial Lecture, Hasluck recounted how in 1973, when Prime Minister Whitlam was wondering whom to nominate to succeed him as Governor-General, he had written down some names meant "to be suggestive of various classes of persons who might be considered".[38] Hasluck wrote:[39]

> The categories I discussed were: Ministerial; judiciary; academic; big business and men prominent in public movements; trade unions. In our previous conversations any idea of making an appointment from among the Governors of the States or from military circles had been discarded so those two categories were omitted.

The suggestion has more recently been made that the best Governors-General are former military personnel or former judges. It is possible that the basis of this [unpersuasive] judgment includes a survey of the occupants or former occupants of state Governorships as well as the Governor-Generalship. To consider this judgment would require comparing the Governors-General who are Australians and who have been judges or career military personnel (Isaacs, Kerr, Stephen, Deane, Jeffery, and now Cosgrove) and those who have not (McKell, Casey, Hasluck, Cowen, Hayden, Hollingworth, and Bryce).

Other issues that arise regarding whom to appoint include whether there is advantage in appointing a former state Governor (Michael Jeffery and Dame Quentin Bryce are the only Australians to have been appointed Governor-General after serving as a state Governor, as some of the British Governors-General also were); whether to appoint former politicians (such

---

[38] Hasluck, op. cit., p. 44.
[39] Ibid., pp. 44-5.

as Isaacs, McKell, Casey, Hasluck, and Hayden,[40] and several of the British Governors-General, some of whom returned to active political life in the United Kingdom after serving in Australia); whether it is appropriate or wise to appoint clergy (Archbishop Peter Hollingworth being the only clergyman appointed Governor-General of Australia, with precedents at the state level in Australia such as Pastor Sir Douglas Nicholls in South Australia and Rev Dr Davis McCaughey in Victoria, and Archbishop Sir Paul Reeves in New Zealand); and whether to appoint a member of the Royal Family as Governor-General (the Duke of Gloucester providing the precedent, but the opposition to the appointment of Prince Charles as Governor-General decades later suggesting this is unlikely in future, even with as popular a figure as Prince William).

In addition to the attributes which Sir Paul Hasluck described, it is now likely to be thought desirable to emphasise that a nominee for the Governor-Generalship be someone able to engage the Australian community, and "interpret the nation to itself". Sir Zelman Cowen is a clear exemplar of this; he had for many years been prominent in Australian public life, including through extensive media and public speaking engagements.[41] Hasluck's warning against partisanship (which does not preclude past political service) and the narrow advocacy of particular causes remains apposite. Clearly in the selection of the person to nominate to the Queen, some Prime Ministers will be more concerned than others to use the office to reflect the diversity of modern Australia; Governors-General of Australia appear to have come from less diverse backgrounds than those of Canada and New Zealand.[42] We have heard little in recent times of the notion, once considered traditional and necessary, that in the selection of the Governor-General there be informal conversations between the Prime Minister and the Queen.[43]

---

[40] Three of the five have been Foreign Minister. Interesting evidence of Sir Robert Menzies's sustained opposition to appointing a person direct from active politics is in Heather Henderson (ed.), *Letters to My Daughter: Robert Menzies, Letters, 1955-1975*, Pier 9, 2011, pp. 206-9.

[41] Markwell, "*Instincts to lead*", op. cit., p. 88.

[42] See Boyce, op. cit., p. 197.

[43] For a recent addition to knowledge of Menzies's approach, see Henderson, op. cit., p. 29. A valuable discussion of the appointment process is in Boyce, op. cit., pp. 121-4.

Sources of advice

Since the 1975 dismissal, there has been considerable controversy about the appropriate sources of advice for a Governor-General in the exercise of his or her discretions. During the 1975 constitutional crisis, the Governor-General consulted both the Chief Justice of the High Court, Sir Garfield Barwick, and another High Court judge (later Chief Justice), Sir Anthony Mason.[44] Both encouraged the Governor-General in his decision that, if the Prime Minister did not advise the dissolution of the House of Representatives, he should be dismissed and a caretaker Prime Minister appointed who would advise a dissolution and the holding of an election. The propriety and wisdom of these consultations have been much debated, even fiercely so.

It is interesting to consider attitudes prior to 1975 on the appropriateness of the Governor-General consulting judges. Sir Paul Hasluck wrote that in 1972 he "asked a friend eminent in the law to read the manuscript" of his Queale Memorial Lecture "lest I had made any gross errors".[45] My understanding is that this was Sir Garfield Barwick, then Chief Justice of the High Court. It is likely that Hasluck knew that Barwick had advised the Governor-General, Lord Casey, in December 1967 about whom to appoint as Prime Minister after the disappearance of Prime Minister Holt. Hasluck said that in a situation where the Prime Minister requests a premature dissolution of the House of Representatives:[46]

> [i]t is open to the Governor-General to obtain advice on the constitutional question from other quarters – perhaps from the Chief Justice, the Attorney-General or eminent counsel – and then a solemn responsibility rests on [the Governor-General] to make a judgment on whether a dissolution is needed to serve the purposes of good government by giving to the electorate the duty of resolving a situation which Parliament cannot resolve for itself.

In the recurrent controversy since 1975 over the appropriateness of the Governor-General consulting High Court judges, reference has been made to research showing the very extensive consultation of early High Court judges, specifically Chief Justice Sir Samuel Griffith and Sir Edmund Barton, by

---

[44] The involvement of Sir Anthony Mason was revealed in January 1994 by Sir Garfield Barwick and Mr Gerard Henderson. The publication of Jenny Hocking, *Gough Whitlam: His Time – The Biography*, Miegunyah Press, Melbourne, 2012, vol. II, pp. 304-7, discussing Kerr's consultation of Mason, added less to public knowledge than was claimed by some. [See ch. 6 of this book.]

[45] Hasluck, op. cit., p. 1.

[46] Ibid., p. 15.

successive Governors-General.[47] These instances included occasions in 1904 and 1909 when the Prime Minister had lost the confidence of the House of Representatives and advised the dissolution of the House, and the Governor-General rejected this advice and, on the resignation of the incumbent Prime Minister, appointed a new Prime Minister. It also included, amongst many other cases, the 1914 dissolution of both houses of parliament, and the abortive suggestion that this double dissolution be reversed (and the old parliament restored) on the outbreak of World War I. Research on these and several other cases of advice from judges to Governors-General and Governors was in part inspired by private comments of Sir Zelman Cowen to the current writer.[48]

In 2009, the current Chief Justice of the High Court, Chief Justice Robert French, quoted extensively from this and other research before concluding a discussion on "The Chief Justice and the Governor-General" in these terms:[49]

> it is difficult to conceive of circumstances today in which it would be necessary or appropriate for the Chief Justice to provide legal advice to the Governor-General on any course of action being contemplated by the holder of that office, whether such advice were tendered with the prior consent of the government of the day or otherwise. If, in some constitutional crisis requiring consideration of the possible exercise of reserve powers, the Governor-General felt the need to seek independent legal advice, there are plainly sources other than the Chief Justice to whom he or she could resort. Indeed, it might be that some agreed mechanism could be established against the rare event that it is thought desirable to have access to independent counsel. A small group of independent experts, perhaps even including one or more retired Justices of the High Court, could be established for the purpose.

Chief Justice French quoted a eulogy for Sir Garfield Barwick in 1997 in which Sir Gerard Brennan, then Chief Justice, said of Barwick's tendering of advice to Sir John Kerr: "It was, and remains, a controversial matter but, if only on that account, will not happen again".[50] Chief Justice French said that he agreed with "that sentiment".[51]

---

[47] Don Markwell, "Griffith, Barton and the Early Governor-Generals: Aspects of Australia's Constitutional Development", (1999) 10 *Public Law Review* [reprinted in ch. 4 of this book].

[48] Markwell, "*Instincts to lead*", op. cit., pp. 91-4.

[49] Chief Justice Robert French, "The Chief Justice and the Governor-General", *Melbourne University Law Review*, vol. 33, 2009, p. 656.

[50] Ibid., quoting "The Late Sir Garfield Barwick" (1977) 187 CLR, p. viii.

[51] Chief Justice French, op. cit., p. 656.

Nothing has come of the suggestion, made by Chief Justice French and by others from time to time, that a panel of advisers for the Governor-General be nominated. It should be evident from the frequency with which Governors-General have felt the need for independent advice (very many times in the early decades of federation, from time to time over subsequent decades, and at least twice in the case of Governor-General Bryce, in August 2010 and June 2013, as will be discussed below) that this is not necessarily best characterised as being a "rare" need.

The fact that unexpected circumstances can arise on which the Governor-General reasonably believes that they need independent advice was illustrated in August 2010 when the federal election produced a hung parliament. A Parliamentary Secretary in the incumbent government was the Governor-General's son-in-law, Bill Shorten. On 23 August 2010, two days after the election, the Governor-General wrote to the Solicitor-General, Stephen Gageler SC,[52] in these terms:[53]

> Dear Solicitor-General
>
> Matters have arisen which have given me considerable concern about the exercise of very important obligations of my office under the Constitution.
>
> It has been suggested in some quarters that the fact that my daughter is married to the Honourable Bill Shorten MP creates some sort of conflict of interest that might impugn my ability to carry out the functions of my office.
>
> The issue of integrity and trust in the office is obviously of the utmost importance not only to me but to the Australian people.
>
> I am therefore seeking your urgent advice as to whether these circumstances create any constitutional or other legal impediment to the proper exercise of my functions, particularly in the current circumstances where the outcome of Saturday's election remains to be determined and may involve me as the Governor-General playing some role.
>
> Yours sincerely,
>
> Quentin Bryce.

---

[52] Later appointed a Justice of the High Court of Australia.
[53] Letter from Quentin Bryce to Stephen Gageler, 23 August 2010 <https://www.gg.gov.au/media-release/advice-solicitor-general-governor-general-her-excellency-ms-quentin-bryce-ac>.

On 26 August 2010, the Solicitor-General provided an opinion to the Governor-General saying that "the marriage of her daughter to Mr Shorten gives rise to no constitutional or other legal impediment to the proper discharge of her functions of office".[54] He observed, however, that "connections and relationships" between a Governor-General and members of parliament "fall to be managed as a matter of prudence, not of legal obligation or legal impediment".[55] Mr Gageler pointed out that the functions of the Governor-General could be temporarily vested in an Administrator,[56] or a Deputy whom the Governor-General could appoint.[57]

The next day, the Governor-General's letter and the Solicitor-General's opinion were made public on the Governor-General's website. It is a matter for judgment as to whether the Governor-General asked the right question of the right person, whether she received the most appropriate advice in the circumstances, and whether she acted most prudently in the circumstances in herself handling the commissioning of the Prime Minister in a hung parliament in which her son-in-law was a frontbencher, rather than leaving the matter to an Administrator or a Deputy. In the event, it became clear through the statements of the Independent and Green members of parliament as to which leader could command the confidence of the House, and the Governor-General commissioned that leader, Ms Gillard, as Prime Minister.

In June 2013, Prime Minister Gillard was defeated by her predecessor, Kevin Rudd MP, in a ballot for the leadership of the Australian Labor Party. Ms Gillard, whose minority government depended on the votes in the House of Representatives of a number of Independent and Green members of parliament, advised the Governor-General to commission Mr Rudd as Prime Minister.[58] That evening, 26 June 2013, the Governor-General's Official Secretary wrote to the Acting Solicitor-General, Robert Orr QC, in these

---

[54] Stephen Gageler, "In the Matter of the Governor-General", Opinion, SG No 33 of 2010, 26 August 2010, p. 4 [7] <https://www.gg.gov.au/sites/default/files/files/media/2010/SG_Letter_26_8_2010.pdf>.

[55] Ibid., p. 4 [5].

[56] Typically the most senior state Governor.

[57] Gageler, op. cit., p. 3 [4].

[58] [Ms Gillard's letter to the Governor-General "recommend[ed]" that she appoint Mr Rudd. Any such recommendation or advice from a resigning Prime Minister as to her successor cannot be binding. See chs. 2 & 3 of this book.]

terms:[59]

> Dear Mr Orr
>
> This is to confirm the meeting that took place at Government House this evening, at the Governor-General's request, in which she sought your advice as to the course of action she should take in responding to the Prime Minister's letter recommending that the Governor-General commission the Honourable Kevin Rudd MP as Prime Minister.
>
> I would be grateful if you would confirm in writing your oral advice to Her Excellency that the Governor-General should commission Mr Rudd as Prime Minister based upon the Prime Minister's tendered advice.
>
> I confirm the Governor-General's view conveyed to you, that it would be her intention, if your advice is to commission Mr Rudd as Prime Minister, that she seek an assurance that he will announce his appointment at the first possible opportunity to the House of Representatives in order to give the House the opportunity for whatever, if any, action it chooses to take.
>
> Yours sincerely,
>
> Stephen Brady
>
> Official Secretary to the Governor-General

The Acting Solicitor-General replied by letter that same evening. He confirmed that in his opinion the Governor-General should commission Mr Rudd as Prime Minister. He further stated that, though the Governor-General could seek an assurance from Mr Rudd that he would announce his appointment to the House of Representatives, it was his opinion that she could not require such an assurance nor make the appointment conditional on it; these latter views are, in my view, open to question. Mr Orr stated that he had consulted the Solicitor-General, Justin Gleeson SC, who "agrees with this advice".[60]

The letters between the Governor-General's Official Secretary and the Acting Solicitor-General were placed on the Governor-General's website.

It is striking that the Governor-General should, at least twice in three years, seek the counsel of the Solicitor-General or Acting Solicitor-General, and that in the second case she should handle this in part through correspondence

---

[59] Letter from Stephen Brady to Robert Orr, 26 June 2013 <https://www.gg.gov.au/mediarelease/advice-acting-solicitor-general-governor-general-honourable-quentin-bryce-ac-cvocommissioning-new-prime-minister>.

[60] Letter from Robert Orr to Stephen Brady, 26 June 2013 <https://www.gg.gov.au/mediarelease/advice-acting-solicitor-general-governor-general-honourable-quentin-bryce-ac-cvocommissioning-new-prime-minister>.

through her Official Secretary. It should be noted that the "advice" from the Acting Solicitor-General to which Mr Brady referred was "advice" in the sense of informal counsel rather than official "advice" such as given by ministers and ordinarily regarded as ultimately binding on (though open to question by) the Governor-General. The wording of the Official Secretary's letter which expressed the Governor-General's intention "if your advice is to commission Mr Rudd as Prime Minister" should not be taken as meaning that she was in any way bound to act on the Acting Solicitor-General's advice; she most certainly was not. Nor, in my view, should it be treated as a settled matter that the optimal or necessary source of informal "advice" to the Governor-General is the Solicitor-General.[61] The Governor-General retains an independent discretion on sources of advice on matters on which she or he has an independent discretion.

In his Queale Memorial Lecture, Sir Paul Hasluck stressed his view that staff at Government House were not in any sense sources of advice on constitutional matters: "If he [or she] wishes for guidance on any legal or constitutional points that may arise he [or she] will seek it from the Attorney-General or from eminent authorities of his [or her] choosing, and not from any staff of his [or her] own".[62] It is an interesting contrast, reflective of the growth of the significance of the role of the Official Secretary to the Governor-General in the intervening decades, that on her retirement as Governor-General in 2014, Dame Quentin Bryce paid a warm public tribute in these terms:[63]

> Stephen Brady, Official Secretary, has given first rate leadership and professionalism as adviser, sounding board and confidant to me.
>
> I have learnt much from his acumen, experience and diplomatic skills.
>
> Stephen has built the Office of the Official Secretary into an exemplary small agency where efficiency, accountability and transparency are hallmarks of performance.

---

[61] [Indeed, the view that it should not is argued briefly in the "Introduction" to this book.]
[62] Hasluck, op. cit., p. 21.
[63] Dame Quentin Bryce, "Speech on the Occasion of Reception Hosted by the Prime Minister", Canberra, 25 March 2014. The growth of "the Governor-General's establishment" is discussed in Boyce, op. cit., pp. 140-3. [See also "Introduction" in this book.]

Conclusion

Sir Zelman Cowen set out as Governor-General to bring "a touch of healing" to a divided nation after the 1975 constitutional crisis, including to restore the public standing of the position of Governor-General after much controversy. Dame Quentin Bryce set out as Governor-General 31 years later to balance the traditional and the contemporary in the office of Governor-General. That both individuals succeeded in these goals has contributed to what I have here suggested has been the consolidation of the office of Governor-General into a mature and modern de facto headship of state exercised in distinctively Australian style, and handed on in 2014 in good shape. Time will tell whether the continuing evolution, modernisation and Australianisation of the office of Governor-General enables it to fulfil the hopes of an evolving Australia with its evolving Australian national identify, or whether the office of Governor-General is succeeded in time by the office of President. Sir Zelman Cowen and Dame Quentin Bryce are two who have held the office of Governor-General who have believed that such a change, on appropriate terms, would be a positive development for Australia.

APPENDIX 1

MONARCHS, GOVERNORS-GENERAL, CHIEF JUSTICES OF THE HIGH COURT, AND PRIME MINISTERS SINCE 1901

Monarchs

Queen Victoria (1837-1901)

King Edward VII (1901-1910)

King George V (1910-1936)

King Edward VIII (1936)

King George VI (1936-1952)

Queen Elizabeth II (1952-)

Governors-General of Australia

Lord Hopetoun (1901-1903)

Lord Tennyson (1903-1904, Acting Governor-General 1902-1903)

Lord Northcote (1904-1908)

Lord Dudley (1908-1911)

Lord Denman (1911-1914)

Sir Ronald Munro Ferguson (1914-1920)

Lord Forster (1920-1925)

Lord Stonehaven (1925-1931)

Sir Isaac Isaacs (1931-1936)

Lord Gowrie (1936-1945)

The Duke of Gloucester (1945-1947)

Sir William McKell (1947-1953)

Sir William Slim (1953-1960)

Lord Dunrossil (1960-1961)

Lord De L'Isle (1961-1965)

Lord Casey (1965-1969)

Sir Paul Hasluck (1969-1974)

Sir John Kerr (1974-1977)

Sir Zelman Cowen (1977-1982)

Sir Ninian Stephen (1982-1989)

Mr W.G. Hayden (1989-1996)

Sir William Deane (1996-2001)

Rt Revd Dr Peter Hollingworth (2001-2003)

Major General Michael Jeffery (2003-2008)

Dame Quentin Bryce (2008-2014)

General Sir Peter Cosgrove (2014-)

Chief Justices of the High Court of Australia

Sir Samuel Griffith (1903-1919)

Sir Adrian Knox (1919-1930)

Sir Isaac Isaacs (1930-1931)

Sir Frank Gavan Duffy (1931-1935)

Sir John Latham (1935-1952)

Sir Owen Dixon (1952-1964)

Sir Garfield Barwick (1964-1981)

Sir Harry Gibbs (1981-1987)

Sir Anthony Mason (1987-1995)

Sir Gerard Brennan (1995-1998)

Murray Gleeson (1998-2008)

Robert French (2008-)

Prime Ministers of Australia

Sir Edmund Barton (1901-1903)

Alfred Deakin (1903-1904)

J.C. Watson (1904)

George Reid (1904-1905)

Alfred Deakin (1905-1908)

Andrew Fisher (1908-1909)

Alfred Deakin (1909-1910)

Andrew Fisher (1910-1913)

Joseph Cook (1913-1914)

Andrew Fisher (1914-1915)

William Morris Hughes (1915-1923)

Stanley Melbourne Bruce (1923-1929)

James Scullin (1929-1932)

Joseph Lyons (1932-1939)

Earle Page (1939)

Robert Menzies (1939-1941)

Arthur Fadden (1941)

John Curtin (1941-1945)

Frank Forde (1945)

Ben Chifley (1945-1949)

Robert Menzies (1949-1966)

Harold Holt (1966-1967)

John McEwen (1967-1968)

John Gorton (1968-1971)

William McMahon (1971-1972)

Gough Whitlam (1972-1975)

Malcolm Fraser (1975-1983)

Bob Hawke (1983-1991)

Paul Keating (1991-1996)

John Howard (1996-2007)

Kevin Rudd (2007-2010)

Julia Gillard (2010-2013)

Kevin Rudd (2013)

Tony Abbott (2013-2015)

Malcolm Turnbull (2015-)

APPENDIX 2

GLIMPSES OF TWO MODERN GOVERNORS-GENERAL: DR PETER HOLLINGWORTH AND DAME QUENTIN BRYCE

The short pieces below are included to reflect the backgrounds and activities of some of those Australians chosen to serve as Governor-General in recent times – Dr Peter Hollingworth (2001-2003), and Ms (later Dame) Quentin Bryce (2008-2014). These snippets are from events at which the author, as Warden of Trinity College at the University of Melbourne, and later Warden of Rhodes House, Oxford, has introduced or spoken about Dr Hollingworth and Dame Quentin.

These short pieces in part reflect why Dr Hollingworth and Dame Quentin were considered by the Prime Ministers who nominated them (John Howard and Kevin Rudd, respectively) as strong choices for an office in which the Governor-General "interprets the nation to itself". The backgrounds of several Australian Governors-General in politics and the law (and in one case as a lawyer Vice-Chancellor) are reflected in the earlier pieces in this book on Sir Paul Hasluck, Sir John Kerr, and Sir Zelman Cowen. Two more recent Governors-General (Major General Michael Jeffery and General Sir Peter Cosgrove) made their earlier careers primarily in the military. As Sir Paul Hasluck pointed out in a passage quoted in chapter 8 of this book, an important issue for a Prime Minister in nominating a Governor-General is their knowledge and experience "of the Australian constitutional background and the Australian administrative structure".[1]

These snippets also reflect issues and activities on which modern Governors-General have provided leadership. The activities mentioned here – especially education and international linkages – were, of course,

---

[1] Sir Paul Hasluck, *The Office of Governor-General*, Melbourne University Press, 1979, pp. 21-2.

only some of the many issues and activities with which Dr Hollingworth and Dame Quentin Bryce and other modern Australian Governors-General have concerned themselves. They must, of course, exercise this community leadership role with careful judgment: there was, for example, criticism of Sir William Deane for what some perceived as an excessive focus on advocacy of his views on Indigenous reconciliation, while his emphasis on this was warmly applauded by many others.

Dr Peter Hollingworth

The Rt Revd Dr Peter Hollingworth (born 10 April 1935) served as Governor-General from June 2001 to May 2003. He came to the position from being Anglican Archbishop of Brisbane (1989-2001), and is the only minister of religion to serve as Governor-General of Australia, though some have served as state Governors and in other Commonwealth countries. Dr Hollingworth's term as Governor-General was adversely affected and ultimately curtailed because of criticism of his handling of child sexual abuse cases brought to his attention when he was Anglican Archbishop of Brisbane.

Valedictory Ceremony for Trinity College Foundation Studies[2]
Melbourne Town Hall
4 December 2002

In completing and graduating from Trinity College Foundation Studies, you become alumni – past students – of Trinity College in the University of Melbourne. We are delighted tonight to welcome one of the most distinguished alumni of Trinity College, the Governor-General of Australia, Dr Peter Hollingworth, and Mrs Ann Hollingworth.

Dr Hollingworth was a resident student, living in and studying at the College, from 1955 to 1959. Mrs Hollingworth is also a graduate of the University of Melbourne, training and later working as a physiotherapist, and one of their daughters, Deborah, has also been a resident student of the College. Dr Hollingworth has said that he was shaped both spiritually and intellectually at Trinity, and I believe that he dates his commitment to work to

---

[2] Trinity College Foundation Studies is an academic programme undertaken by Trinity College, the University of Melbourne, to prepare international students for entry to the University of Melbourne and other universities.

overcome injustice and suffering to his time at Trinity. He trained to become an Anglican priest, and served for 25 years with the Brotherhood of St Laurence, an Anglican body committed to social welfare and social justice. Over those years, including throughout the 1980s as Director of the Brotherhood of St Laurence, Dr Hollingworth became very prominent in Australia as an advocate for the poor and disadvantaged.

In 1989, Bishop Hollingworth became Archbishop of Brisbane, and he continued to play other significant roles of leadership and service in Australian public life. In 1997, Archbishop Hollingworth was elected by the College Council to be a Fellow of Trinity – the highest honour the College can bestow. He was formally installed as a Fellow in the Chapel in November 1998, and he wrote afterwards: "It was a most memorable experience which above all other things reminds one of the obligation to give back some of what we have received."

Last year, Dr Hollingworth became Governor-General of Australia, the second member of this College, after Lord Casey in the 1960s, to hold Australia's highest office, playing important roles under the Australian Constitution and representing Australia, both overseas and to its own people.

It is very fitting that the Governor-General of Australia should congratulate students who have come to Australia from many countries around the world to study here. It is also very fitting that Dr Hollingworth, an alumnus of Trinity College, should welcome you as new alumni of the College – which he will do later in this ceremony. Dr and Mrs Hollingworth have both over many years been very active supporters of Trinity College, and we are deeply grateful that they are with us tonight to express their support and encouragement for the students and staff of Trinity College Foundation Studies.

Welcome to Abdurrahman Wahid[3] at a Global Foundation luncheon
Trinity College, University of Melbourne
12 December 2004[4]

It is an immense honour and pleasure for me – as Warden of Trinity College in the University of Melbourne, and as a member of the Global Foundation – to welcome you to Trinity College today, and especially to welcome one of

[3] Abdurrahman Wahid, often known as Gus Dur (1940-2009): President of Indonesia (1999-2001); leader of Nahdlatul Ulama, Indonesia's largest Islamic Organisation.
[4] Previously published in Donald Markwell, *"A large and liberal education": higher education for the 21st century*, Australian Scholarly Publishing, 2007, pp. 216-7.

the most significant advocates of liberal Islam and religious tolerance in the world today, Abdurrahman Wahid. Sir, you are warmly welcome, and we are honoured that you are here.

We are honoured also that speaking on behalf of the Global Foundation today, and formally introducing Mr Wahid, will be another liberal religious leader who, like Mr Wahid, has devoted himself to serving the community and who has also held his country's highest public office – Dr Peter Hollingworth.

In April 2002, an article by Mr Wahid was published in a number of Australian newspapers discussing how to defeat terrorism. In it, he spoke of the value of young Muslims obtaining a liberal arts education in the west, and of the dangers of their obtaining too narrow and un-nuanced an education. This article drew much attention and admiration here at Trinity College. We are committed to a philosophy of what we call "large and liberal education", and this philosophy infuses the university preparatory programme we run for overseas students, Trinity College Foundation Studies. The many hundreds of students who undertake this academic programme each year include well over 100 from Indonesia, and very many Muslim students. We are delighted also to welcome Indonesian students each year into residence as undergraduates in this College.

In the 2002 issue of the College magazine, we repeated some of Mr Wahid's argument – which has had a profound impact here – and, in the same issue of our magazine, we featured a photograph of Dr Hollingworth, a Fellow of this College, and then Governor-General of Australia, meeting with Trinity College Foundation Studies students from several countries, including Indonesia. I might mention that with us today is another Anglican priest, the Revd Kim Cruickshank, who serves as Chaplain in Foundation Studies, and who offers support and encouragement to students of all faiths, including – most obviously – to both Christian and Muslim students.

The chair of our proceedings today, Dr Peter Hollingworth, was educated at the University of Melbourne and in this College, where he was a resident student for several years. Ordained an Anglican priest, he served for some 25 years at the Brotherhood of St Laurence, gaining national prominence as an advocate of social justice and of solutions to poverty, before being elected Archbishop of Brisbane in 1989, and then serving as Governor-General of Australia from 2001 to 2003. It is my privilege to invite Dr Hollingworth to speak and to preside on behalf of the Global Foundation.

Dame Quentin Bryce

Ms (later Dame) Quentin Bryce (born 23 December 1942) served as Governor-General from September 2008 to March 2014. The only woman so far to serve as Governor-General of Australia, she came to the position from serving as Governor of Queensland (2003-2008). She and her immediate predecessor as Governor-General, Major General Michael Jeffery (2003-2008), who had served as Governor of Western Australia (1993-2000), are the only Australians to have served as state Governors also to become Governor-General; some of the early Governors-General were British aristocrats who had also served as Governors of Australian states. Dame Quentin Bryce had made her earlier career as a legal academic, leader in social justice advocacy, and university college head.

Welcome to Ms Quentin Bryce AC and Mr Michael Bryce
Rhodes House, Oxford
28 April 2011[5]

It is an immense privilege for all your fellow Australians here today to welcome Your Excellencies to Oxford, which has educated and is educating so many Australians, and specifically to welcome you to Rhodes House, the home of the Rhodes Scholarships. I am delighted that you have had the chance today to talk with so many outstanding Australian students and academics who will contribute, indeed in many cases are contributing, to the future of our country and the wider world, in diverse fields, as Australian Oxonians have been doing for generations.

Australian Oxonians who have done so – and indeed who have met, talked, partied, and dined, in this very Hall – in years past include Nobel Laureates Howard Florey and Sir John Eccles, public figures such as Sir Zelman Cowen – a dear friend of yours and of mine – and Bob Hawke, and countless others. Sir Zelman Cowen famously said that the role of the Governor-General is to represent the nation to itself, and, Your Excellency, your experience as law teacher and as a leader in collegiate education, as an advocate for women and for children, for human rights and equal opportunity, and as Governor of Queensland, have equipped you to play this role superbly.

---

[5] Previously published in Donald Markwell, *"Instincts to lead": on leadership, peace, and education,* Connor Court, 2013, pp. 102-3.

To welcome you here is a particular personal pleasure for me. Governor-General, not only do you and I both hail from tiny towns in western or central western Queensland; but who would have imagined over 30 years ago, when you were my long-suffering tutor in administrative law at the University of Queensland, that I would one day welcome you here today? It is a great privilege and pleasure to do so, and all of us here in this Hall are delighted to welcome you and Mr Bryce. I am also glad to have this opportunity, as Warden of Rhodes House, to thank you for your much-valued contribution to the Rhodes Scholarships, as Governor of Queensland and as Governor-General.

APPENDIX 3

TWO CONSTITUTIONAL SCHOLARS:

SIR KENNETH WHEARE AND

DR EUGENE FORSEY

Sir Kenneth Wheare (1907-1979)

Extract from "British Social Science and Humanities"
in T.B. Millar (ed.), The Australian Contribution to Britain
Australian Studies Centre, University of London
1988

I know Mr. Wheare personally and have read the Essay for which he obtained the Cecil Prize last year, and feel able without hesitation to express my conviction of his fitness to undertake research in Colonial History, and notably into the evolution of the British Commonwealth. It seems to me that he has acute insight into constitutional distinctions...[1]

Those were the words with which, in 1932, one Australian nearing the end of his career, Oxford's Regius Professor of Greek, Gilbert Murray, began a testimonial for another Australian, Kenneth Wheare, then a Rhodes Scholar embarking on his career. Wheare was applying for the Beit Senior Research Scholarship in Colonial History that would set him on the path to become, little more than a decade later, Gladstone Professor of Government and Public Administration in Oxford.[2]

If Sir Keith Hancock's greatest contribution to Commonwealth history was to move the focus from constitutional to economic questions,[3] perhaps

---

[1] MS Gilbert Murray 504 fols. 11-2, Bodleian Library, Oxford; see also ibid. 60 fols. 92-3.

[2] See, e.g., *Dictionary of National Biography 1971-1980*, pp. 894-6. Sir Norman Chester, "Sir Kenneth Wheare, 1907-79", *Political Studies*, vol. 28, 1980. Geoffrey Marshall, "Kenneth Clinton Wheare 1907-1979", *Proceedings of the British Academy*, vol. 67, 1981.

[3] [On Hancock, see Markwell, "British Social Science and Humanities", op. cit., and *"Instincts to lead": on leadership, peace, and education*, Connor Court, 2013, pp. 227-30.]

Sir Kenneth Wheare's was to give the continuing constitutional discussion greater rigour and precision. He was regarded as the leading authority on the constitution and government of Britain and the Commonwealth. Wheare once described himself as "not a lawyer but only a political scientist";[4] but, where Hancock wrote of the Commonwealth as a historian, Wheare wrote of it as, in effect, a lawyer.

Wheare, born in 1907, was, like Hancock, both an undergraduate at Melbourne University, where his interest in Politics was encouraged by Professor Macmahon Ball, and a Rhodes Scholar; he read Philosophy, Politics, and Economics at Oriel, taking a First in 1932. Wheare was Beit Lecturer in Colonial History at Oxford from 1935 to 1944, when he became Gladstone Professor of Government and Public Administration and a Fellow of All Souls. Wheare became Rector of Exeter College, Oxford, in 1956, and died in 1979, seven years after his retirement from Exeter. He is commemorated in Oxford with a gargoyle on the Bodleian Library; the gargoyle depicts his benign face, with next to it a kangaroo.[5]

In successive editions of Wheare's *The Statute of Westminster and Dominion Status* (1938) and in his *The Constitutional Structure of the Commonwealth* (1960) may be traced the constitutional development of the Commonwealth through the 20th century – of self-governing colonies in the Empire, to Dominions in a Commonwealth and Empire with shared allegiance to the Crown, and then to independent states in a Commonwealth unified by little more than shared acceptance of the monarch as its Head. Perhaps Wheare's most notable contribution is the concept of "autochthony"[6]: many member states of the Commonwealth wished to assert, not only that they were autonomous states "in no way subordinate to the government of the United Kingdom", but also that "their constitution has force of law ... within their territory through its own native authority and not because it was enacted or authorised by the parliament of the United Kingdom; that it is ... 'home grown', sprung from their own soil, and not imported from the United Kingdom." To convey this, Wheare used the word "autochthony" – from the Greek, meaning "sprung from that land itself". As Sir Zelman Cowen has shown, it is a term of enduring relevance, including for recent developments in Canada and

---

[4] K.C. Wheare, *Maladministration and Its Remedies*, Stevens & Sons, London, 1973, p. 1.

[5] There is a photograph of it in Howard Morphy & Elizabeth Edwards, *Australia in Oxford*, Pitt Rivers Museum, Oxford, 1988, p. 88.

[6] K.C. Wheare, *The Constitutional Structure of the Commonwealth*, Clarendon Press, Oxford, 1960, ch. 4.

Australia.[7]

In his 1932 testimonial, Gilbert Murray had spoken of Wheare's "acute insight into constitutional distinctions". Murray was directly responsible for Wheare's writing one of the books in which this constitutional insight was revealed. In 1948, Murray, acting as an editor of the Home University Library series, suggested to Wheare that he write a book on constitutions.[8] The result, *Modern Constitutions*, was first published in 1951, and remains of great value. Wheare's interest in comparative political institutions, especially "federalism in its various incarnations",[9] is also evident in his work on *Federal Government*, first published in 1946, and on *Legislatures*, published in 1963.

Those political scientists who stress the social and economic interests at work in politics might think that Wheare focussed solely on the elaborate façade of constitutional government, and not on the real workings within. But this criticism would be a mistake. Lord Beloff, a later occupant of Wheare's chair, has written:[10]

> [Wheare's] writings combined three principal strands – a respect for the legal and constitutional framework of political action in all democratic systems, an understanding of the historical roots of the different Anglo-Saxon polities and institutions, and above all an awareness of how men actually behave in the political and administrative context – an awareness solidly based on his own practical experience in getting things done.

Nowhere is Wheare's appreciation of the reality of politics clearer that in his comments on bureaucracy and in his most original book, *Government by Committee* (1955). In his Inaugural Lecture in 1945, Wheare declared: "The form of government which exists in this country today may be described with substantial accuracy as a parliamentary bureaucracy"[11] – a system in which there is a legislature less powerless than is often thought, and bureaucracy which was, and needed to be, on massive scale. The two were "organically integrated and controlled by a cabinet system", and Wheare stressed the importance of this political control of the bureaucracy. Given such control, Wheare regarded "parliamentary bureaucracy" as "the ideally best form of democratic government for a modern industrial state". His concern for

---

[7] Vernon Bogdanor (ed.), *The Blackwell Encyclopaedia of Political Institutions*, Blackwell, Oxford, 1987, p. 36.
[8] MS Gilbert Murray 411 fols. 82-4, 98-9; see also fol. 24.
[9] *Dictionary of National Biography 1971-1980*, p. 895.
[10] Ibid.
[11] K.C. Wheare, *The Machinery of Government: An Inaugural Lecture*, Clarendon Press, Oxford, 1945, pp. 4-5.

the control of administration was reflected in his 1973 Hamlyn lectures on *Maladministration and its Remedies.*

Wheare had his own practical experience of bureaucracy. He played an active role in Oxford University, College, City Council, and other administration.[12] He was a superb committee member. "'Over my dead body, Mr Vice-Chancellor,' he was once heard to say, of some proposal that displeased him, 'if I may take up a moderate position in this matter.'"[13]

Wheare also served in the 1950s on the Franks Committee on administrative tribunals and inquiries, and he had earlier acted as constitutional adviser to conferences and conventions on Newfoundland and on Central African Federation. He is credited with the authorship of some of the new Commonwealth constitutions which he analysed in *The Constitutional Structure of the Commonwealth*; and it is said, though perhaps the story is apocryphal, that he would sometimes come into a meal in College as civil war or a coup was breaking out in some distant land, and say, rather whimsically, "well, it seems they've torn up another of my constitutions."

Wheare's interests – especially the Commonwealth, federalism, and constitutions – seem to me to be entirely natural for an Australian student of government working in Britain – someone, that is, from an old Commonwealth country with a written and federal constitution. And, of course, these topics have attracted the interest of other Australians in Britain, such as Hancock, R.T.E. Latham, Bruce Miller, Sir Zelman Cowen, John Finnis, and others.[14]

---

[12] [Wheare also chaired the Rhodes Trustees, 1962-1969. Lady (Gill) Williams told me that of the five Chairs of the Trustees during the Wardenship of her late husband, Sir Edgar Williams (Warden of Rhodes House, Oxford, 1952-1980), Wheare was the most understanding and best.]

[13] Marshall, op. cit., p. 494.

[14] [His sustained interest in Australian constitutional matters was evident in his defence of Sir John Kerr in "Australia's Constitutional Crisis", *The Parliamentarian*, vol. 59, 1978. See J.R. Poynter, "Wheare, Sir Kenneth Clinton (1907-1979)", *Australian Dictionary of Biography*, vol. 16, Melbourne University Press, 2002.]

Dr Eugene Forsey (1904-1991)[15]

> *Review of* A Life on the Fringe
> *by Eugene Forsey (1990)*
> *Published as "Canada's Best"*
> The Round Table: The Commonwealth Journal of International Affairs
> *October 1991*

Dr Eugene Forsey, the Canadian socialist and constitutionalist who died early in 1991 at the age of 86, was a man of great charm. He was also a man of great acuity and unwavering principles, and a fearless, tenacious fighter. These qualities adorn the pages of the memoirs he was finally persuaded to write in his 80s, and which appeared only months before his death. In them, he depicts his life, as "a Christian of the Left", as one on the fringe, rather than at the centre, of affairs: "in scholarship, in trade unionism, in politics, in religion". But, as usual, he is too modest.

Born in 1904, Forsey was proud of his Newfoundland origins and West Country English ancestry. But he spent most of his life in Ottawa and Montreal (he was perfectly bilingual). The son of a Methodist minister *manqué* who died when Forsey was under six months old, he was bought up in his maternal grandparents' household in Ottawa, within walking distance of the House of Commons. His feel for constitutional conventions undoubtedly owed much to his grandfather's 60 years of service to Canadian parliaments, where he became a great authority on parliamentary procedure. Forsey could remember "every Prime Minister who has held office since 1894 except Sir Charles Tupper".

As a teenager, and then an undergraduate at McGill, Forsey became fiercely devoted to Arthur Meighen, the Conservative leader. But neither his Conservatism nor his aim to enter the Methodist ministry survived McGill. When he went to Balliol College, Oxford, in 1926 as a Rhodes Scholar for Quebec, he soon became active in the Labour Party and the Quakers. His socialism was a Christian socialism based on a commitment to "the Social Gospel". "It was grounded in the British, not the continental European, socialist tradition: it was evolutionary, parliamentary, pragmatic, and closely linked with the trade unions." Oxford confirmed Forsey's pride in England and its constitutional government. It also exposed him to the British institution of

---

[15] There are further reflections on Dr Forsey in Markwell, *"Instincts to lead": on leadership, peace, and education*, Connor Court, 2013, pp. 139, 318. See also Helen Forsey, *Eugene Forsey: Canada's Maverick Sage*, Dundurn, 2012.

letters to the newspapers (above all, of course, *The Times*): to the horror of family and friends who thought that only "cranks" wrote such letters, Forsey, back in Canada, embarked in the 1930s on a "long and often turbulent career of writing letters to newspapers". It is for such letters that many Canadians will best remember him.

Forsey returned to Canada in 1929, to a non-tenured post at McGill, where he stayed until 1941. His account of these years stresses his frosty relations with the university administration, and his work through the Depression years in the Co-operative Commonwealth Federation (C.C.F.), which he helped to found in 1932, and in other parts of "the movement for social change" such as the League for Social Reconstruction (L.S.R.), and the Fellowship for a Christian Social Order (F.C.S.O.). It was through student Christian activities that he met Harriet Roberts, whom he married in 1935.

A short visit to the Soviet Union in 1932 left him optimistic for its future. He favoured a united front against Fascism, and in support for the League of Nations. He toyed with ways to reconcile Christianity and communism. But he fought vigorously against the influence of communists in the F.C.S.O. (which died at their hands), and later in the trade unions. He left the Quakers during the Spanish Civil War, because he believed that he would fight if he were in Spain. But sufficient of his earlier pacifism and isolationist nationalism had clung to him that, to his later regret, he did not volunteer during World War II. After a year at Harvard in 1941-1942, Forsey was "eager to work for the labour and socialist movements", and in the summer of 1942 he became Director of Research (or "general handyman") at the Canadian Congress of Labour. He stayed with it and its successor body until his "retirement" in 1969.

Forsey was awarded a doctorate from McGill for the study that was published in 1943 (and again in 1968, and 1990) as *The Royal Power of Dissolution of Parliament in the British Commonwealth*. This work remains a classic study of part of the reserve powers of the Crown, alongside *The King and His Dominion Governors* (1936) by the Australian socialist Dr H.V. Evatt. *The Royal Power* contains a strong defence of Lord Byng and Arthur Meighen in the constitutional crisis of 1926, attacking the ill-informed orthodoxy which favoured Mackenzie King. Forsey regarded King as ignorant of parliamentary government and, *inter alia*, massively egotistical. Work on *The Royal Power* led to renewal of Forsey's friendship with Meighen, who became "perhaps my closest friend". He provides a fine portrait of Meighen here, describing his as "perhaps the most unpretentious man I have ever known", and as "incomparably the greatest parliamentarian of my time, probably the greatest Canada has ever had", and disputing the "caricature" of him as an "arch-reactionary".

Forsey's commitment to constitutional principles and conventions was evident over many years in other ways: not least in his vigorous defence of the action of the Governor-General of Australia, Sir John Kerr, in dismissing a government unable to obtain parliamentary Supply in 1975. Forsey and Kerr subsequently became firm friends. They died within weeks of each other, having both greatly valued what they knew would be their final telephone conversation between Canada and Australia.

Forsey's innumerable tasks during his 27 years with the Labour Congress included taking an often conciliatory role in collective bargaining, and writing a major history of the Canadian labour movement from 1812 to 1902. He stood on four occasions for election to public office as a C.C.F. candidate, including twice for the House of Commons (1948 and 1949). On all occasions he was a substitute candidate, and on all occasions he was soundly defeated. Given his active social radicalism, it is extraordinary that he won and retained the friendship and admiration of men and women across the political spectrum. His radicalism was, however, not so far removed from traditional Canadian Conservatism as it was from free market ideology; and he believed that the C.C.F. had a considerable *indirect* impact for "social justice" through inspiring "some Liberals and some Conservatives". John Diefenbaker (Conservative), Pierre Trudeau (Liberal), and Ed Broadbent (N.D.P.) all asked him to stand for parliament for *their* parties.

Though he accepted some government positions (such as on the Board of Broadcast Governors from 1958 until his resignation in 1962), he declined other offers (including, from Trudeau, the Ambassadorship to the Vatican: Forsey was a Protestant). In 1970, he accepted from Trudeau appointment to the Senate. With his long years of C.C.F. commitment, Forsey might have been expected to sit as an N.D.P. senator. But he had been bitterly disillusioned with the N.D.P. at its founding convention in 1961 (which he attended) over its acceptance of the doctrine that Canada was "two nations", politically as well as culturally. He saw this doctrine as unhistorical and dangerous. Though he was – as he proves – a strong supporter of the rights of French Canadians, this 1961 fight marked the beginning of his 30-year battle against what he regarded as the excesses of Quebec nationalism, and against the appeasement of it by what he saw as gullible English-speaking Canadians.

A strong (but not uncritical) admirer of Trudeau, especially over Trudeau's handling of national unity, he sat in the Senate as a Liberal. When Trudeau had stood for the Liberal leadership, Forsey, still with the Labour Congress, wrote to promise to "'support you by any means in my power, even to the point of total silence' (which I thought might be the best gift I could give him)". He writes here that "in my judgement Pierre Trudeau kept Quebec in Canada when no one else could have done it. In my judgement also, he saved us from Baader-Meinhof gangs and Red Brigades."

As a senator, however, Forsey acted very much as an Independent, and he came to regret his decision to sit as a Liberal. He gave particular attention to the Canadian constitution, and, above all, to his work as Senate Chairman of a joint parliamentary committee to review subordinate legislation. He helped kill off what he regarded as an ill-conceived attempt by Trudeau in 1978 to replace the Senate with a "House of Federation", and to codify what purported to be, but were not, constitutional conventions relating to the monarchy. His memoirs provide a dazzling account of the legal incompetence he encountered in Canadian bureaucracy – and the failure, even by lawyers, to understand that the rule of law must, for the sake of individual freedom, prevail over administrative whim or convenience. Forsey had for decades been a champion of civil liberties (including of trade union rights against some astonishingly vague and arbitrary legislation, and of Aboriginal rights). His commitment to the rule of law and to constitutional conventions fitted logically, he believed, with his commitment to social change.

His memoirs are written with great wit and elegance, and many anecdotes and literary allusions (many to the Anglican *Book of Common Prayer*, which Forsey loved). It displays his fairness of mind, and his remorseless pursuit of precision and logic. Unsurprisingly, many of his judgments are controversial (and there are some trivial errors). Though some parts may be too detailed for non-Canadians to digest readily, the volume gives fascinating accounts of many of the major figures and events of 20th-century Canadian academic, political, and trade union life. Other portraits include one of his tutorial partner at Balliol, Harry Hodson, as "a philosophical genius" who read Kant on the bus.

A Life on the Fringe reflects the nature of "Englishness" and "Frenchness" in Canada, and the role of religion in politics. It shows that one could be a strong Canadian nationalist while supporting the retention of symbols of

Canada's history. In 1965, when the flag was changed, Forsey argued for one that was "bicultural, with symbols – both British and French – to remind us of the origins of our nation. Instead, what we have is not even multi-cultural or agricultural; it is silvicultural."

This volume gives insights into Canadian federalism in action – from Forsey's fights for the disallowance of oppressive provincial legislation, to his views on a succession of constitutional proposals to "appease" Quebec. It contains a strong defence of the work of the Canadian Senate (though supporting some Senate reform), an attack on Meech Lake,[16] and constructive suggestions for constitutional change. It regrets the widespread ignorance among Canadians of their constitutional heritage and history (including of "the great struggles between King and Parliament in seventeenth- and early eighteenth-century England"). It touches on Canada's relations with the U.S., including Forsey's opposition to Canada's joining the Organisation of American States, and the tensions between international trade unionism and Canadian nationalism.

Eugene Forsey was, as Hedley Bull said of John Anderson, "a greater man than many who are more famous". He has, in a phrase he used of others, "gone to his reward". These memoirs are a fitting memorial to him, and a most engaging and enjoyable read.

---

[16] [The Meech Lake Accord of 1987 was an ultimately unsuccessful agreement between Prime Minister Mulroney and provincial Premiers for constitutional reform aimed, as Forsey saw it, at appeasing Quebec.]

INDEX

www.ingramcontent.com/pod-product-compliance
Lightning Source LLC
Chambersburg PA
CBHW070446100426
42812CB00004B/1222

* 9 7 8 1 9 2 5 5 0 1 1 5 5 *